MW00776135

KENNETH R. PHILP

Termination Revisited

AMERICAN INDIANS ON THE TRAIL TO SELF-DETERMINATION, 1933–1953

University of Nebraska Press
Lincoln and London

© 1999 by the University of Nebraska
Press. All rights reserved. Manufactured
in the United States of America ∞
First paperback printing: 2002
Library of Congress Cataloging-in-Publi-
cation Data. Kenneth R. Philp, 1941–,
Termination revisited: American Indians
on the trail to self-determination, 1933–1953
/Kenneth R. Philp.   p.   cm. Includes
bibliographical references and index.
ISBN 0-8032-3723-5 (cl: alk. paper)
ISBN 0-8032-8769-0 (pa: alk. paper)
1. Indian termination policy.   2. Indians of
North America—Government relations—
1934.   I. Title. E93.P55   1999
323.1'197073'09041—dc21   98-39667 CIP

For my family,
Marjory and Chris

CONTENTS

ILLUSTRATIONS

Photographs following page 112

TABLES

PREFACE

This book was written to fill a void in the historiography of Native Americans during the twentieth century. It covers the period from the Indian New Deal to termination in the early 1950s, when plans were made to rapidly assimilate Indians, end the trust on their tax-free land, and place them under state jurisdiction. Scholars generally have viewed termination as a regressive era when Native Americans lost important rights and were placed on the road to dispossession.

Standard historical interpretations of termination provide valuable insights. They trace the origins of this policy to the collapse of New Deal reform, the impact of World War II on Indian life, the rapid economic development of the West, and shifts in postwar liberalism. In addition, termination has been portrayed as a modern war of conquest where intolerant federal officials victimized Indians by seizing their property, making them displaced urban refugees, and ceding tribal authority to states.

These important accounts illuminate how coercive federal power was used to harm Indian communities. Nonetheless, historians have glossed over Native American responses to termination. They have generally ignored the interactive relationships between the descendants of European settlers and tribal people during this era.

Closely linked to tribal organization during the New Deal, termination meant different things to different groups of Indians. For some Alaskan Indians and for the Mescalero Apaches, Paiutes, and Blackfeet, termination seemed to offer an opportunity to fulfill promises of tribal self-rule under the 1934 Indian Reorganization Act (IRA). The Navajos, on the other hand, saw in termination a chance to jettison unpopular New Deal programs. Aspects of termination also appealed to pan-Indian groups in California and Oklahoma because it provided pathways to escape federal wardship.

Termination was a broadly based social movement in the United States to assimilate Indians and liberate them from federal supervision. It reflected the conservative and nationalist mood of the Cold War era that resonated with the ideologies of individualism and capitalism. Congress responded to these trends in 1946 by creating the Indian Claims Commission so Native Americans would have the financial resources to successfully run their own affairs.

President Harry S. Truman used the authority of the executive branch to redirect federal Indian policy. Truman had little interest in New Deal community programs such as the Indian Reorganization Act. Instead, he wanted to uphold the civil rights of Native Americans and other minorities, reorganize the Indian Bureau, and help tribal people find jobs in an expanding capitalist market economy.

This drive to end the segregation of Indians and give them equality as citizens of states lost momentum by 1953. Unexpected controversies in the postwar era and the emergence of a group of articulate Native American leaders made the Truman years a pivotal turning point where Indians sought alternatives to termination. In its place, they formulated concepts of self-determination that differed from the melting-pot views of Euro-American settlers.

The origins of this unforeseen development were complex. Native Americans and federal officials held divergent views toward possessory claims, tribal autonomy, and water rights, which led to conflict. Furthermore, deep cleavages and growing differences were revealed in controversies over the right of tribes to hire independent legal counsel, state jurisdiction in Indian country, and the authoritarian policies of Indian Commissioner Dillon S. Myer.

Recently, scholars have emphasized the importance of rethinking the past from the perspective of an Indian-centered reality. The result has been a New Indian History that brings Native Americans to the center of the historical stage. I have followed that approach by showing that Indians did not remain on the periphery of events during termination.

This study is an external account of the early termination period by a non-Indian historian. The narrative of the text does not represent the inner voice of a Native American author. The organization of the book and fragmentary historical evidence also made it impossible to depict the diverse reactions of more than three hundred Indian nations to termination. Nonetheless, a conscious effort has been made to recognize the role of Native Americans who worked to redesign an antiquated reservation system, end human degradation, and dismantle colonial rule by the Indian Bureau.

An exceptional group of Native American leaders came forward during the postwar era to provide a more secure future for their people. These political activists testified before Congress, met with state and federal officials, hired attorneys to prosecute claims and represent their other interests, used publicity to air grievances, were involved in civil disobedience, and joined pan-Indian organizations to coordinate their activities.

Rarely did these leaders speak for entire groups because of divisions within Indian communities. They also were limited in the amount of influence that they could assert at the federal level as members of advisory committees, consultants to the Interior Department, and lobbyists before Congress. Nevertheless, they influenced local communities and made their voices known to federal authorities as well as the general public at a critical juncture in Native American history.

The National Congress of American Indians (NCAI) was in the vanguard of this movement toward more self-determination. It provided Indians with a national political structure that transcended IRA tribal councils. Important leaders of this pan-Indian organization in the early postwar years were Ruth Muskrat Bronson, Cherokee; Frank George, Nez Percé; Napoleon Bonaparte Johnson, Cherokee; John C. Rainer, Taos Pueblo; Will Rogers Jr., Cherokee; and Avery Winnemucca, Pyramid Lake Paiute.

The NCAI leaders did not always agree on common objectives. They did, however, take bold steps to encourage independence for Indian people. For instance, Johnson and Rogers called for the progressive liquidation of the Indian Bureau and a staged federal withdrawal. Bronson militantly defended the timber and fishing rights of Alaskan Indians as well as the power of the Mescalero Apache IRA tribal council to remove a superintendent. Rainer and Winnemucca took the lead in upholding the right of tribes to hire attorneys without federal interference, while Bronson and George insisted that Congress obtain Indian consent prior to imposing state jurisdiction and ending the trust.

Adam Castillo, president of the California Mission Indian Federation, was another effective pan-Indian spokesperson. Castillo bitterly opposed the IRA because it reimposed wardship on acculturated Native Americans in Southern California. He repeatedly asked Congress to abolish the Indian Bureau, place California Indians under state jurisdiction, and approve a per capita distribution of claims awards and tribal funds so they could become self-reliant citizens.

Sam Ahkeah, chair of the Navajo Tribal Council, was troubled by racial bigotry, human suffering, and federal paternalism. He helped Navajos determine their own destiny by devising strategies to alter the structural circumstances of reservation poverty. Furthermore, Ahkeah took important civil rights initiatives and used treaty rights to guarantee the universal education of Navajo children.

Under Ahkeah's direction, the Navajos reaffirmed their government-to-government relationship with the United States. They bypassed the Indian

Bureau and met directly with congressional appropriation committees, rejected state jurisdiction over their affairs, and approved a long-range federal program to rehabilitate their homeland. The Navajos chose a parliamentary rather than IRA form of tribal government to confirm their right to self-rule.

George Pambrun, the chair of the Blackfeet Business Council, was another leader who brought about significant change. He successfully defended the constitutional authority of the tribe's IRA government to prevent the imposition of termination by administrative fiat. Pambrun also cooperated with the pan-Indian Montana Inter-Tribal Policy Board, state officials, and the NCAI to counter federal power that threatened tribal dissolution.

Blackfeet factionalism impeded Pambrun's efforts. Louis Plenty Treaty and other full-blood leaders did not want their tribal government patterned after the United States Constitution. Their definition of self-determination included respect for traditional values, continued social services guaranteed by treaty, and federal oversight to protect their trust property from mismanagement by the IRA Business Council.

These and other Native Americans responded with encounter and resolution during the Truman years to influence the circumstances of their lives. They used political activism, protest, and reform to break the crust of apathy and alienation caused by the absence of Indians from the pinnacles of decision making at the federal level. The variety of their responses to empower both individuals and tribal governments made the uniform national policy of termination an outmoded concept. It marked the beginning of a Native American movement for increased self-determination that would reverberate throughout the twentieth century.

This book has had a long incubation. Consequently, it is difficult to acknowledge all of the people who provided assistance at one stage or another of this project. I owe special thanks to George Miles and his excellent staff, who on short notice made available the facilities of the Beinecke Rare Book and Manuscript Library at New Haven. Janet Kennelly, an archivist at the National Anthropological Archives at the Smithsonian Institution, also provided helpful finding aids and gave countless leads. Furthermore, I am indebted to Robert Kvasnicka, who assisted my research at the National Archives and Washington National Records Center.

This book also benefited from the contributions of other individuals. Donald L. Fixico offered valuable suggestions for revision and comments on the role of Native American leaders. Tom Cowger shared information concerning the records of the National Congress of American Indians and recent scholarship on termination.

Every research project of this scope is a collective enterprise. I am deeply indebted to the many librarians and archivists at several institutions who gave invaluable advice in locating material in their holdings. This volume would not have been possible without assistance from the Harry S. Truman Presidential Library, Library of Congress, National Archives, Montana State University Library, Nebraska State Historical Society, Princeton University Mudd Manuscript Library, Smithsonian Institution, South Dakota State University Library, University of Montana Archives, University of North Dakota Library, University of Oregon Library, University of Texas at Arlington Library, University of Utah Marriott Library, University of Wyoming Archives, Washington National Records Center, Wisconsin State Historical Society, and Yale University Beinecke Manuscript Library.

The University of Texas at Arlington provided important financial support. Grants from the Organized Research Fund at the Graduate School made it possible to visit archives scattered throughout the United States. President Robert Witt and Provost George Wright approved a sabbatical for the 1995–96 academic year, which allowed release time from administrative duties to finish research and writing.

A number of colleagues and staff at the University of Texas at Arlington were very supportive. Special thanks go to Stanley Palmer, a good friend, who served as chair of the Department of History in my absence. I am also grateful to Ben Agger for his encouragement and interest in faculty development. Richard Francaviglia, the director of the Center for Greater Southwestern Studies and the History of Cartography, offered assistance on a number of occasions. Especially helpful were Center secretaries Darlene McAllister and Lois Lettini, who prepared the entire manuscript with amazing accuracy and speed. Jackie Stempel and Nancy Whitted, administrative assistants for the History Department, also took time from their busy schedules to locate photographs.

Portions of this volume have appeared in somewhat different form in the *Western Historical Quarterly*. Permission to publish copyrighted material from this journal is greatly appreciated.

Finally, I would like to express my appreciation to Marjory, my wife and special companion for over thirty years. She encouraged me to complete this research project even though for her it meant taking on additional family responsibilities. I am deeply thankful for Marjory's patience and good humor during my absence at our Torch Lake cottage to finish writing this book. My son, Chris, also deserves recognition for putting up with his father's preoccupation with the history of American Indians.

TERMINATION REVISITED

1

ON A NEW TRAIL:
THE PROMISE OF SELF-RULE

To say today that the record of Indian wardship is disgraceful is an under-statement. It has been disgraceful from the beginning. With rare interludes, it has been disgraceful through all administrations. The horrors of today may be paralleled by the horrors of the past. The past is irrevocable. The present and future is in our hands. The bonds of Indian wardship must be broken forever. STATEMENT BY ADAM CASTILLO, PRESIDENT, CALIFORNIA MISSION INDIAN FEDERATION, 1945

In 1941, President Franklin D. Roosevelt told Budget Director Harold D. Smith that if one agency should not reside in Washington DC during World War II, it was the Indian Bureau. Roosevelt was convinced that the bureau had relied too much on Southwestern data when it emphasized tribal self-rule during the New Deal. At Smith's initiative, the bureau's national office was moved one year later to the Merchandise Mart in Chicago. There, isolated government officials found it more difficult to communicate effectively with Congress concerning federal Indian policy.[1]

After Pearl Harbor, coordination between the executive and legislative branches of government in the management of Indian affairs reached a low ebb. Key personnel shifted almost constantly between Washington DC and Chicago. The bureau lost 40 percent of its experienced personnel when over eight hundred employees left for military service or transferred to war-related activities. The loss of so many people not only adversely affected the morale of those who remained behind, but it also led to a breakdown in the bureau's medical, educational, and social welfare programs.[2]

During World War II, Congress reasserted the responsibility for Indian affairs that it had relinquished to the executive branch during the Great Depression. In 1943, the Senate Subcommittee on Indian Affairs, chaired by Oklahoma

Democrat Elmer Thomas, issued Senate Report 310, which warned that the 1934 Indian Reorganization Act (IRA) had created tribal communes that condemned Indians to perpetual wardship. This vitriolic report recommended that Congress abolish the bureau, transfer its services to other federal agencies, end the trust over Indian property, and make states responsible for the universal education of Indian children. More moderate in tone were hearings held by South Dakota Republican Karl E. Mundt before the House Committee on Indian Affairs to determine if the changed status of Indian servicemen and citizens required new congressional legislation.[3]

In November 1944, delegates from fifty tribes met in Denver to found the National Congress of American Indians (NCAI). Scholars have observed that this event marked a turning point in Indian affairs. A group of political activists appeared with a supratribal consciousness that originated from common experiences in the non-Indian world. These Native American leaders advocated new forms of self-determination that differed from the melting-pot concept favored by most Euro-Americans.[4]

The emergence of the NCAI came at a time when Indian policy was in disarray. Federal officials had ignored solicitors' rulings about the inherent sovereign powers of tribes, had broken promises under the 1934 Indian Reorganization Act, and had stereotyped Native Americans as countercultural socialist heroes. Other disturbing realities were the failure of Congress to settle tribal claims, to fully protect Indian civil rights, and to provide adequate funds for reservation economic development.

It came as no surprise that in January 1945 a beleaguered John Collier resigned as Indian commissioner. When Napoleon Bonaparte Johnson, the NCAI president, learned about Collier's departure, he sent President Roosevelt a telegram that recommended the appointment of a Native American as commissioner. This request was ignored by Secretary of the Interior Harold L. Ickes, who stood by his nomination of William Brophy, an attorney for the Pueblo Indians.[5]

Instead of consulting with Indians, Ickes contacted members of the Senate Committee on Indian Affairs to obtain support for Brophy's candidacy. At confirmation hearings, the senators told Brophy they wanted a commissioner who would not work at cross purposes with Congress. When Brophy attempted to discuss his philosophy toward Indians, Senator Joseph O'Mahoney indicated that the nominee's views were irrelevant. He noted that Congress, not the executive branch, would be responsible for setting the direction of Indian policy.[6]

Several distinguished Indians testified at Brophy's confirmation hearings. Ben Dwight, the counsel for the Choctaw Nation; Dan Madrano, the secretary of the National Congress of American Indians; W. W. Short, president of the Choctaw and Chickasaw Federation; Robert Yellowtail, superintendent of the Crow Reservation; and Oglala Sioux delegates all requested that a qualified Indian head the bureau. Yellowtail also criticized Ickes for rushing Brophy's nomination while President Roosevelt had been talking with Joseph Stalin at Yalta. This prevented Indians from consulting with the White House about who should be the next commissioner.[7]

Senator O'Mahoney did not follow this advice. Instead, he upheld congressional authority by referring to a document prepared at his request by the Legislative Service of the Library of Congress. It summarized recent congressional reports that called for the repeal of IRA, abolition of the Indian Bureau, settlement of tribal claims, and universal education for Indian children. At the conclusion of this hearing, committee members met in executive session and voted unanimously in favor of Brophy's nomination, which the Senate confirmed on 6 March 1945 (pl. 1).[8]

Indian affairs had reached a crisis by the end of World War II because of widely divergent definitions of Indian self-determination. For New Deal reformers, self-rule meant that dependent Indian nations retained inherent powers of sovereignty and the legal right to a separate existence under permanent federal guardianship. Many members of Congress viewed this definition with skepticism. They wanted to jettison the IRA, which increased the government's supervision of the entire Indian population, so it would be possible to place tribes under state jurisdiction and emancipate them from federal wardship.

The controversy over Indian self-rule began when officials in the Roosevelt administration reopened the discussion about the legal and political status of Native Americans. John Collier, then the newly appointed Indian commissioner, sought to preserve tribal cultures because he thought they provided examples of harmonious communal life that would benefit the rest of society. Collier was determined to recognize the bilateral contractual relationship that existed with Indians before 1871 when Congress prohibited treaty making.[9]

Secretary Ickes agreed with Collier that tribes were distinct, independent political communities with exclusive authority to manage their internal affairs. Consequently, he chose Nathan R. Margold, a New York attorney, as solicitor of the Interior Department (pl. 2). Prior to his appointment, Margold had served as legal adviser on Indian claims at the Institute for Government Research and offered legal advice to Pueblo Indians. It was Margold who persuaded Felix S. Cohen, a personal acquaintance, to come to Washington DC (pl. 3). Cohen's assignment as assistant solicitor was to draft legislation that would give Indians greater political and economic autonomy.[10]

Both attorneys were deeply influenced by Felix's father, Morris Raphael Cohen. A distinguished professor of philosophy at City College of New York (CCNY) and staff member of the New School for Social Research, the elder Cohen had encouraged Margold and other students to think critically by using Hebraic and Marxist perspectives to point out the flaws of capitalism, militarism, and nationalism. In 1913, Cohen organized the Conference on Legal and Social Philosophy to demonstrate how law intersected with economics, social science, and public policy. A leader in American thought and life, Cohen convinced many attorneys, including Louis D. Brandeis and other Supreme Court justices, to become legal realists and practitioners of sociological jurisprudence.[11]

Felix Cohen closely identified with his father's effort to unite the discipline of law with a passion for social justice. In 1933, he published *Ethical Systems and Legal Ideals*, which recognized the importance of law as an instrument for building a better society. He also joined the Socialist Party and along with Margold became a member of the National Lawyers Guild, a leftist organization that rivaled the conservative American Bar Association.[12]

In an article written for the *American Socialist Quarterly*, Cohen discussed how to use law to reconstruct society. He believed that a revolutionary interpretation of existing legal forms would destroy the foundations of capitalist law that resulted in oppression and class violence. For Cohen, the ideals of equality, liberty, and democracy found in the United States Constitution and Declaration of Independence provided a theoretical justification for a second American Revolution that would usher in a socialist democracy to replace the chaos of capitalism during the Great Depression.[13]

Cohen cited examples of how the political ideology of the Founding Fathers could be used to create a new utopian social order. The division of sovereignty between the nation and states provided socialists with an opportunity to initially seize power at the local level. There, it would be possible to appeal to the masses and build a socialist framework for American society. In much the same spirit, Cohen proposed to transform capitalist corporations into instruments for democratic management that allowed workers to keep the wealth they produced.[14]

Cohen convinced Commissioner Collier and Solicitor Margold that constitutional and corporate law could be used by tribal communities to create socialist democracies. In January 1934, Collier sent a memo to tribal councils stating that a speedy settlement of Indian claims would depend on whether tribes formulated plans for self-rule that included constitutions and federally chartered cooperative associations. Collier did not envision that tribes would immediately manage their own affairs. Instead, the Indian Bureau under a system of indirect colonial rule would gradually transfer authority to Indian communities.[15]

For Collier and other Interior Department officials, self-rule meant that Indian groups would need to organize and adopt municipal ordinances. This would enable them to use tribal police and courts for law enforcement, control the expenditure of tribal funds, provide detailed budget recommendations to Congress, and have the power to remove undesirable federal employees. In his memo on Indian self-government, the commissioner warned that he would transfer authority only to tribes that established a communal system of land tenure ensuring equality in the ownership of community assets.[16]

Collier relied on legislation drafted by Cohen to restructure federal Indian policy. Introduced in Congress during February 1934 as the Wheeler-Howard Bill, this measure proposed to end land allotment and give tribes sweeping authority to manage their own affairs. Indian groups that incorporated under federal law would have all powers not inconsistent with the U.S. Constitution. Tribes would be responsible for managing the mandated collective ownership of allotted, heirship, and trust land. They could also borrow money from a credit fund, purchase property for landless Indians, and have a separate legal status under a special federal court of Indian affairs.[17]

Commissioner Collier convened several Indian congresses in March 1934 to obtain support for this legislation. At these meetings, Collier and other government officials promised to end the bureau's absolute power over Indian life. The delegates who attended these congresses welcomed the opportunity to manage their own affairs. Nonetheless, they wanted the government to protect their private ownership of property, honor treaties, and settle claims before walking down the trail that led to more tribal autonomy.[18]

In June 1934, Congress passed the Indian Reorganization Act. This statute ended land allotment and authorized funds to purchase tax-exempt land set aside for tribal homelands. Native Americans were eligible for positions at the Indian Bureau without regard to civil service laws. Congress also authorized funds for loans to Indian students and tribal organizations and established a revolving credit fund to encourage economic development.

Section 16 of the IRA permitted tribal home rule. Indians had the right to organize for their common welfare and adopt constitutions and bylaws. In addition to all powers vested in them by existing law, tribes, with the approval of the interior secretary, were allowed to employ legal counsel, prevent the sale of land without tribal consent, and negotiate with federal, state, and local governments for services. The interior secretary also was required to consult with tribes before submitting budget requests to Congress.[19]

Disappointed with this narrow congressional definition of tribal authority under IRA, Solicitor Margold interpreted section 16 to allow the executive branch to use constitutional law in a revolutionary way. This extraordinary assertion of authority on behalf of tribes opened the door to extended and bitter conflict with Congress, the Justice Department, and acculturated Indians over the scope of tribal sovereignty. It explains why Congress in subsequent years would attempt to repeal the IRA, terminate the trust, and emancipate Indians from federal wardship.

On 25 October 1934, Margold submitted an eighty-seven-page legal opinion entitled "The Powers of an Indian Tribe" at the request of Secretary Ickes. The preparation of this document was largely the responsibility of Assistant Solicitor Cohen. The occasion for Margold's ruling was wording in section 16 of the IRA that guaranteed to tribes that adopted constitutions all powers vested in an Indian tribe or tribal council by existing law. Ickes asked the solicitor to examine the meaning of this statement so Indians and government officials would have guidelines as they drafted IRA constitutions and charters.[20]

Margold ruled that tribes had unrestricted powers of self-government. The solicitor held that section 16 did not refer merely to delegated powers that Congress had granted under previous statutes and treaties. Instead, "all powers vested in an Indian tribe" made reference to a whole body of inherent powers that had not been surrendered by virtue of original tribal sovereignty.[21]

For Margold, the most basic principle of Indian law was that tribes did not have powers delegated by Congress but rather had the inherent powers of a limited sovereignty. He noted that Chief Justice John Marshall in *Samuel A. Worcester v. The State of Georgia* (1832) had recognized that tribes were distinct political communities with exclusive authority over their domestic affairs. The solicitor concluded that three fundamental principles marked the entire discourse of judicial decision on the nature of tribal powers: tribes originally possessed the powers of sovereign states; conquest terminated external sovereignty; this restriction did not affect the internal sovereignty of the tribe and its powers of local self-government.[22]

Margold ruled that the IRA merely provided statutory recognition of the inherent powers of tribal self-rule. These powers included the prerogative of tribes to determine their own form of self-government, define the conditions of membership subject to the supervision of the secretary of interior, regulate domestic relations, prescribe rules of inheritance except for allotted lands, levy taxes, and exclude nonmembers from tribal territory except for authorized government officials. Tribes could also regulate the use and disposition of property, administer justice unless Congress had transferred civil or criminal jurisdiction to state or federal courts, and supervise the conduct of federal employees subject to the discretion of the Interior Department.[23]

Some administrators at the Indian Bureau considered Margold's views novel, radical, and heretical. They kept the solicitor's opinion from public view because they feared that it would encourage Indians to do too many things for themselves. Margold's ruling also raised the question of whether Indian Bureau or congressional oversight was necessary if tribes had the inherent sovereign power to manage their own affairs.[24]

Margold's legal opinion, "Powers of an Indian Tribe," was used by the bureau's tribal organization unit to help prepare IRA constitutions. Drafts of these proposals were forwarded to the Interior Department for approval. Solicitor Margold told Secretary Ickes that most of these constitutions were unexceptional in design, inconsistent with the federal government's definition of justice, and often in conflict with existing laws.[25]

To remedy this situation, the solicitor asked Cohen to review the constitutions and propose amendments to those that did not meet with departmental approval. This created ill will among Indians who were asked to reconvene their constitutional conventions. Several tribes had to modify constitutions that automatically conferred membership on future generations of children, because of residency and other restrictions under section 19 of the IRA. On the Pine Ridge and Fort Belknap Reservations, tribal councils tried to assert their inherent power to supervise local government employees, only to learn that this was outside their province.[26]

Interior Department attorneys drafted boilerplate constitutions and charters to speed up tribal organization and resolve the dilemma over what powers Indians actually possessed. These documents listed important tribal responsibilities while recognizing the overall authority of the secretary of interior to regulate Indian affairs. This procedure contradicted Margold's earlier opinion that Indians had an unfettered right to self-rule. Well-intentioned government officials had assumed a task that should have been completed by Indians themselves.[27]

In 1935 Margold took another important initiative on behalf of Indian self-determination. He ruled that tribes could administer their own system of justice unless Congress had transferred civil or criminal jurisdiction to state courts. This interpretation of law, like Margold's "Powers of an Indian Tribe," was at odds with the intent of Congress. The previous year, the House and Senate had eliminated provisions for a separate Native American judiciary from the final draft of the IRA.[28]

In his "Memorandum on the Power of the Secretary of Interior to Make Regulations Governing the Conduct of Indians," Margold ruled that the power of forty-one Courts of Indian Offenses did not rest solely on the authority of the Interior Department to create them. These courts also represented the inherent powers of tribes to govern their own members. This legal opinion made it possible for Cohen to redesign the framework of tribal courts.[29]

In January 1935, he sent superintendents the draft of a new legal code that permitted tribes to establish their own judicial systems similar to Courts of Indian Offenses. Under Cohen's proposal, tribal councils instead of the secretary of interior would appoint Indian judges. They would also have civil and criminal jurisdiction over thirty-eight common offenses such as assault, kidnapping, forgery, reckless driving, and bribery.[30]

Because this reform was the first step in giving tribes substantial authority in the field of law and order, Cohen asked superintendents to carefully review the proposed code. Only twenty-two out of sixty superintendents thought this law code suited their jurisdictions. Sixteen superintendents opposed it for one or more of the following reasons: state jurisdiction was essential in California, Oklahoma, the Dakotas, and other areas where land allotment, small reservations, and the loss of tribal authority made it impossible to maintain separate courts; traditional law enforcement still worked well among the Florida Seminoles, New York Indians, and New Mexico Pueblos; and certain tribes unaccustomed to modern legal forms could not effectively administer their own courts.[31]

Most superintendents expressed a willingness not to interfere with the functioning of Indian courts, but they insisted on the right to command tribal police. Under Cohen's law code, superintendents could issue search and seizure warrants to any person, based on reliable information concerning an unspecified offense against the tribe. This authorization underscored the reality that, despite the promise of self-rule, Indians were still under the domination of the federal government.[32]

Cohen responded to the concerns of superintendents by creating a two-tiered system of forty-one tribal courts. In November 1935, he issued a revised law code that prevented superintendents from acting as judge, jury, and prosecuting attorney for Courts of Indian Offenses. Tribes that organized under the IRA, with constitutional authority to maintain law and order, could establish their own courts. This enabled IRA tribes to pass ordinances, rather than relying on administrative regulations to settle civil disputes. If tribal funds were available, IRA governments could appoint and remove judges without the Indian commissioner's approval and could employ their own police force.[33]

The IRA constitutions and tribal ordinances provided a uniform legal framework for self-government. After Secretary Ickes approved IRA constitutions and bylaws, he signed a document that forever relinquished his authority over the enumerated powers of these tribes. Ickes then ordered employees under his supervision to respect the authority of IRA governments and courts.[34]

This well-intentioned policy did not resolve numerous problems associated with tribal organization and economic development. For instance, in 1936 the Interior Department hired James E. Curry, an idealistic lawyer from Chicago who would later serve as legal counsel to the NCAI, to assist with organizing cooperatives on reservations.[35] In April, Curry consulted with Indians at seven New Mexico pueblos and encouraged them to reorganize their handicraft industry and to incorporate for community-based economic activity.[36]

Curry soon discovered that Pueblo Indian villages were not utopian socialist democracies. In a letter to Cohen, he indicated that individual tribesmen owned a disproportionate number of animals. Grave inequalities also existed in the assignment of agricultural land. Curry even doubted whether Secretary Ickes had legal authority to regulate stock grazing because the Pueblo Indians had fee simple title to their Spanish land grants.[37]

For Curry, credit associations and cooperatives were a key ingredient of Indian self-rule. These tribal corporations were not controlled by outside capital or predatory economic interests. They democratically used the one-share, one-vote principle instead of allowing wealth to flow unevenly to a single stockholder.[38]

In 1937 Curry joined the Indian Bureau's extension division. Much of his time was spent in Oklahoma, where one-third of the Indians in the United States resided. There, Curry encouraged groups of Comanche, Cherokee, Cheyenne, Arapaho, and Creek Indians to set up cooperatives to market poultry, strawberries, cattle, and other commodities.[39]

Nonetheless, he made little headway with the Five Civilized Tribes because of opposition from Joseph Bruner, a successful Creek businessman from Sapulpa. Bruner was president of the American Indian Federation, which attracted individuals who disliked the IRA because they thought it encouraged segregation, the revival of outmoded customs, and socialism. Bruner and his followers were more interested in a claims settlement than belonging to federally chartered credit associations and cooperatives.[40]

In March 1937, Cohen made a special visit to Oklahoma City to review some of the tribal organization problems that Curry and other bureau employees had encountered. Ben Dwight, a Choctaw principle chief and attorney, told Cohen that the Five Civilized Tribes did not want to divert tribal funds and future claims awards to pay the high administrative cost of federally supervised self-rule. These Indians also feared that tribal organization would give Negro freedmen and non-Indian intermarried citizens too much political power.[41]

The difficulty in organizing Oklahoma's Indians did not prevent Cohen from accepting an invitation in 1939 to head an Indian Law Survey funded by the Department of Justice. The purpose of this one-year project was to codify and analyze some five thousand statutes and treaties, two thousand judicial decisions, and numerous executive rulings for use by government attorneys. More than ten solicitors, as well as several law clerks and typists, were assigned to this ambitious research project. Eventually, they compiled a forty-six-volume set of legal documents. Cohen used this material to prepare his *Handbook of Federal Indian Law*, which summarized the findings of this survey.[42]

Officials at the Justice and Interior Departments viewed this project from different perspectives. Assistant Attorney General Norman M. Littell wanted to use law to integrate Indian citizens into mainstream society and to defend the federal government against tribal lawsuits before the Court of Claims and Supreme Court. Cohen intended to use the Indian Law Survey to buttress Margold's rulings on the inherent powers of tribes to manage their own affairs.[43]

On 31 October 1939, a dramatic showdown occurred that revealed deep fissures in the Roosevelt administration over the direction of tribal self-rule. At two o'clock in the afternoon, Norman Littell called Felix Cohen into his conference room and announced that the Department of Justice had decided to terminate the Indian Law Survey. With considerable irritation, Littell expressed dissatisfaction with Cohen's attitude and the quality of his legal interpretations.[44]

The assistant attorney general handed Cohen twenty-three pages of detailed criticism concerning the preliminary drafts of the Indian law handbook. Littell objected to Cohen's defense of the Quilleute and Quinaielt Indians' right to operate boats for hire on the Queets River in Washington State. He then cited errors in the handbook that gave the federal government rather than the states the responsibility for educating Indian children. Littell also chided Cohen for inferring that a law of Indian affairs existed apart from specific treaties and statutes, as well as for devoting too much attention to Pueblo litigation against the United States.[45]

On 1 November at 10:30 A.M., Littell once again requested a conference with Cohen. The assistant attorney general humiliated Cohen in front of staff members by publicly announcing the termination of his work for the Justice Department. A short time later, Littell belittled Cohen's scholarship and character before senators and officials at the Interior Department.[46]

Solicitor Nathan Margold agreed that the Justice Department had the right to end the Indian Law Survey because it funded this project. Neither he or Secretary Ickes, however, thought that Cohen's legal work lacked merit. They rebuffed Littell by having the Interior Department accept financial responsibility for publishing *The Handbook of Federal Indian Law* in 1942. The handbook upheld tribal sovereignty and political equality, as well as the principle of federal jurisdiction in Indian affairs.[47]

The impact of Cohen's legal interpretations of tribal authority depended on whether Indians voted for and made use of the IRA. Cohen had alienated many Indians, created administrative confusion, and offended members of Congress when he formulated complicated regulations that made tribal organization a prerequisite for obtaining IRA loans. Cohen's rules required Indians to vote in favor of the IRA, draft constitutions, and write charters of incorporation before they could borrow money from the revolving credit fund.[48]

This economic incentive encouraged some Indians to politically organize for their common welfare. It discriminated against landless Indians and individuals who resided in California, the Eastern United States, Oklahoma, and the Great Plains, where tribal authority had diminished. It meant that the $10 million IRA loan fund authorized by Congress for impoverished Indians would not be fully utilized.

By 1944, a total of 258 elections had been held on the IRA. This did not include Indian groups in Oklahoma or natives of Alaska, who were included under most provisions of the IRA in separate legislation. Ultimately 192 tribes, with a population of 130,704, voted to accept the IRA. This represented only 35 percent of the total Indian population of 368,819 because large tribes such as the Crow, Iroquois, and Navajos voted no. Eighty-eight tribes with a population of 100,445 wrote constitutions, whereas 68 tribes numbering 69,753 adopted charters of incorporation.[49]

Historians have shown that IRA tribal organization did not meet the needs of the diverse Indian population. Nor did it provide substantial economic progress, or create a durable political framework for the future. Instead, the IRA left a bitter legacy that led to new directions in federal Indian policy.[50]

Disillusioned with federally managed economic development and tribal self-rule, Indians left their reservations in record numbers during World War II. By the early 1940s, forty-three thousand Indians had moved from their homelands to find jobs in war-related industries, and another twenty thousand were serving in the armed forces. The Indian Bureau estimated that approximately 25 percent of the total Indian population had migrated away from reservations.[51]

This out-migration, Indian service in the military, and the loss of one million acres in Indian-held resources for wartime purposes further undermined New Deal efforts to promote a tribal alternative to assimilation. Under the Selective Service Act, Indians no longer were classified as a separate group of citizens. Secretary of War Henry S. Stimson confirmed their equal status when he dismissed Commissioner Collier's request to establish a separate Indian infantry division.[52]

Not only did World War II weaken Indian Bureau authority; it transformed Indian affairs. The experience Indians encountered on the homefront and in military service stimulated their interest in education and industrial training. Returning veterans worked for the resolution of tribal claims and equal citizenship rights, and they provided new perspectives on self-determination.[53]

The New York–based Association on American Indian Affairs (AAIA) responded to the renewed momentum toward assimilation generated by Indian participation in the war. In 1942, it recommended in a report to its board of directors that Congress should immediately settle tribal claims; otherwise, it suggested, Indians would continue to regard the government with skepticism. The AAIA report called for a radical reorganization of the Indian Bureau, with a transfer of its responsibilities to tribal leaders at all levels of administration. Furthermore, it called for educated Indians to assume leadership positions among their own tribes instead of at faraway reservations.[54]

Oliver LaFarge, AAIA president, emphasized that events surrounding World War II had fundamentally changed Indian life as hundreds of people entered the army or accepted war-related jobs. Unfortunately, out-of-step government officials still planned for the day before yesterday. They mistakenly assumed that a growing Indian population could live primarily on reservation resources.[55]

In 1944, the AAIA recommended a comprehensive reform program to encourage self-determination. It suggested that the key to understanding the current status of Indian citizenship was the acknowledgment that Indians had both tribal and individual rights. Tribal rights, based on treaties and occupancy of homelands, included self-rule, tax-free land, and federal protection from outside interference. Significant individual rights were the right to vote as citizens and the right of expatriation as wards or the freedom to abandon tribal relationships.[56]

In reference to the Indian New Deal, the AAIA warned against magic cure-all approaches to Indian policy. Contemporary Indians were the descendants of nations with diverse cultural patterns, and the AAIA suggested that the federal government should design its programs to meet the needs of particular groups. The AAIA asked government officials to respect the integrity of individual Indians, consult with them to encourage self-reliance and independence, and provide tribes with federal assistance to overcome economic, political, and social problems.[57]

In order to complete its trust obligation and encourage tribal self-rule, the AAIA called for the Indian Bureau to plan for its own liquidation. To encourage this process, the AAIA advocated the creation of a Planning and Development Branch to identify tribes that no longer required federal trusteeship and that could safely relinquish some federal controls, and those tribes that needed to retain their present relationship to the federal government. States also were encouraged to provide health, education, and law enforcement services to Indians as long as state authority did not jeopardize Indian rights.[58]

The Home Missions Council of North America, a New York–based interchurch group representing twenty-three denominations, agreed that it was time to redesign an outmoded reservation system. In 1943, the council had distributed two thousand copies of a booklet entitled *Indian Wardship*. Ghostwritten by G. E. E. Lindquist, an authority on Protestant mission work, it emphasized that wardship deprived Indian citizens in Arizona and New Mexico of their right to vote and Social Security benefits.[59]

Lindquist criticized self-styled friends of the Indian who sentimentally thought tribes should live forever in an idyllic communal paradise. He emphasized that Chief Justice Marshall's opinion that tribes resembled domestic dependent nations did not apply to contemporary society. IRA tribal governments bore no resemblance to pre-Columbian systems. Instead, they perpetuated wardship, reimposed federal control over acculturated Indians, and allowed the interior secretary to supervise every detail of tribal life.[60]

At House Committee on Indian Affairs hearings, Commissioner Collier acknowledged that tribal organization under the IRA had been unnecessarily complicated. The Indian Bureau also had failed to resolve Indian claims, problems with heirship land, and the plight of seventy-five thousand landless Indians. Furthermore, the 1933 Johnson-O'Malley Act, which authorized the Indian Bureau to contract with state governments for health, educational, and other social services, had not worked well on the Navajo Reservation.[61]

Collier urged Congress to restudy the entire trust relationship. He observed that approximately one-third of the Indian population could be removed from federal supervision. At the request of Representative Karl Mundt, Collier presented statistical information that divided Native Americans into three categories: 151,000 predominantly acculturated individuals, 124,000 semi-acculturated tribespeople, and 94,000 predominantly nonacculturated Indian persons. This testimony would encourage those individuals who wanted to emancipate Indians from wardship.[62]

After these hearings ended, Collier consulted with Indians about how to proceed. During the spring of 1944, Cherokee Ruth Muskrat Bronson, Rosebud Sioux Charlie Heacock, Nez Percé Archie Phinney, and other Native Americans employed at the Chicago Indian Bureau office worked to establish a national tribal association to better represent Indians before Congress. They met regularly with D'Arcy McNickle, a Cree, who had recently discussed the idea of a new pan-Indian organization with leaders of Southwestern tribes.[63]

Bronson publicized many of their concerns in a book, *Indians Are People Too,* in which she emphasized that federal wardship was debilitating on reservations where government officials intruded into all aspects of segregated Indian life. Bronson called on Congress to help Indians escape federal domination so they could enjoy the birthright of other Americans (pl. 4).[64]

Bronson was convinced that IRA tribal councils and cooperative enterprises had encouraged Indian initiative and self-confidence. Nevertheless, this revolutionary law had not lived up to its promise because Indians still lived on reservations run for—not by—them. She concluded that Native Americans must do their own thinking about the future and assume responsibility for high-level positions at the Indian Bureau.[65]

Mark Burns, a field representative from Minnesota, helped Bronson and other Indian leaders reach this goal. He drafted a provisional constitution for the National Congress of American Indians and notified these tribal leaders in October 1944 that this organization would hold its first meeting in Denver. Burns also made it clear that Indians who opposed the IRA were welcome to join the NCAI.[66]

In November, eighty Indian delegates from twenty-seven states attended the first NCAI convention in Denver. Many delegates were from an elite middle class that valued hard work, individual liberty, and private property. Successful participants in the non-Indian world, they wanted all Native Americans to have first-class citizenship, education, and material goods that enriched their lives. The delegates also represented acculturated tribes on the Great Plains. Only 25 percent had ties to the Indian Bureau.[67]

Four distinguished individuals influenced by Oklahoma pan-Indian movements served in early NCAI leadership positions: Ruth Muskrat Bronson; Dan Madrano, a Caddo member of the state legislature; Ben Dwight, a former chief of the Choctaw Nation who worked as special assistant to Governor Robert S. Kerr; and Napoleon Bonaparte Johnson, a Cherokee judge. In the NCAI keynote address, Dwight asked the delegates to unite behind common Indian concerns instead of Democratic, Republican, or Socialist agendas.[68]

The delegates responded by adopting a constitution and platform that emphasized both tribal and individual rights. The NCAI's mission under the constitution was to preserve Indian cultural values, uphold treaties, and promote the common welfare of all Native Americans. The platform recommended the protection of trust property, first-class citizenship, and the settlement of tribal claims. It also asked federal officials to consult with Native Americans and strictly follow the legal provisions of IRA charters.[69]

Napoleon Bonaparte Johnson, an attorney from Claremont, Oklahoma, was selected as the first NCAI president. A boyhood chum of Will Rogers, the well-known American humorist, Johnson earned his LL.B. degree from Cumberland University in Tennessee. His goals were to end romantic stereotypes of Native Americans, to achieve the progressive liquidation of the Indian Bureau, and to establish joint federal-state programs to help Indian citizens better manage their own affairs (pl. 5).[70]

Shortly after the convention adjourned, Ruth Muskrat Bronson accepted the position as NCAI executive secretary. Raised a Presbyterian, she taught English at Haskell Institute before moving to Washington DC to direct the Indian Bureau's guidance and placement program for college-age students. Under Bronson's able leadership, the NCAI established a legal aid service for tribes and lobbied before Congress on legislation that affected Indians.[71]

Johnson and Bronson helped redefine what Indian self-determination meant in the postwar era. But they did not repudiate the IRA or solicitors' rulings that reaffirmed the inherent sovereign powers of Indian communities to organize tribal governments and courts to survive modernity. Both valued sociological jurisprudence because it guaranteed tribes a measured separatism on their reservation homelands under federal protection.[72]

Yet by 1945, it was clear to almost everyone that the New Deal promise of self-rule was still not a reality. The birth of the NCAI, the recommendations of the AAIA, and Collier's difficult relations with Congress brought about a growing awareness that continued federal trusteeship over all Indians was inappropriate. Especially troublesome was the continued federal paternalism associated with wardship, widespread poverty in Indian country, and disrespect for rights guaranteed by treaties. Only tribal activism, an awakened public conscience, and a responsive Congress could overcome this impasse. The first major effort to address this issue was a successful drive by Indian groups, the NCAI, and federal officials to create an Indian Claims Commission.

2

SETTLING TRIBAL CLAIMS

The basis of these claims settlements emanates from solemn treaties entered into between the government and Indian tribes. . . . The existence of $1.6 billion in claims . . . serves to hold the Indian in his present status on the reservation through fear that separation from the tribe might deprive him of any share he might have in a settlement. The disposition of these claims will go a long way toward solving the problem of wardship. STATEMENT OF NAPOLEON BONAPARTE JOHNSON, PRESIDENT, NATIONAL CONGRESS OF AMERICAN INDIANS, 28 MARCH 1945

At the conclusion of World War II, a diverse group of tribal leaders, claims attorneys, members of Congress, and government officials joined forces to secure passage of the Indian Claims Commission Act. As one historian has observed, there were those who believed this legislation would enhance tribal authority and force the United States to honor treaty obligations. Other people, however, viewed a claims settlement as the final step toward detribalization and the termination of federal wardship.[1]

On 13 August 1946, representatives from several tribes attended an impressive White House ceremony to watch President Harry S. Truman sign a bill that created the Indian Claims Commission. Distinguished guests who worked for years to redress historic grievances attended this event: Lawrence Appah, Ute; Peter Beauchamp, Arikara; Reginald Curry, Ute; James Frechette, Menominee; Boyd Jackson, Klamath; Peter H. Kennerly, Blackfeet; D'Arcy McNickle, Cree; and Julius Murray, Ute.[2]

Napoleon Bonaparte Johnson, the president of the NCAI, also witnessed the signing of the claims bill. After returning home to Claremore, Oklahoma, he sent an open letter to tribes throughout the United States, warning that this important law would be worthless unless tribal attorneys coordinated their claims work. He also emphasized the importance of presenting cases that did not jeopardize subsequent claims by setting bad precedents.[3]

The NCAI addressed this problem at its November 1946 convention in Oklahoma City. There, tribal delegates passed a resolution that authorized Johnson to accept grants and voluntary contributions to establish a Legal Aid Service at the nation's capital. It helped attorneys locate archival evidence to prepare claims for indigent tribes.[4]

Between 1945 and 1951, the NCAI received $32,000 from the Robert Marshall Civil Liberties Trust. This money was used to send Ruth Muskrat Bronson, the NCAI executive secretary, to Alaska to defend Indian possessory rights and to retain James E. Curry as legal counsel. The NCAI promised the Marshall Trust that its Legal Aid Service would also prepare a model constitution and charter to help organized tribes use their claims awards more efficiently.[5]

The NCAI balanced this commitment with support for Indian groups in California, Oklahoma, Oregon, and elsewhere that viewed the Indian Claims Commission Act as an opportunity to end their wardship status, distribute tribal funds on a per capita basis, and use money from claims awards to manage their affairs under state jurisdiction. The bipartisan coalition in Congress that endorsed claims legislation favored this second approach to self-determination. President Truman also was convinced that a claims settlement would encourage Indian citizens to more actively participate in the civic and economic life of postwar America.

As early as 1855, Congress gave Indians the right to bring cases before the Court of Claims, which reviewed litigation based on federal law or contract. Congress withdrew this right for Indians to sue the government in 1863 because several tribes had joined the Confederation of American States during the Civil War. Indian claims remained unresolved until 1881, when Congress permitted the Choctaws and other tribes to request separate jurisdictional bills that enabled them to adjudicate their grievances before the Court of Claims.[6]

Indians and their attorneys gained valuable legal experience before this tribunal. They were frustrated, however, by delays of more than ten years in persuading Congress to pass jurisdictional bills prior to presenting their cases. The court also dismissed meritorious claims based on moral fraud, loss of wildlife, and lawsuits predicated on the immemorial possession of aboriginal land because of technical lack of jurisdiction.[7]

The number of claims increased dramatically after 1924 when Congress passed the Indian Citizenship Act. During the next three years, tribes submitted thirty-seven cases before the Court of Claims. Congress responded by appropriating additional funds so the General Accounting Office could set up an Indian Tribal Claims Section to compile data on new litigation against the United States.[8]

In 1928, the Institute of Government Research published the Meriam report, which criticized the handling of Indian claims. This report emphasized that unsettled claims had a negative psychological effect on Indians' ability to run their own affairs. Many individuals refused to work, cooperate with federal officials, or make future plans as long as their claims remained unresolved. The Meriam report tried to end this impasse by recommending that the secretary of interior appoint a staff of nonpartisan legal experts to investigate all remaining claims and identify which cases Congress should forward to the Court of Claims.[9]

Congress did not follow this advice, but it upheld the principle that treaties were legal contracts. In 1929, Congress permitted twenty-five thousand California Indians to submit a claim of $12.8 million for land lost after the Senate refused to ratify eighteen treaties in 1852. In subsequent years, F. G. Collett, a leader of the Indians of California, Inc., raised $180,000 for the prosecution of these claims. Collett and Adam Castillo, president of the Mission Indian Federation, worked sixteen years before the Court of Claims awarded California Indians $5 million in December 1944. Castillo then filed another lawsuit to secure over $17 million in claims for nontreaty Indians.[10]

The Blackfeet, Klamath, Paiute, Shoshone, and Ute tribes hired Ernest Wilkinson, a Washington DC attorney, to present their cases before the Court of Claims. In 1935, the Blackfeet won a claims award of over $6 million, but gratuitous offsets for federal administrative services lowered the amount to $622,000. In 1938, the Klamath of Oregon won a settlement of $5.3 million for reservation land conveyed to a third party without their consent. This and other court decisions, which included back interest payments, shocked officials at the Department of Justice. In 1939, they initiated the Indian Law Survey to provide a more vigorous defense against future tribal claims.[11]

In Oklahoma there was widespread support among sixty-one thousand Indians from thirty-two tribes for a claims settlement. Many of these groups wanted the federal government to compensate them for the loss of land, removal, and mismanagement of tribal funds. In 1934, the Five Civilized Tribes established the National Indian Confederacy and selected Joseph Bruner, a Creek, as its chief. Bruner was well known for his work on behalf of Indian claims in Oklahoma.[12]

Bruner was also elected president of the American Indian Federation (AIF) at Gallup, New Mexico. The AIF recruited about four thousand members from thirty-three tribes throughout the United States. Its constitution called for intertribal cooperation to defend the rights of Indian citizens. Bruner spent much of his time in the nation's capital lobbying before the House and Senate Indian Affairs Committees to settle over $1 billion in tribal claims.[13]

In April 1939, the AIF persuaded Senator Elmer Thomas of Oklahoma and Congressman Usher L. Burdick of North Dakota to introduce bills that provided a claims settlement for approximately thirty thousand enrolled individuals who owned land allotments and their heirs. Under this legislation, each Indian and his or her heirs were entitled to $3,000 and had to agree to accept the full responsibilities of American citizenship. Under the Thomas bill, money could also be claimed for dead ancestors.[14] The Department of Interior estimated that if Congress passed this legislation, the government would be liable for nearly $10 billion.[15]

Indians had one year to register for this proposed settlement. The AIF immediately began a campaign to collect $1 for each $3,000 claimed to help eligible Indians apply for benefits. Nearly five thousand people in Oklahoma alone gave money to the federation.[16] These bills, which did not pass Congress, were also popular in North and South Dakota, where the Sioux had instituted twenty-two lawsuits for awards of more than $278 million before the Court of Claims. Undeterred by this legislative setback, the AIF continued to petition President Roosevelt and the chairs of the House and Senate Indian Affairs Committees for an immediate and final claims settlement with all tribes.[17]

The extraordinary persistence by Indians to resolve their claims had a positive outcome. As early as March 1935, claims bills sponsored by the Interior Department were introduced in the House and Senate. In 1940, both the Democratic and Republican platforms called for a final settlement of Indian claims. Senator Elmer Thomas responded to this bipartisan sentiment by introducing legislation to create a claims commission that functioned as an agency independent of the executive branch of government. This initiative failed because of the refusal of the Department of Justice to exclude offsets for gratuitous government expenses, opposition from the Budget Bureau, and continued resistance from President Franklin D. Roosevelt, who favored federal social programs for contemporary and future generations of Indians as a way to compensate them for past wrongs.[18]

The issue of Indian claims surfaced again in March 1943 when a bipartisan coalition from the House Indian Affairs Committee held hearings on House Resolution 166 to determine what laws were required to reflect the changed status of American Indians. Henry M. Jackson, a Democrat from Washington, James O'Connor, a Democrat from Montana, and Karl E. Mundt, a Republican from South Dakota, disagreed with the position taken by President Roosevelt after an investigation of Indian affairs. They were convinced that a claims bill, rather than an expanded federal guardianship, was the best way to address the concerns of veterans and other Indians living in the modern world.[19]

This assessment was based on the knowledge that sixty-eight tribes had filed $1.4 billion in claims before the Court of Claims. The court had allowed recoveries for thirty-two tribes and awarded $37 million in net judgments that included substantial back interest payments. Eleven other tribes also had cases pending before the court totaling $56 million.[20]

During the summer of 1944, Jackson, O'Connor, and Mundt spent four weeks visiting states with large Indian populations to hear the testimony of over 250 Indian leaders. They learned that many tribes had gained valuable experience under the IRA even though all important decisions by tribal governments were subject to approval by the secretary of interior. Indian progress toward self-determination also had been slowed by inadequate land resources and economic opportunities, educational policies that perpetuated tribal life instead of promoting acculturation, the diversion of appropriations for tribes into administrative channels, and the failure to train and recruit Indian superintendents.[21]

One of the questions that Mundt, Jackson, and O'Connor asked was whether Congress should resolve litigation through the Court of Claims or a commission. Most Indians favored a special tribunal because of how long it took to adjudicate cases before the Court of Claims. This testimony convinced committee members that outmoded claims procedures kept Indians on reservations waiting for future cash awards. They believed the path to Indian independence would be blocked for the next one hundred years unless Congress mandated a different way to settle claims.[22]

In December 1944, the committee published House Report 2091, which called on the Seventy-ninth Congress to create a claims commission with at least one Indian representative. This commission would file and consider all moral and legal claims submitted prior to a December 1950 deadline, determine and forward all legal claims with offsets to the Court of Claims for final settlement, and send meritorious claims with recommendations for cash awards to Congress.[23]

The National Congress of American Indians supported this recommendation. Shortly after the NCAI's November 1944 meeting in Denver, Napoleon Bonaparte Johnson asked the interior secretary to call a conference because of widespread dissatisfaction with the administration of Indian affairs. The NCAI Executive Council also met with the House and Senate Committees on Indian Affairs, the General Federation of Women's Clubs, Association on American Indian Affairs, and other groups to discuss the issue of tribal claims.[24]

At its first meeting, the NCAI executive council drafted an Indian Claims Commission bill. Congressman William Stigler, of Choctaw-Chickasaw ancestry, introduced this legislation. H.R. 1198 would create an Indian Claims Commission, which had the authority to determine tribal claims of every nature against the United States. These claims could not be excluded by any rule of law, statue of limitations, or laches. The commission, in determining the merits of any claim, had to offset previous gratuitous payments made by the United States.[25]

A chief commissioner and two associate commissioners appointed by the president would administer the Indian Claims Commission. Under this legislative proposal, one member of the commission had to be a member of the bar in good standing and at least one person an enrolled member of a recognized group of Indians. Tribes had five years to file claims, could select attorneys of their own choice, and appeal all questions of law to the United States Supreme Court. The commission was required to terminate its proceedings within ten years to encourage the prompt resolution of all claims.[26]

Stigler not only supported claims legislation but also worked behind the scenes to discredit tribal self-rule under IRA and encourage Indian emancipation from wardship. Stigler approved an article before it was submitted by O. K. Armstrong to the *Reader's Digest* entitled "Set the American Indians Free." This essay also was endorsed by Representative Francis Case of South Dakota and by Senators Dennis Chavez of New Mexico, Harlan J. Bushfield of South Dakota, and Albert Grorud, the clerk of the Senate Committee on Indian Affairs.[27]

Armstrong sharply criticized the IRA because it revived ancient customs, imposed a collectivist economic system on tribes, and subjected them to regulations that increased federal paternalism. He recommended that Congress declare that the twenty-two thousand Indian veterans, persons of less than one-quarter Indian blood, and high school graduates were competent to run their own affairs. Furthermore, Armstrong called for the bureau to help Indians become self-supporting citizens during the time it remained in existence.[28]

The House Indian Affairs Committee recommended a claims commission for two basic reasons. First, there was the expectation that once claims were settled, the federal government could downsize the Indian Bureau, remove Indians from federal guardianship, and let them independently manage their own affairs.[29] Members of the House were constantly being asked to introduce jurisdictional bills that allowed tribes to appear before the Court of Claims. The General Accounting Office had spent over a million dollars to prepare Indian claims legislation, and members of Congress were reluctant to approve these complicated bills without additional information. It was simply much easier to authorize a commission to determine the obligation of the federal government toward Indians.[30]

Furthermore, the NCAI endorsed the creation of a claims commission. Johnson, the NCAI president, reminded the House Committee in a letter that claims emanated from solemn treaties. At a time when the world was fighting a war to uphold national and international integrity, he thought it appropriate to carry out legal and moral obligations on the home front. For Johnson, the obstacle of federal guardianship over Indian wards would never be removed unless the government dealt with this issue. Unresolved claims also had the undesirable effect of tying Indians to reservations while they waited patiently for large cash awards.[31]

Other Indians from Oklahoma attended hearings of the House Indian Affairs Committee to testify in favor of Stigler's claims bill. W. W. Short, president of the Choctaw and Chickasaw Confederation, emphasized that enrolled members of the Five Civilized Tribes should have the opportunity to settle claims before they died. Short believed that only 10 percent of the restricted Chickasaw full-bloods and 15–20 percent of the enrolled Choctaws were still under the rules and regulations of the Interior Department. Therefore, it made sense to settle claims and release Indians who wanted to join mainstream society.[32]

Ben Dwight, an Indian attorney for the Choctaw Nation, told the House Indian Affairs Committee that unsettled claims had hamstrung the Indian Bureau. Older Indians especially were upset that the federal government had broken its promise to settle claims after they accepted land allotment and state jurisdiction. Dwight agreed with Short that once claims were resolved, Congress could release large numbers of Indians from wardship. He estimated that only twenty-five hundred out of twenty-two thousand enrolled Choctaws required government supervision.[33]

Paul N. Niebell, the attorney for the Creek and Seminole Nations, complained to the committee about his experience before the Court of Claims. Since 1930, he had filed twenty-six claims for erroneous survey of land, the value of land excluded from treaties, and maladministration. In most cases, it was impossible to adjudicate these claims because of technical defenses of law used by the Justice Department.[34]

Felix Cohen, the assistant solicitor of the Interior Department, then used a map to show committee members tribal land cessions. He indicated that except for parts of California, Louisiana, and eastern Texas, where Indian rights had been taken away prior to U.S. sovereignty, there were either treaties or other agreements for obtaining every square mile of the country.[35] He estimated that Indians received between $500 million and $1 billion for this property. Cohen thought that, by and large, Indians had made reasonable transactions. The issue of claims arose after the transfer of this real estate because of subsequent government violations of treaties and other agreements.[36]

After Cohen completed his presentation, Ernest L. Wilkinson, a Washington DC claims attorney, testified that Congress had no alternative but to establish a claims commission. Wilkinson, who represented the Northwestern Shoshone tribe of Idaho, cited a recent Supreme Court decision to illustrate his point. The court had voted 5–4 against the Shoshone appeal from the Court of Claims to receive compensation for land taken subsequent to a 1863 treaty that allowed immigrants and gold miners right-of-way through their territory. Three justices held that the treaty of 1863 was not a recognition of Indian title. Two other justices, in a concurring opinion, did not consider treaties contracts and asked Congress to resolve this matter.[37]

Secretary of the Interior Harold L. Ickes also endorsed the claims bill. He cited the 1928 Meriam report to remind committee members that the expectation of large claims awards made it extremely difficult for the government to secure Indian cooperation. The secretary urged Congress to find an alternative to the unsatisfactory procedure where the Court of Claims dismissed Indian moral claims based on alleged fraud and duress for technical reasons (pl. 6.).[38]

Ickes offered several amendments to H.R. 1198, the most important of which required the claims commission to notify tribes, bands, and other recognizable Indian groups of the bill's provisions, to ask all known Indian groups to file claims, and to create an Investigation Division, which would thoroughly search for evidence concerning each tribal claim and make this data available to Indians. Claimants were also allowed the right to appeal questions of law to the Court of Claims instead of the Supreme Court to ensure a speedy resolution of claims disputes.[39]

One of these amendments would later cause considerable controversy. Ickes insisted that under the Indian Reorganization Act tribes were entitled to select legal counsel of their choice. Nonetheless, the interior secretary by law had to approve the attorney contracts of those tribes not organized under IRA.[40]

The committee accepted these amendments along with others made by Cohen and Wilkinson after a two-day conference. The first revision eliminated language in the bill that made the commission subject to the jurisdiction of the executive branch. Wilkinson believed it was inappropriate for either the Interior or Justice Departments to tell the commission how to decide particular cases. Under this amendment, the Indian Claims Commission was structured as a court so it would follow an adjudicated rather than negotiated settlement of claims.[41]

Cohen and Wilkinson also inserted in the bill a provision calling for offsets that used the same standard for Indian and non-Indian claimants. In previous cases, the Court of Claims had discriminated against Indians by deducting gratuitous expenditures. Henry Jackson, chair of the committee, warned that members of Congress might object to this amendment because it encouraged large claims settlements. Wilkinson replied perceptively that the reasonableness of claims would be determined by the persons President Truman appointed to run the Indian Claims Commission.[42]

That raised the important question of whether one member of the commission should be an Indian. North Dakota Representative Charles R. Robertson doubted whether there were any Indian attorneys in his state who could qualify for an appointment. Arizona's John Murdock indicated that this problem existed in the Southwest but not in Oklahoma, where important public officials were of Indian ancestry.[43]

At this critical juncture, Cohen contradicted his own commitment to the principle of Indian self-determination. Instead of vigorously supporting the idea of having an Indian on the commission, Cohen pointed out that in Oklahoma persons born since the final roll sometimes were not considered tribal members. He also believed that successful Indian attorneys probably would prefer to remain in private practice.[44]

After listening to Cohen's testimony, the House committee struck the provision that required an Indian to serve on the commission. It did mandate, in a bipartisan spirit, that no more than two commissioners could belong to the same political party. These and other amendments were incorporated into a revised claims bill that was introduced as H.R. 4497 for future consideration.[45]

In the meantime, Secretary Ickes put pressure on Harold D. Smith, director of the Budget Bureau, to approve establishment of a claims commission. This would be Ickes's last major effort on behalf of Indians before he resigned on 16 February 1946 in a dispute with President Truman over the appointment of Edwin Pauley as Undersecretary of the Navy.[46] Ickes sharply criticized Smith for repeatedly blocking efforts to reach a claims settlement, even when it was obvious that Indians had been exploited by worthless treaties. He argued that it would be a national disgrace to place the stigma of presidential disapproval on legislation that brought justice to the country's oldest national minority.[47]

Shortly after Ickes's departure, Smith explained to Truman why he opposed previous claims bills and the reason for changing his mind. He warned the president that if Stigler's bill passed, it would cost the government millions of dollars. On the other hand, the House Rules Committee recently had approved Resolution 511, which authorized the entire House to consider H.R. 4497. Smith responded to this political development by proposing amendments to the bill that dealt with offsets and the character of claims to limit cash awards.[48]

Truman told Smith to draft necessary amendments to the claims bill and make it part of the administration's program. The president, however, requested a careful analysis of this measure prior to congressional approval because he did not want the federal government to reopen settled claims. Truman also asked for reassurance that the government was not going to "unloose a Frankenstein" and create unintended havoc in Indian affairs.[49]

On 26 May 1946, the House convened as a Committee of the Whole to reach a final determination on H.R. 4497. Congressmen Jackson, Mundt, and Stigler from the Committee on Indian Affairs led the discussion on this bill. They made a tacit alliance with the NCAI, Indians in California and Oklahoma, as well as with other tribes that favored a claims settlement to end or lessen their dependence on the federal government.[50]

Jackson observed that treaties signed prior to 1871, when the Senate treated tribes as domestic dependent nations, were a version of international law. Nonetheless, he showed antipathy toward contemporary tribal self-determination by not mentioning Margold's 1934 opinion that tribes still had inherent powers of self-government, Cohen's *Handbook on Federal Indian Law*, or the numerous tribal constitutions ratified under IRA. Jackson did note that it cost Congress $30 million annually to fund the Indian Bureau and only $26 million for the legislative branch of the U.S. government. He was convinced that once Congress settled claims, thousands of Indians would abandon their tribal heritage, leave impoverished reservations, and enjoy the substance instead of the shadow of citizenship.[51]

Mundt believed that Indians would refuse to detribalize unless there was a just and permanent solution of their claims. For him, it made no sense to spend millions of dollars each year for the salaries of paternalistic government employees who were doing for Indians what they should do for themselves. Once tribes had their day in court, Congress could sharply curtail appropriations for the Indian Bureau and end supervision over people who were ready to become "self-respecting citizens instead of puppets of an endless bureaucracy."[52]

Stigler thought a claims settlement would bring the dawn of a new era for American Indians. H.R. 4497 guaranteed them citizenship rights under the Fifth Amendment to the U.S. Constitution, which states that no person shall be deprived of life, liberty, or property without due process of law. The passage of this claims bill also would enable many Indians to follow the example of the Klamath Indians, New York Indians, and Wind River Shoshone. After these tribes won cash awards from the Court of Claims, Congress lessened their dependence on the federal government by minimizing or eliminating gratuitous appropriations.[53]

Persuaded by these arguments, House members approved the Indian Claims Commission bill and sent it to the Senate Committee on Indian Affairs. Most of the testimony before the Senate committee during July 1946 concerned technical matters of law and amendments proposed by the Department of Justice and the Budget Bureau. Commissioner William Brophy also was given an opportunity to discuss his views about Indian claims.

Brophy linked a claims settlement to the gradual withdrawal of federal services for Indians who were willing to surrender their tribal membership. He also gave a deferential reply when Oklahoma Senator E. H. Moore wondered whether it would be possible to abolish the Indian Bureau after Congress created a claims commission. The commissioner did not envision this scenario in the foreseeable future but acknowledged that Congress, not the executive branch, must answer this question.[54]

Next, committee members considered amendments proposed by Attorney General Tom C. Clark, who feared that H.R. 4497 made the United States liable for large sums of money. The attorney general recommended that the Senate eliminate the phrase that no claim should be excluded because it was barred by law or any rule of equity. He also wanted Congress to reject litigation based on moral grounds and adhere to a 1935 statute authorizing the government to offset the gratuitous expenditures in claims awards.[55]

Brophy tried to block these amendments by asking whether Congress should mandate the appointment of an Indian on the claims commission to help determine awards. Senator Elmer Thomas, the chair of the committee, ignored Brophy's question. Furthermore, he abruptly adjourned the Senate hearings to show contempt for the Indian Bureau and limit its influence.[56]

When the committee reconvened, senators listened to the testimony of two individuals who favored emancipation from federal wardship. Wade Crawford, a Klamath Indian and former superintendent, warned that in the past, government officials had used tribal funds for political patronage. He asked Congress to carefully regulate attorney claims contracts and prohibit the secretary of interior from using tribal funds to prosecute claims without prior Indian approval.[57]

F. G. Collett, who represented the Indians of California, Inc., disliked section 6 of the claims bill, which directed the federal government to deposit cash awards in the U.S. Treasury. The Indian Bureau then could use the money for land purchase, home construction, and other federal services. Collett reminded the members of Congress that California Indians had won a $5 million settlement in the Court of Claims. They favored per capita payments and the freedom to manage their own financial affairs.[58]

Collett also thought it was important to protect the legal rights of one-half to two-thirds of the nontreaty Indian population of California. He asked if nontreaty Indians could file a claim under the proposed bill. Government solicitors, who attended this hearing, gave a tentative but favorable reply.[59]

The Senate committee then reviewed amendments proposed by the Justice Department. No formal decision was reached before the committee went into executive session. At this closed meeting, the committee made several amendments to House Resolution 4497 that limited the rights of Indians before the claims commission. This necessitated the convening of a conference committee between the managers of the House and Senate during July 1946.[60]

The conferees agreed to amendments, in response to Senate concerns, that worked to the disadvantage of Indians. The most important ones limited claims to those arising in law or equity and reduced six classes of claims to five by making it impossible to file claims for breach of duty committed by officers and agents of the United States. They also made available to the U.S. government all defenses, except statute of limitations, laches, and claims based on standards of fair and honorable dealings.[61]

The House and Senate conferees did take Indian interests into consideration by defining what offsets could be used in claims awards. They prohibited the Indian Claims Commission from deducting government money spent on Indian removal, as well as health, education, and other administrative expenses. The commission, however, was authorized to offset expenditures for direct Indian benefits such as land purchase.[62]

In the House-Senate proposed bill, the Court of Claims was allowed to dispose of all pending cases, but it had to consider tribal claims on the basis of fair and honorable dealings and had to follow the rules of the new claims commission concerning offsets. Indians could appeal commission rulings to the Court of Claims if the rulings contained errors in law or were not supported by substantial evidence.[63]

The members of the House and Senate joint committee encountered a chilly reception when they met with the president at the White House to discuss the Indian Claims Commission bill. Truman, who indicated that he still had not made up his mind whether to sign this legislation, wanted more information about how much an Indian claims settlement would cost the U.S. government.[64]

In August 1946, Wyoming Senator Joseph O'Mahoney met with Truman to convince him to not veto the bill. The senator emphasized that it was unwarranted in the light of past experience to conclude that the claims commission would give Indian claimants extravagant amounts of money. O'Mahoney told the president that a claims commission would encourage Indians to become less dependent on the federal government. He also predicted that it would enable Congress to drastically reduce the size of the Indian Bureau.[65]

President Truman also listened to his new interior secretary, Julius A. Krug, who had little background or experience in Indian affairs. Krug was raised by a Wisconsin immigrant family that settled in the United States to escape authoritarian rule in Bismark's Germany. A tactful but firm administrator, Krug showed more interest in efficient government than social reform.[66]

In the spring of 1946, Krug received hundreds of letters from Indians who favored a claims settlement. This intense lobbying effort by the National Congress of American Indians persuaded Krug to support H.R. 4497.[67] The secretary of interior believed that claims awards would provide many tribes with the financial resources to run their own affairs without federal assistance. He also thought Congress would cut appropriations for tribes in proportion to the size of their claims settlements.[68]

Krug told Truman that during the last fifty years the Court of Claims had awarded tribes $47 million. These claims settlements were not an unnecessary expenditure. Congress had used claims awards to purchase land and livestock to help tribes support themselves.[69]

Krug also reminded Truman of important political realities. Members of Congress from western states generally viewed this measure as the most significant Indian legislation enacted in more than a decade. It fulfilled platform pledges made by both parties. The international community viewed the bill as the touchstone of U.S. sincerity in dealing fairly and honorably with small nations. Furthermore, Commander Clark M. Clifford, a member of the White House staff, had arranged a signing ceremony so the president could support his good friends in Congress.[70]

President Truman signed the Indian Claims Commission bill on 13 August 1946. He told the American people that this legislation removed a lingering discrimination against First Americans. Since the Northwest Ordinance of 1787, the government had pledged respect for Indian rights. Instead of confiscating Indian property, it had purchased, for approximately $800 million, 90 percent of the land from tribes that once owned the continent. Truman believed it would have been a miracle, in the largest real estate transaction in history, if mistakes were not made in carrying out the precise terms of treaties. To correct this situation, the United States would submit all controversies to the judgment of an impartial tribunal (pl. 7).[71]

Truman predicted the Indian Claims Commission Act would inaugurate a new era for Indian citizens. They had proved by their loyalty during World War II the wisdom of a national policy built on the principle of fair dealing. The president hoped that a final claims settlement would encourage Indians to find community in the nation instead of the tribe and to fully share in the prosperity of America's postwar capitalist market economy.[72]

Whether the Indian Claims Commission marked a new era depended to a great extent on the persons President Truman appointed to the commission. In November 1946, Napoleon Bonaparte Johnson wrote an open letter to NCAI tribes that discussed this important issue. He warned that a tragedy would occur if Truman chose men ignorant of Indian matters. Johnson encouraged tribal leaders to contact the president and urge him to appoint commissioners of unquestioned honesty with a thorough knowledge of Indian administration, law, or history.[73]

The NCAI president sent this letter because rumors had appeared in newspapers that President Truman would appoint claims commissioners without experience in Indian affairs. Two months later, Ruth Muskrat Bronson, the NCAI executive secretary, once again reminded tribal leaders to get in touch with the president before he selected people with no understanding of Indian treaties. The claims commission, like any other court, would be governed by precedent. A series of bad decisions by inexperienced commissioners would nullify the whole purpose of the claims law.[74]

By January 1947, the White House staff had compiled a list of thirty nominees for the claims commission. Cohen was the front-runner, with letters of recommendation from all the major Indian rights organizations, the NCAI, Secretary of the Interior Krug, Undersecretary of the Interior Oscar L. Chapman, and Indian Commissioner William Brophy. In second place was Johnson, who received endorsements from Senator James E. Murray of Montana, Joseph Bruner, head of the American Indian Federation, and numerous people from Oklahoma.[75]

President Truman turned down an historic opportunity to appoint an expert in Indian law or a distinguished Cherokee attorney to head the claims commission. Instead, he followed Speaker Sam Rayburn's advice and chose Texas Democrat Edgar Witt, a lawyer who had recently chaired the Mexican Claims Commission, which had made settlements favorable to the United States. The president followed Senator Hugh Butler's recommendation in picking William McKinley Holt, an attorney from Lincoln, Nebraska, for the required appointment of a republican commissioner. Truman's other choice, Louis O'Marr, the attorney general of Wyoming, was nominated by Senator Joseph O'Mahoney.[76]

The Senate unanimously confirmed Truman's three appointments. During its first year of existence, the Indian Claims Commission hired employees and formulated administrative guidelines. It had a light workload because most tribal attorneys waited for the commissioners to set legal precedent before filing their claims. Consequently, the commission used only $64,000 of its $150,000 budget.[77]

When Congress authorized the commission to organize an Investigation Division as part of the claims process, it recognized that Indian claimants had legitimate grievances against the government. Witt did not use this division to reach a negotiated settlement with tribes. Instead, he structured the commission as a court and followed administrative policies used by the Court of Claims. This decision encouraged Indians and their attorneys to develop an adversarial relationship with the Justice Department.[78]

The first case before the Indian Claims Commission involved the Western Cherokees of Oklahoma, who asked for compensation because government negotiators had not acted honorably in the drafting of a treaty. The commissioners cited the principle of *res judicata* to make the Western Cherokees' prior judgment before the Court of Claims binding in a second lawsuit. This attempt to limit Indian claims was reversed on appeal before the Court of Claims. The court ruled that the 1946 claims law created new causes of action against the United States.[79]

In 1948, Attorney General Tom Clark asked Mastin G. White, the solicitor of the Interior Department, to interpret the term "identifiable group of Indians" within the meaning of the Claims Act to limit grounds for litigation. White ruled that "identifiable" meant tribes or bands whose political existence was recognized by Congress or the executive branch.[80]

This legal chicanery violated the rights of approximately one hundred thousand people who were not notified of their right to file claims as required by law. It prevented officials at the Indian Bureau from using a 1945 survey by the Library of Congress that identified Indians residing in the eastern half of the United States. This survey listed over sixty Indian groups—on the Atlantic seaboard, on the gulf coast from Florida to Texas, and in certain midwestern states—that still maintained varying degrees of cultural identity after three hundred years of war, disease, and miscegenation.[81]

White's opinion had far-reaching consequences. The commissioners relied on this ruling to dismiss the claims of Apaches who alleged unfair treatment at Fort Sill because of the actions of Geronimo. In a precedent-setting decision, the commission dismissed Apache claims on jurisdictional grounds. It sided with Justice Department solicitors by ruling that the commissioners would consider only the grievances of recognized tribes or bands. This allowed the claims commission to sidestep its obligation to review individual claims cases based on moral considerations and litigation concerning the negative impact of land allotment.[82]

The commission also tried to dismiss the claims of nontreaty Indians of California because they were not a single identifiable group. In this case, the commission ignored the significance of tribal organization by small California bands under IRA. The Mission Indian Federation and other California pan-Indian organizations protested this unpopular decision. In 1950, the Court of Claims reversed the commission's ruling on appeal. The court found that under the 1946 statute it was the intent of Congress to enlarge the number of tribal groups entitled to present claims.[83]

Most claims were filed a few months before August 1951, the end of the five-year registration period. The commission had the formidable task of hearing 852 claims cases. These lawsuits alleged that the United States had failed to honor its treaty commitments, bought Indian land below market value, and mismanaged tribal funds. By the time President Truman left office, the commission's narrow interpretation of the law had resulted in the dismissal of 34 of these claims and the approval of only five awards worth $6.4 million to Choctaw, Chickasaw, Creek, and Kaw claimants.[84]

This legal tactic angered Indians, who had spent over $1 million in preparing claims cases. Their expectations included the appointment of an Indian to the commission to investigate and determine claims, scrupulous respect for treaty rights, and generous cash settlements to remedy past wrongs. Only if this happened would tribes have the financial means to eliminate wardship and become self-reliant.[85]

The efforts by Bruner, Collett, Crawford, Johnson, and other persons to usher in a new era for tribal people lost momentum when President Truman refused to appoint an Indian to the Indian Claims Commission, ensuring that federal officials would continue to formulate policies without Indian consent. Furthermore, once it became clear that awards would be dismissed, delayed, or smaller than expected, the U.S. government encountered growing criticism from Indians.

The promise of self-determination was broken when Congress withheld final claims payments. Federal officials, not Indians, would decide when and how to distribute cash awards. This caused friction between people who favored per capita payments so that individual Indians could become independent citizens and those who intended to use claims money to encourage tribal self-government and economic development.

The Utes in Utah encountered this problem. In July 1950, the Court of Claims awarded these Indians $32 million based on litigation concerning unsold tribal land. Senator Arthur V. Watkins insisted that the Utes not spend their cash awards for tribal self-determination under an antiquated reservation system. The senator used his legislative power, as chair of the Indian Affairs Subcommittee, to withhold the distribution of claims money until the Utes severed their ties with the federal government. This intolerant policy of forced assimilation violated the spirit of the Indian Claims Commission Act. It made the Utes more rather than less dependent on other people for their survival.[86]

The resolution of claims meant different things to different people. Ickes, Cohen, and other New Deal administrators anticipated that Indians would use their cash awards to subsidize the cost of operating modern tribal governments. For President Truman, Senator Watkins, and NCAI leaders, the settlement of claims was an attractive alternative to centralized planning by the Indian Bureau. They believed that this agency would never have adequate resources to properly support the administrative overhead of tribal governments or provide a growing Indian population with a decent standard of living.

There were other events besides the Ute experience that confirmed President Truman's prediction that a claims settlement would bring unforeseen consequences. Instead of filing claims before the commission, the Navajos insisted that the government honor the Treaty of 1868, which promised schools for their children. James Curry, the NCAI legal counsel, not only assisted tribes with claims litigation, but he also signed general counsel contracts to defend the inherent power of tribes to self-determination. Another unexpected development was the solicitation of claims contracts by rival law firms and a controversy over the right of Indians to choose independent legal counsel. This dispute raised complex questions about tribal authority and the federal government's proper role as guardian.

A controversy also arose over section 2 of the Claims Act, which directed the commissioners to hear and determine the claims of identifiable groups of Indians in Alaska. Claims were allowed for the U.S. government's taking of land that was owned or occupied by Indians without payment or just compensation. The commission relied on the 1941 Supreme Court decision *United States v. Santa Fe Railroad Company*, which ruled that exclusive occupancy and tribal use in a definable territory from time immemorial was required by Indians to prove aboriginal possessory rights.[87]

The NCAI used its Legal Aid Service to defend the rights of Alaska's Haida and Tlingit Indians. At stake was Indian control of offshore fishing grounds, access to timber in the Tongass National Forest, and the question of whether additional reservations should be created under the 1936 Alaska Reorganization Act (ARA). The Indian Claims Commission could not resolve these complex issues because of its limited jurisdiction. This worked to the advantage of high-level government officials who valued resource development by private enterprise more than Indian legal rights under ARA constitutions and charters. Their disregard of the inherent power of Indian communities to control local economic resources would put self-determination in a deep freeze for all of Alaska's native people.

3

ALASKA:
SELF-DETERMINATION IN A DEEP FREEZE

Why are we suddenly to be made what you called displaced persons. . . .
We are asking for men and women in the States who will dare raise their
voices on our behalf to insist that their public servants in Washington shall
not enrich their friends by giving away our trees, our trap lines, our lands,
our homes. With God's help, we still hope that what our parents passed on
to us we may in turn pass on to our children and our children's children
forever. AMY HOLLINGSTADT, PRESIDENT, ALASKA NATIVE SISTERHOOD, 19
DECEMBER 1947

During mid-August 1946, Secretary of the Interior Julius A. Krug flew from
Washington DC to Anchorage. One of the highlights of this trip was meeting with
five hundred Inuits on the shores of the Arctic Ocean. Krug told village residents
that he was committed to the maximum development of Alaska's resources that
had commenced during World War II. Fred Ipalook, the chair of the village
of Barrow, was especially pleased with the secretary of interior's promise to
improve local services and health care. The visit ended with a ceremonial feast,
tribal dances, and a reindeer blanket toss—a traditional way of celebrating a
gala occasion.[1]

After he left Barrow and returned to the nation's capital, Krug asked officials at
the Indian Bureau and other federal agencies to justify their policies in terms of
economic growth for Alaska. He also made arrangements with Congress to cut
timber in the Tongass National Forest to encourage the production of newsprint.
On several occasions, Krug met with representatives from the salmon industry
to draft legislation that protected their use of fish traps.

Krug anticipated widespread support for these initiatives. Instead, he encountered stubborn resistance from leaders of the National Congress of American
Indians. In 1946, Napoleon Bonaparte Johnson, the NCAI president, sent Ruth

Muskrat Bronson to Alaska to inform native groups of their rights under the Indian Claims Commission Act. After she returned home, Bronson persuaded James E. Curry, the NCAI legal counsel, to aggressively defend the possessory claims of Haida and Tlingit Indians to timber in the Tongass National Forest and fish traps built by absentee owners adjacent to their property.

Other political activists joined this movement for self-determination by reaffirming their legal rights under the 1936 Alaska Reorganization Act. Frank G. Johnson, an Indian leader, used the village of Kake ARA constitution and bylaws to hire attorneys who made arrangements with a private corporation to cut and market timber in defiance of the authority of the Forest Service. Cyril Zuboff and Amy Hollingstadt, as well as other members of the Alaska Native Brotherhood and Sisterhood, also blocked legislation in the Eightieth Congress to repeal the ARA, which authorized federal loans to native-owned cooperatives.

In yet another act of defiance, NCAI leaders opposed legislation that proposed to extinguish Indian possessory claims in return for trust patents to land allotments. Bronson used her influence on the National Advisory Committee on Indian Affairs at the Interior Department to discredit this idea. Curry and Cyrus Peck of the Alaska Native Brotherhood assisted Bronson by asking members of Congress and White House officials to safeguard Haida and Tlingit property rights.

Secretary Krug encountered protest and dissent because he did not consult regularly with native spokespersons in Alaska. Instead, he relied on advice from Solicitor Warner W. Gardner, who disliked the sociological jurisprudence practiced by Nathan Margold. In 1942, former solicitor Margold had encouraged Indians in southeastern Alaska to identify possessory claims to land that from time immemorial they had used for agriculture, hunting, and seed gathering. Margold also had ruled that aboriginal fishing rights in ocean waters or below high tide remained unaffected by common law.[2]

In 1943, Secretary of the Interior Harold L. Ickes used this legal opinion to set aside by executive order, under section 2 of the Alaska Reorganization Act, four large reservations for Aleuts, Inuits, and Athabascan Indians. Two years later, after departmental administrative hearings, Ickes recognized 8 percent of Haida and Tlingit possessory claims at the villages of Hydaburg, Kake, and Klawock.[3]

The interior secretary also closed fish traps operated by the salmon industry at eleven sites where Indians, by right of aboriginal occupancy, had rights of fishery. These floating traps consisted of a wire lead running from the shore for a distance of three hundred yards. The lead opened into two wire enclosed hearts that directed the fish into a holding area, where they were harvested by cannery workers. Non-Indians who wanted to utilize these sites were required to secure leases from native owners.[4]

These efforts on behalf of Indians created an atmosphere of hysteria in southeastern Alaska. At Ketchikan, Sitka, and Juneau, Euro-American settlers held mass meetings to protest giving Alaska back to the natives. More importantly, attorneys from Seattle who represented nonresident canneries challenged the authority of the Interior Department to unilaterally decide complex legal issues. They insisted that only Congress, or a tribunal of competent jurisdiction, could determine the merit of native possessory claims.[5]

Gardner concurred with the position taken by settlers and Seattle attorneys. Early in 1947, he persuaded Secretary Krug to reverse departmental policy that set aside water rights for exclusive native use. Gardner emphasized that besides looking after native interests, the interior secretary had an overall responsibility to develop the immense and untouched natural resources of Alaska.[6]

In June 1946, Solicitor Gardner took bold steps to move the Interior Department in that direction. He informed Alfred W. Widmark, the mayor of Klawock, that private attorneys had initiated lawsuits challenging the authority of the interior secretary to validate Indian possessory claims and that government officials had responded by reaching a compromise with representatives of the salmon industry postponing litigation for one year. Under this agreement, the P. E. Harris Company would deliver the entire production of its fish trap 124 to the Indian cannery at Hydaburg. In return, the Indians were prohibited from operating the eleven trap sites set aside for their use or to build their own fish traps during the 1947 season.[7]

The Indians had little choice but to accept this one-sided agreement. The threat of litigation by the salmon industry also made it impossible for them to build fish traps on the one hundred sites they claimed in other parts of southeastern Alaska. This was a serious matter because the courts had determined the question of ownership on who first built the fish trap.[8]

In another departure from the past, Gardner advised Secretary Krug not to use section 2 of the Alaska Reorganization Act to create reservations in southeastern Alaska to protect Indian possessory rights. Gardner disapproved of reservations because they set natives apart from the white community, protected tax-exempt property, and would result in the uncertain application of territorial laws as well as health and educational systems. However, he did see valid reasons to set aside small areas for Inuits who were exploited during World War II.[9]

Gardner believed that Indians had a legally protected right to lands in actual and exclusive use, including Haida and Tlingit unextinguished rights to timber in the Tongass National Forest. Nonetheless, he was willing to recommend the condemnation of these timber rights because he felt the establishment of pulp mills in Alaska would bring a larger public benefit to settlers, Indians, and the nation. The solicitor was certain the Haida and Tlingit people would drop their possessory claims in the Tongass National Forest for a guaranteed percentage of timber receipts.[10]

Persuaded by Gardner's arguments, Secretary Krug canceled Interior Department administrative hearings scheduled for October 1946 to determine the possessory rights of Indians other than those at the villages of Hydaburg, Kake, and Klawock. Krug also doubted whether Congress or the courts would accept a scholarly report on native possessory claims written by Dr. Walter R. Goldschmidt, an employee of the Bureau of Agricultural Economics, and Theodore H. Haas, the Indian Bureau's chief counsel. Based on field investigations that Krug authorized during the summer of 1946, the Goldschmidt-Haas report used the testimony of Indians to determine land use at twelve villages.[11]

Goldschmidt and Haas stated that the Haida and Tlingit people each formed nations, even though many elements associated with nationality in the modern world were absent, such as centralized political organization. Both nations were unified by a common language, traditions, and religious beliefs. Prior to European contact, they had developed the highest forms of civilization in America north of Mexico. Despite epidemics and outside encroachment, these Indians had adjusted to modern conditions while preserving many of their ancient customs.[12]

This report concluded that Haida and Tlingit Indians had continuously used and occupied the lands and waters of southeastern Alaska since time immemorial. They had a well-defined system of property ownership held in the name of the clan or with joint usage by extended families. Title to land was obtained by inheritance and never bought or sold. Goldschmidt and Haas delineated on maps where Indians claimed possessory rights to almost two million acres, including land that anchored twenty-seven salmon traps. They recommended that the federal government safeguard without further delay the lands still under Indian use and occupation.[13]

In February 1947, Charles M. Wright, an NCAI attorney, reminded Krug that the Haida and Tlingit Indians regarded as a pioneering effort the Goldschmidt-Haas report and earlier departmental administrative hearings to determine the extent of their claims in southeastern Alaska. His clients anticipated that a similar procedure would be used at Aleut and Inuit villages. Wright warned the secretary of interior that the NCAI would contest any effort to disregard legitimate Indian rights.[14]

Krug ignored this pointed criticism. He was far more disposed to working with business interests that wanted to establish a multimillion-dollar pulp industry in southeastern Alaska. The interior secretary also wanted Seattle-based corporations, rather than Indians, to control Alaska's waters, which produced 60 percent of the world's salmon with an annual pack of six million cases valued at $50 million.[15]

Early in 1947, Krug forwarded legislation to the Senate Committee on Interstate and Foreign Commerce and the House Committee on Merchant Marine Fisheries that threatened Indian fishing rights. The secretary of interior was authorized by this bill to lease salmon traps after 1948 for fifteen years. These nonrenewable leases would be issued on a preferential basis, with 100 percent approval to salmon operators with twenty or fewer sites and 75 percent approval for companies with more than forty trap sites. Forty-two surrendered trap sites would be auctioned in sealed bids, with preference given to Alaskan communities.[16]

Salmon corporations that controlled excess trap sites could sell abandoned canneries at fair market value after five years. The P. E. Harris Company and Pacific American Fisheries agreed to option the Kake and Kasaan canneries, where twenty-four traps were anchored adjacent to Indian villages. They also were willing to surrender four traps near the villages of Hydaburg and Klawock.[17]

Operators who leased trap sites from the federal government had to pay a royalty of 5 percent of the first five hundred thousand salmon and 7 percent of the fish caught in excess of that amount. Leases to fish traps anchored on land subject to the possessory rights of Haida and Tlingit Indians would continue for fifteen years. The Indians were not allowed to collect royalties from these leases unless the courts or Congress recognized their possessory rights.[18]

Gardner appeared before the Senate Subcommittee on Interstate and Foreign Commerce in June 1947 to testify on behalf of S.R. 1446. He asked Congress to postpone consideration of this bill and wait for the outcome of a referendum scheduled by the territorial legislature of Alaska to determine whether to abolish fish traps. He also recommended that Congress consult with Indians about the decision to put their royalties in escrow because the Alaska Native Service had reported mixed Indian reactions to this bill.[19]

Krug's salmon trap proposal was blocked in January 1948 at joint hearings before the House Committee on Merchant Marine and Fisheries and the Senate Committee on Interstate and Foreign Commerce. There, the American Federation of Labor, fishermen who used gear other than fish traps, and E. L. Bartlett, the territorial delegate to Congress, protested against this legislation. So did the Haida and Tlingit Indians, who retained the Washington DC law firm of James Curry, Henry Cohen, and Jonathan Bingham to represent their interests.[20]

Frances Lopinsky, an attorney from this firm, appeared before the Senate committee at the end of January 1948. She indicated that the Curry, Cohen, and

Bingham firm had signed contracts with eighteen town councils and Indian cooperative associations incorporated under the Alaska Reorganization Act. The firm also represented the Alaska Native Brotherhood and Alaska Native Sisterhood.[21]

Lopinsky testified that the salmon trap legislation sponsored by the Interior Department was an illegal restraint of trade that allowed federal bureaucrats to create exclusive rights on the public domain. It contained loopholes and weasel words that permitted salmon packers to assign excess traps to friendly companies instead of Indians. Lopinsky stated that this legislation also provided for royalty rates that bore no resemblance to the actual value of fishing sites and ignored sacred Indian possessory rights recognized in 1945 at Interior Department administrative hearings.[22]

Furthermore, she emphasized that the trap site bills set her clients back a generation in their economic development. It gave the secretary of interior more rather than less control over their lives. Lopinsky stressed that Indian citizens had the inalienable right to decide whether to use or lease their property. She warned that it was unconstitutional to treat Indians as serfs, let salmon packers operate canneries on their unpatented land, and lease property for a minimal fee without judicial process or just compensation.[23]

According to Lopinsky, the Indians were divided into two camps. Five native villages favored this legislation because they gained access to canneries and fish traps. A much larger group, however, refused to endorse any measure that perpetuated outside control of Alaska's natural resources. These Indians were embittered because the P. E. Harris Company wanted to sell its cannery at Kake for $575,000. They could not afford this ludicrous asking price because the total catch from eleven nearby fish traps had declined from 3.6 million fish in 1941 to 162,000 in 1947.[24]

The salmon trap legislation, which did not pass Congress, was part of a broader effort to develop Alaska's natural resources at the expense of Indians. After visiting fourteen native villages during October and November 1946, Ruth Muskrat Bronson concluded that the Haida and Tlingit Indians were an unwanted and despised people. Local settlers subjected them to racial discrimination, whereas government officials treated their wards with contempt. The Indians were fighting against tremendous odds to avoid becoming propertyless citizens who lived a marginal existence on the Alaskan frontier.[25]

The NCAI executive secretary was upset with Solicitor Gardner's decision to hold numerous interdepartmental conferences in January 1947 without Indian input. At these meetings, officials from the Agriculture and Justice Departments expressed their dislike of the Goldschmidt-Haas report, which recorded Haida and Tlingit claims to almost two million acres of timberland. Instead of a negotiated settlement, they wanted Congress to extinguish Indian title using precedents established by the Supreme Court in the settlement of the continental United States.[26]

Bronson responded to this ominous development by asking Curry, the NCAI legal counsel, to protect Indian possessory rights. Curry replied that big money was involved and that the NCAI lacked the financial resources to properly defend Alaska's Indians. To resolve this problem, he agreed to provide free legal services for each village that signed a general counsel contingency contract with his law firm. If there was a favorable settlement, the Indians would have to provide reasonable compensation for fees and expenses approved by the secretary of the interior.[27]

In April 1947, Curry wrote an urgent letter to Haida and Tlingit Indians, explaining that President Harry Truman and other high-ranking people were behind an effort to persuade private corporations to invest $200 million for the construction of pulp and paper mills in southeastern Alaska. Curry also told the Indians that he had spoken for them on behalf of the NCAI at recent meetings with officials from the Forest Service and Interior Department. Everyone agreed that it was desirable to develop Alaska's resources and at the same time safeguard Indian rights.[28]

After much discussion, it was decided that Felix Cohen, a solicitor at the Interior Department, would draft a bill that authorized the Forest Service to cut timber in the Tongass National Forest and to set aside small parcels of land for the pulp mills. In return, the Forest Service would pay the Indians 10 percent of the gross proceeds from timber sales. Curry encouraged the Indians to accept this legislation because it provided an immediate source of income to hire attorneys to defend their possessory claims.[29]

A short time later, Curry met with Bronson and Lopinsky. They decided that Bronson should make a second trip to Alaska to determine Indian views of this proposal. Beginning in May 1947, she met with representatives from each village and solicited general counsel contracts for Curry.[30]

The 10 percent bill met with general Indian approval, but it did not have widespread support elsewhere. Attorneys for the salmon and pulp industries, as well as Governor Ernest Gruening of Alaska, found it unacceptable. The Justice Department also refused to endorse this measure because officials there took the position that Indians should appear before a federal court to prove their possessory claims.[31]

Secretary Krug scheduled a conference at the Interior Department to end this impasse. Present were Gardner, Cohen, and E. L. Bartlett, Alaska's congressional delegate. Under pressure from Krug, they wrote a bill that removed Indians as active participants in the legislative process. As one historian has noted, it made Indians more rather than less dependent on federal officials and provided no alternative but expensive litigation to determine their possessory rights.[32]

Krug's legislative proposal was introduced in the Eightieth Congress in April 1947 as House Joint Resolution 205. This measure gave the secretary of agriculture and secretary of interior a free hand to appraise and sell timber on vacant, unappropriated, and unprotected land in the Tongass National Forest. It did not recognize or deny the validity of native property rights based on aboriginal occupancy. Until Congress determined the ownership of this disputed land, all receipts from the sale of timber would be deposited in a special U.S. Treasury account.[33]

Secretary Krug strongly supported H.J.R. 205 in a letter to Speaker Joseph W. Martin. For Krug, the Haida and Tlingit Indians were not distinct political communities or domestic nations with well-defined boundaries. Instead, they were a major obstacle to the development of the pulp industry in southeastern Alaska. The secretary viewed this legislation as an interim solution that permitted the processing of timber for newsprint and paper products. The next session of Congress would have to consider the more controversial question of native possessory claims against the United States.[34]

The House Committee on Agriculture met during May and July 1947 to consider H.J.R. 205. At these hearings, Ohio congressman Cliff Clevenger asked Gardner if he was familiar with the Menominee Reservation in Wisconsin, where Indians managed their own sawmill. Gardner replied that it was impossible to duplicate this native-owned timber operation in Alaska because of uncertainty over who owned land and timber in the Tongass National Forest.[35] Unlike Margold, he thought it was unclear whether two recent Supreme Court decisions (*U.S. v. Santa Fe Railroad* [1941] and *Alcea Band of Tillamooks v. U.S.* [1946], which upheld Indian possessory rights in the continental United States) applied to the territory of Alaska. He continued to defend H.J.R. 205 by dismissing the Goldschmidt-Haas report as a hasty survey that only scratched the surface of exceedingly complex legal problems. He also characterized the administrative hearings to determine the claims of Hydaburg, Kake, and Klawock, in which thirty-three lawyers participated, as an abortive procedure that resulted only in nonbinding advisory opinions.[36]

Gardner did acknowledge that the uncertain title to Indian land could be resolved by establishing reservations under the 1936 Alaska Reorganization Act. He was reluctant to recommend this option to Congress because many Indians in southeastern Alaska disliked federal wardship. Furthermore, Gardner did not view reservations in Alaska as homelands. Instead, he characterized them as isolated tax-exempt federal islands with a distinct legal status that thwarted the movement toward Alaskan statehood.[37]

When Curry appeared before the House committee on behalf of the NCAI, he indicated that the Haida and Tlingit Indians had voted unanimously against this legislation. Curry argued that H.J.R. 205 was an unconstitutional taking of private property for private use without just compensation. He compared it to fascist law, which had overused the power of eminent domain to expropriate the property of Jews and other minorities.[38]

Curry then introduced a written statement prepared by Napoleon Bonaparte Johnson. The president of the NCAI warned that H.J.R. 205 repeated one of the worst mistakes in opening up the American West to settlement. It permitted the government to confiscate sacred Indian property and trampled on the Indians' dignity by treating them as children. For Johnson, the pulp mills were not worth the price of pauperizing Indians and making them dependent on federal assistance for generations.[39]

Gardner responded to this critical testimony by asking Don C. Foster, the general superintendent of the Alaska Native Service, to identify Indians willing to appear before the House committee. Foster recommended three members of the territorial legislature, Frank Peratrovich of Klawock, Andrew Hope of Sitka, and Frank G. Johnson of Kake, and also Fred Grant, who represented the village of Hydaburg. Bronson met these four men at Union Station on 24 June 1947. They went directly to Curry's Washington law office, where an agreement was reached to work for an amended bill that protected Indian rights.[40]

Ten days later, the Indian delegates testified before the House committee. They defended ownership to land handed down for generations and expressed a desire to manage their own affairs. Peratrovich thought it was ridiculous for members of Congress and Interior Department officials to tell them that administrative hearings and the Goldschmidt-Haas report were not binding on the federal government. For Johnson, reservations were the only logical way to protect Indian property and operate tribal sawmills.[41]

During the last week of June and July an intensive effort was made to amend H.J.R. 205. After much discussion, Secretary Krug proposed to pay Indians 10 percent of the proceeds from the sale of timber in the Tongass National Forest if they relinquished all possessory rights except for town sites. Negotiations ended when Curry and the Indian delegates rejected this compromise.[42]

This did not prevent the Eightieth Congress from passing the Tongass Timber Bill on 26 July 1947. The Senate Committee on Public Lands, chaired by Senator Hugh Butler of Nebraska, put it on the unanimous consent calendar at 1:00 A.M.

Clifford Hope, the chair of the House Committee on Agriculture, followed the same procedure at 10:00 A.M., when only a handful of the members of Congress were present. According to Governor Gruening, this controversial legislation squeaked through fifteen minutes before the adjournment of Congress. President Truman signed the Tongass Timber Act in August 1947.[43]

After this setback, opponents of the law continued their campaign to protect Indian possessory rights. James Curry worked closely with Felix Cohen to sell Indian timber to interested buyers and to block the government's trespass on Indian land. Both were convinced that the Tongass Timber Act imposed economic colonialism on Indians by allowing absentee corporations to steal their natural resources. To rectify this deplorable situation, Cohen met with Frank G. Johnson, the delegate from Kake who had testified against H.J.R. 205. They decided that Indians should stake out mineral claims, organize under the Alaska Reorganization Act to operate sawmills, and find customers to purchase their lumber.[44]

In September, Curry met with Henry Cohen, the cousin of Felix Cohen, who represented the New York law firm of Cohen, Bingham, and Stone. They signed a contract with the Timber Development Corporation under the control of Milton Zadenburg and other investors. This company agreed to pay the villages of Kake, Kasaan, and Klawock $3,000 in return for a ten-year option on Indian timber, pay $10,000 in attorney fees for Curry, and finance a small sawmill at Kake to vindicate the Indians' right to cut timber without a permit from the Forest Service.[45]

Curry also notified the Daugherty and Foley Pulp Company and Puget Sound Pulp and Timber Company that federal officials were not authorized to sell timber in certain parts of the Tongass National Forest without Indian consent. Curry warned that he would file a lawsuit to challenge the constitutionality of the Tongass Timber Act. The pulp companies responded by refusing to bid on four auctions held by the Agriculture Department.[46]

In early October 1947, Cohen informed Secretary Krug that Kake had found buyers to purchase timber that belonged to Indians. He warned that any effort by government officials to interfere with the independent sale of Indian timber would result in prolonged litigation. This would put the Interior Department in the awkward position of having to oppose its own wards, reverse past departmental rulings, and discourage Indian self-determination.[47]

Cohen reminded Secretary Krug that the Indians at Kake had sent him a telegram requesting a negotiated settlement of their possessory rights. They recommended that the Interior Department use its legal authority under the Alaska Reorganization Act to expand the Hydaburg Town Reserve by 101,000 acres to include the towns of Kake, Kasaan, and Klawock. This proposal also granted the Forest Service control over the cutting of timber in return for cash payments. It gave preference to Indian loggers and waived the possessory rights of these villages to additional land in southeastern Alaska.[48]

Secretary Krug was interested in this proposal and asked Solicitor Mastin G. White, who replaced Warner Gardner, for an opinion on his authority to create reservations. On 16 October 1947, the Interior Department issued a press release, the same day that Krug received a favorable ruling from the solicitor, which announced the signing of a proclamation to increase the size of the Hydaburg Town Reserve. One week later, the department issued a second press release, which reversed this decision, in response to complaints from officials at the Agriculture Department.[49]

In the meantime, the Indians at Kake adopted an ARA constitution and bylaws that authorized them to hire an attorney and operate their own business. In November, the NCAI challenged Krug's decision by announcing that Kake and Kasaan had signed contracts with the Timber Development Corporation to cut $20 million worth of lumber on Indian land offered at auction by the Forest Service.[50]

Cohen lost this showdown over the right of Indians to manage their own affairs. In early December, he received an unsigned letter that charged him with a conflict of interest. It stated that private Indian timber sales at Kake and Kasaan were predicated on advanced information about the prospective order to expand the Hydaburg Town Reserve. This accusation, and lack of support from superiors, led to Cohen's resignation in December 1947 and his decision to open a private law practice in Washington DC.[51]

Native political activists who continued to fight for self-determination after Cohen's unexpected departure encountered harsh treatment from the federal government. At the village of Shungnak, an Inuit who dug for jade on his own land was thrown into jail at the request of a mining company. In southeastern Alaska, a Tlingit Indian who tried to catch fish in a disputed area was arrested and subjected to an FBI investigation.[52]

The Indians at Kake also encountered problems in January 1948 when they began to assemble sawmill equipment that was purchased by the Timber Development Corporation. Secretary Krug responded to this challenge to his authority by asking Solicitor White to issue an opinion in March 1948 on the "Administration of Indian Affairs in Alaska." This opinion prohibited native groups from selling standing timber in the Tongass National Forest without permission from the Interior Department.[53]

One month later, Indian political activists contested this ruling by initiating logging operations at Kake. A crew of sixteen men cut fifty-three hemlock and spruce trees. Thomas Jackson, the manager of this enterprise, also announced plans to expand operations to twenty thousand board feet a day as soon as the village sawmill began operations. Angry government officials responded by threatening Jackson and his followers with imprisonment for this act of civil disobedience.[54]

Hugh Butler, a member of the Senate Public Lands Committee, also fought the Indians. During February and March 1948, he presided over extensive hearings by the Senate Subcommittee on Interior and Insular Affairs. The subcommittee considered two bills: Senate Joint Resolution 162, which repealed section 2 of the Alaska Reorganization Act and rescinded the executive orders in 1943 that established four reservations, and Senate Resolution 2037, which transferred legal jurisdiction over natives to the territorial government and repealed the ARA.[55]

This legislation encountered strong resistance from the Alaska Native Brotherhood and Alaska Native Sisterhood. Grand Presidents Cyril Zuboff and Amy Hollingstadt sent telegrams to the subcommittee in defense of the creation of reservations under ARA. They also indicated that the ARA revolving credit fund made it possible for natives to purchase fishing boats and operate forty-one cooperative stores and two canneries.[56]

Ruth Muskrat Bronson, executive secretary of the NCAI, told Butler's subcommittee that this proposed legislation confiscated native property without compensation and violated a solemn pledge made under section 16 of the Indian Reorganization Act to ask for tribal consent prior to the sale of land. Bronson characterized S.J.R. 162 and S.R. 2037 as vicious racist proposals that, if passed, would propel the country straight toward fascism.[57]

During these hearings, Senator Butler sent Secretary Krug a scornful letter concerning the sale of Indian lumber to the Timber Development Corporation. Butler accused Cohen of collaborating with Curry to break the law and block bids to cut trees in the Tongass National Forest. Butler insisted that in the future Krug should carefully review the contracts of Curry and other lawyers who represented tribes.[58]

Stung by this sharp criticism, Krug told senators that he had authorized Assistant Commissioner William Zimmerman to approve attorney contracts. The secretary defended the right of Indians to pick their own lawyers, even if these lawyers embarrassed government officials. He also testified that Alaska's natives faced virtual destruction without the power to form local ARA municipal councils and borrow money from the federal government.[59]

Krug reminded the subcommittee that he had worked closely with Congress to ensure passage of the Tongass Timber Act. This did not mean that reservations were unnecessary in Alaska. Poachers had threatened the livelihood of natives by indiscriminately killing their game from helicopters. Furthermore, Krug stated that if Congress would amend the ARA to provide for a review process after departmental administrative hearings, it would be possible to quickly negotiate a settlement with Haida and Tlingit Indians that traded their possessory claims for reservations.[60]

The Eightieth Congress did not act favorably on S.J.R. 162 or S.R. 2037. Butler's Committee on Interior and Insular Affairs, however, issued its report in May 1948. Ghostwritten by Albert Grorud, the clerk of the Senate Indian Affairs Subcommittee, the report attacked the legal foundation of native self-rule in Alaska. This report stated that Margold's 1943 opinion was erroneous because Congress did not contemplate setting aside large reservations during its legislative deliberations on the ARA. It noted that the House and Senate, not the executive branch, had exclusive authority to create or extinguish Indian title by purchase, treaty, or the sword.[61]

On the same day that Butler's Senate report was issued, President Truman delivered a message to Congress supporting Alaskan statehood. Truman pointed to the strategic military importance of Alaska, which had oil reserves and other valuable natural resources. The president indicated that the legal question of whether or not natives owned land had hampered the territory's industrial and agricultural development. To resolve this dilemma, Truman recommended that Congress authorize the secretary of interior to grant natives land and fishing rights necessary for their economic livelihood if they waived possessory claims.[62]

Following the president's message, officials in the Truman administration met jointly to draft a bill that was forwarded to the House Public Lands Committee one day before the Eightieth Congress adjourned. H.R. 7002 authorized the secretary of interior to issue patents-in-fee to native communities or individuals for property such as town sites, gardens, smokehouses, fishing camps, missionary stations, and burial grounds. These trust patents would be tax free for a twenty-five-year period. Indians who received patents in the Tongass National Forest were under the administrative control of the Forest Service. They lost the freedom to manage their own property but had the right to a proportionate share of income from the sale of timber minus administrative costs.[63]

Other provisions of this bill reduced natives from a people having property in their own right to a propertyless people partaking of charity. Titles to all oil, gas, and other subsurface minerals were reserved to the U.S. government unless the secretary of interior determined that native communities already had developed these natural resources. All possessory rights were extinguished immediately, whether natives accepted or rejected land patents within six months after

Congress passed the legislation. This method of expropriation and confiscation resembled the Dawes General Allotment Act of 1887.[64]

Curry responded to this crisis by writing a letter in September 1948 to Secretary of State George C. Marshall in which he complained on behalf of the NCAI and the Alaskan Native Brotherhood that seven thousand Haida and Tlingit Indians were being deprived of their land and the right of self-determination. Curry pointed out that since the Tongass Timber Act, the Department of Agriculture had violated the U.S. Constitution by taking his clients' private property without due process of law. This action also violated international obligations under Article 73 in chapter 11 of the United Nations Charter. Curry asked Marshall to bring this matter to the attention of President Truman or the U.N. Committee on Non–Self-Governing Territories.[65]

Curry's letter to Marshall explains, in part, why H.R. 7002 was not reintroduced in the Eighty-first Congress. In December 1948, there were also interdepartmental conferences where government officials discussed whether Indian possessory claims should be resolved by setting aside reservations or through revised legislation. What emerged from these meetings in 1949 was a draft amendment to H.R. 7002 that authorized a $40 million loan fund to help Indians become self-supporting and to provide financial assistance for vocational training on and off their homelands.[66]

Because of the ongoing controversy over possessory claims, this proposal required White House clearance before it was sent to Congress. It immediately encountered resistance from the National Advisory Committee on Indian Affairs established in January 1949 by Secretary Krug. Oliver LaFarge, the president of the Association on American Indian Affairs, chaired this committee, and Ruth Muskrat Bronson from the NCAI served as its secretary.[67]

In March 1949, the advisory committee sent Secretary Krug a memo warning that this bill deprived Alaska's natives of their fundamental rights guaranteed by treaty, judicial decisions, and previous rulings by the secretary of interior. The committee recommended that Krug settle all possessory claims by using his authority to create reservations under the ARA. In cases where agreements could not be reached, an impartial tribunal appointed by the president and ratified by the Senate would make final judgment.[68]

The adverse reaction of the advisory committee to the revised draft of H.R. 7002 was discussed at the highest levels of the White House. Assistant Secretary of the Interior William E. Warne telephoned Charles S. Murphy, a leading presidential adviser, and requested reconsideration of this controversial legislation. Warne was responding to pressure from Cyrus Peck and other members of the Alaska Native Brotherhood, who had sent over six hundred letters opposing H.R. 7002 to newspaper editors, clergymen, labor leaders, government officials, and every member of Congress.[69]

Murphy turned this problem over to Stephen Springharn and Philleo Nash, both members of the White House staff. They decided that the arbitrary confiscation of native land conflicted with President Truman's civil rights program. Nash and Springharn suggested that Krug place more emphasis on conciliation and negotiation by mutual agreement with natives to resolve their claims.[70]

A short time later, David K. Niles, the president's administrative assistant, informed Truman that the National Advisory Committee on Indian Affairs strongly objected to H.R. 7002. Niles warned the president that this bill, if implemented, would arouse a storm of protest from native people, Indian welfare groups, and civil rights organizations. Two days later, Truman told Krug that legislation sponsored by the Interior Department to settle native claims met with his disapproval. The president asked the secretary to draft an alternate proposal that provided for a fair settlement of possessory rights.[71]

Krug then resumed his effort to draft new legislation. Self-determination for Alaskan natives, however, remained in a deep freeze because government officials refused to negotiate in good faith. A few months later, Krug resigned as secretary of the interior.[72]

On 30 November 1949, his last night in office, Krug unexpectedly signed orders designating reservations for the villages of Hydaburg, Barrow, Shungnak, and Kobuk. Assistant Secretary Warne persuaded Krug to sign these documents because he was convinced that reservations, along with an expanded credit fund, would protect natives and provide a way to settle their possessory claims. Warne's plan, which encouraged self-determination, was sidetracked when all of the villages except Hydaburg voted against reservations.[73]

The natives were influenced by white settlers who argued that reservations would restrict their freedom, promote racial discrimination, and jeopardize Social Security benefits and other rights enjoyed by American citizens. Natives also voted no because the reservations were contingent on waiving their possessory claims to fisheries, land, oil, and other valuable subsurface deposits. The order setting aside a one-hundred-thousand-acre reserve for Hydaburg was overruled later by a federal court due to procedural irregularities.[74]

Secretary Krug's vacillation and the native reaction to creating reservations in Alaska were part of a broader reaction against New Deal policies that treated tribes as quasi-sovereign domestic nations. After 1945, Congress, the executive branch, and many Indians no longer viewed tribal self-government and cooperative economic enterprise as the only test of America's democratic faith. The Haida and Tlingit Indians, however, resisted these developments.

They insisted that the U.S. government respect their political autonomy and property rights.

Events in Alaska made leaders of the NCAI more militant in their defense of Indian self-determination. Curry captured this restive spirit at the 1948 NCAI convention in Denver. There he praised the tribal delegates for their ability to organize and agitate for social justice. Their self-sacrifice on behalf of Alaska's natives reminded Curry of the Sinn Feiners, who fought for freedom in Ireland, and Jews who created and protected their homeland of Israel in an inhospitable environment.[75]

Curry did not mention that NCAI political activists had collaborated with Navajos to transform Indian affairs. Led by Sam Ahkeah, the Navajos in the early postwar era fought for the right to vote in state elections, access to Social Security benefits, and a universal education for their children. Furthermore, they convinced Congress to reverse the economic dislocation caused by stock reduction, which took their property without due process of law.

4

A FAIR DEAL FOR NAVAJOS

The Navajos desperately want an education. They want to get out of their condition of extreme poverty, unsanitary housing and living, acute sickness and ignorance. They want their children to become better farmers, more skillful workers. They want to know how to handle money, how to operate their own filling stations, how to be their own middlemen for their own Navajo products. WILL ROGERS JR., 3 FEBRUARY 1948

During early May 1946, twenty-three Navajos left Gallup, New Mexico, on the Santa Fe Railway to visit Washington DC. Their mission was to ask government officials to honor a treaty signed in 1868. The delegation included Chee Dodge, the eighty-six-year-old tribal chair, Sam Ahkeah, vice-chair, representatives from each of the eighteen Navajo districts, and superintendent James M. Stewart.[1] Shortly after their arrival in the nation's capital, the Navajos registered at the Harrington Hotel. There, they held two strategy sessions prior to meeting with Secretary of the Interior Julius Krug, Indian Commissioner William Brophy, representatives from the Budget Bureau, and members of Congress. It was decided that Dodge and Ahkeah would present the tribe's views on Navajo education. The other delegates would discuss livestock reduction, reservation boundaries, a new range survey, and the desirability of decentralized administration.[2]

On 14 May, the Navajo delegation consulted with Secretary Krug after an earlier appearance before the Senate Indian Affairs Committee. Delegate Scott Preston told Krug that the tribe, for the most part, had followed grazing regulations and reduced the number of its livestock. Despite this cooperation, veterans and hundreds of young people had been denied grazing permits and the right to own sheep and goats. Preston believed that some Navajos would starve if the government continued to enforce this restrictive land management program.[3]

Krug defended the need for grazing regulations and reminded Preston that the reservation could support only a certain number of livestock. The secretary, however, did agree to personally look into the question of whether the government had accurate, updated information on reservation resources. He also accepted Preston's invitation to become the first secretary of the interior to visit the reservation.[4]

Delegate Joe Duncan raised another important issue before this meeting ended. He requested a new survey of the reservation boundary east of Shiprock, New Mexico, because a white trader had recently built a fence over the reservation boundary line. Duncan believed that a resurvey would help protect valuable tribal coal deposits in this region. Commissioner Brophy promised Preston that the Indian Bureau would survey this part of the reservation and compile a new inventory of grazing resources as soon as Congress appropriated funds for this purpose.[5]

On 20 May, the delegation held an unprecedented meeting with representatives from the Budget Bureau. Chee Dodge asked the U.S. government to honor article 6 of the Navajo Treaty of 1868. Under this agreement, the government had a responsibility to educate over fourteen thousand children who did not attend school. The tribal chair provided government officials with a list of boarding schools to build, remodel, or enlarge. He also noted that thirteen thousand Navajos who resided off the reservation in the Taylor Grazing District urgently needed hospital facilities.[6]

Dodge recommended compulsory education for Navajo children. This requirement was necessary because after stock reduction most children no longer herded sheep and goats. Veterans and war workers without an education or knowledge of the English language also had reported difficulties in dealing with non-Indians.[7]

The tribal chair concluded his remarks by asking for increased congressional appropriations to solve these and other problems. Dodge called on the government to build new hospitals and construct irrigation facilities on the San Juan River for thousands of people who could no longer make a living from livestock. He also recommended higher salaries for underpaid Navajo police, who sometimes had to beg for food, to help the tribe deal more effectively with law enforcement problems such as alcohol abuse.[8]

Sam Dodd, from the Budget Bureau, asked the tribal chair why so few Navajo children attended the day schools built with Public Works Administration funds between 1935 and 1936. Dodge replied that day schools had a poor academic reputation and that children had to commute long distances from remote communities to reach them. Dodd complimented the Navajos on their presentation and promised to carefully study their needs. He was reluctant, however, to approve the construction of new schools on the reservation before Indian Bureau employees solved the problem of unused classroom space at the Albuquerque, Sherman Institute, and Chilocco boarding schools.[9]

The Navajo confrontation with the U.S. government continued when members of the Native American Church at Cortez, Colorado, sent a petition to President Harry S. Truman on 15 July 1946. They complained that only 124 students out of a total tribal population of fifty-five thousand attended high school. Other serious problems were malnutrition, stock reduction, unfair treatment at trading posts, and exploitation by corporations that paid low wages.[10]

Such problems led to the Navajo confrontation with the federal government during the spring and summer of 1946. Stock reduction and strict grazing regulations imposed during the New Deal had shattered the tribe's subsistence economy. This traumatic experience created a new, if embittered, sense of tribal solidarity.[11]

The experience of World War II transformed Navajo relations with the outside world. Along with thousands of other Indians, the Navajos demonstrated an eagerness to leave their homes to secure high-income jobs in war-related industries. The four hundred Navajo Code Talkers, who served with distinction in the armed forces, also became accustomed to equal treatment when they associated with other citizens.[12]

In the early postwar era, Sam Ahkeah, Howard Gorman, and other Navajo leaders championed self-determination to address complex problems on the reservation. They asked Congress to honor the Navajo Treaty of 1868 to ensure educational opportunity for all children. Navajos also worked with the National Congress of American Indians to stop the enforcement of unpopular grazing regulations, receive Social Security benefits, and secure the right to vote in state elections with other citizens. Furthermore, they persuaded the Navajo Tribal Council to oppose state jurisdiction as a precondition to large-scale federal economic assistance.

Navajo political activism emerged after World War II because conditions on the reservation were a national disgrace. The Navajos did not receive public assistance from state agencies. One Indian Bureau field doctor, nurse, dentist, and social worker served a population of over fifty-five thousand people. The Navajos had the highest tuberculosis rate in the country, an appalling infant mortality rate ten times the national average, and the shortest life expectancy in the United States. Nearly half of the children died before reaching school age. Most of those that survived were illiterate because the government provided only six thousand classrooms for over twenty-four thousand students.[13]

In October 1945, Margaretta Dietrich, the president of the New Mexico Association on Indian Affairs, distributed 12,500 leaflets that described the terrible state of Navajo education. She asked the federal government to build new schools so the Navajos could become self-sufficient citizens. Dietrich also pointed to the shocking need for improved medical services. A recent study of selective service records for four thousand Navajo men revealed that 88 percent were illiterate, 9 percent were rejected because of tuberculosis, 10 percent had serious eye impairment, and 12 percent suffered disqualifying ear defects.[14]

Ruth Kirk, the chair of the board of directors of the New Mexico Department of Public Welfare and the wife of a Gallup trader, also was upset by the extent of Navajo illiteracy and poverty. In March 1946, she traveled to Philadelphia and New York to organize a national campaign to improve conditions on the Navajo reservation. She met with representatives of the Association on American Indian Affairs, the General Federation of Women's Clubs, the Home Missions Council, and Indian Rights Association. They decided to organize a Navajo Coordinating Committee and hold a symposium to develop a long-range rehabilitation plan acceptable to the Navajos, Indian Bureau, and Congress (pl. 8).[15]

Federal officials discussed the Navajo crisis at a Post-War Resources Institute sponsored by the Department of Interior. There, James M. Stewart, who helped organize the Navajo trips to Washington DC, asked his colleagues to reexamine the philosophy behind the Indian Reorganization Act. He emphasized that vastly changed conditions in the United States required new policy initiatives.[16]

Stewart argued that the federal government had a responsibility, even under treaties, to determine when its legal and ethical trust for Indians should end. He recommended that the federal government concentrate on meeting the needs of the Navajos and a few other tribes. Otherwise the Indian Bureau would become a gigantic welfare service devoting its activities to large groups of rural people with only a limited degree of Indian blood.[17]

Commissioner Brophy responded to this presentation by asking Ward Shepard, an Indian Bureau consultant, to submit a report on current Navajo problems. During the New Deal, Shepard had designed the tribe's soil conservation and stock reduction program. He also helped develop the Navajo day school curriculum where teachers taught students grazing management, subsistence farming, rural vocational training, and the importance of maintaining their native culture.[18]

In November 1946, Shepard sent Brophy a confidential memo that lacked specific information about range surveys, grazing regulations, or education. Instead, it suggested that the commissioner protect the Navajos from "the cancer of an atheistic, nihilistic, and materialist modern world." Shepard also told

Brophy to ignore the Navajo request for new boarding schools because the curriculum at these institutions would be loaded with the "atomic fission of white materialism" that transformed Navajos into "Lowgrade Okies."[19]

The commissioner ignored Shepard's quixotic report. Instead he asked the Senate Appropriations Committee for funds to educate fourteen thousand Navajo children who did not attend school. Congress responded by authorizing $850,000 for the construction of school dormitories at Shiprock and Toadlena, as well as the renovation of other obsolete boarding school facilities.[20]

Congress did not appropriate all the money that Brophy requested because off-reservation boarding schools remained under-utilized throughout the United States. During the summer of 1946, Commissioner Brophy met with the Navajo Tribal Council, Superintendent Stewart, and George Boyce, the director of Navajo education, to address this problem. They decided to create a Special Navajo Education Program at Sherman Institute in Riverside, California, for students older than twelve years without past school experience or knowledge of English. Willard Beatty put Hildegard Thompson, an educator at Window Rock, in charge of this project.[21]

The Navajos took advantage of this educational opportunity. In September, 225 students, 75 over the enrollment limit, assembled at Fort Wingate for the trip to California. They received bilingual instruction at the Sherman Institute and learned vocational skills in shop and home economics classes for employment on or off the reservation. Most of these Navajo students accomplished three years' work during the 180-day term, spoke five hundred words of English, made outstanding progress in social development, and adjusted well to their new environment.[22]

In the meantime, Secretary Krug kept his promise to become the first secretary of interior to visit the reservation. On 16 September 1946, he inspected Ganado Mission, Hunter's Point Day School, a typical hogan, the tribal sawmill, Fort Defiance Hospital, and a trading post. During this tour, Krug complained to government employees that he had inherited a complex and politically difficult problem (pl. 9).[23]

In the evening the secretary spoke to the Navajo Tribal Council. He noted that four months previously Chee Dodge and other Navajos had presented their problems with clarity, conviction, and deep sincerity. Krug told the Navajos that it took only one day to confirm their need for new schools. The secretary also believed that the tribe required additional hospitals, roads, and irrigation projects. He expressed a willingness to work with the tribal council to formulate a long-range plan for economic development. Krug concluded his remarks by pledging to treat the Navajos the same as other American citizens.[24]

To help keep this promise, Commissioner Brophy asked Dr. George I. Sanchez, a specialist in bilingual education at the University of Texas, to determine whether the government should convert Navajo day schools into boarding institutions. In 1948, after a two-year delay, the Haskell Institute published Sanchez's report, *The People: A Study of the Navajos*, which seriously damaged the bureau's credibility to act as the Indians' guardian. It led to the inescapable conclusion that the federal government must reform Indian affairs.

Sanchez characterized Navajo education as a record of bungling, neglect, and shame. During the 1930s, the Indian Bureau had implemented progressive education policies that sounded good in theory but did not work in practice. The disturbing reality was that 2,274 Navajo students attended schools with crude sanitation facilities, contaminated water supplies, and hazardous fire escapes. Only thirty-seven out of fifty Navajo day schools remained open for a few months each year. Many students did not attend these educational centers because buses could not reach classrooms due to impassable roads, flash floods, snow, and drifting sand.[25]

Sanchez thought the makeshift hogans adjacent to day schools were an inadequate substitute for modern boarding facilities. The crowding of a dozen children and adult supervisor into one of these smoky hovels with a dirt floor and bugs, for even part of the year, bordered on the sadistic. Sanchez recommended that the federal government provide Navajos with the same kind of centralized educational services available to other citizens.[26]

The Sanchez report strengthened the position of government officials who wanted to emancipate Indians from federal wardship and the limitations of reservation life. In May 1949, Senator Arthur V. Watkins, with support from Interior Secretary Krug, persuaded Congress to appropriate $3.7 million to convert the Bushnell Army Hospital complex at Brigham City, Utah, into a Navajo boarding school for two thousand elementary and high school students. The Intermountain Indian School also served as a center to train adults for off-reservation employment and permanent relocation.[27]

In another important initiative, Krug directed Interior Department employees to develop plans to alleviate Navajo poverty. In February 1947, Acting Commissioner William Zimmerman participated in a symposium sponsored by the Navajo Coordinating Committee at the New York Museum of Natural History. Sam Ahkeah, the chair of the Navajo Tribal Council, and 125 delegates prominent in the fields of Indian health, education, welfare, and reclamation attended this important event. They adopted resolutions that asked Congress to increase funding for emergency relief, education, and the San Juan irrigation project.[28]

During the spring and summer of 1947, officials at the Interior Department considered several different rehabilitation proposals. A. L. Wathen, the Indian Bureau's chief engineer, recommended spending $98 million for Navajo health, education, and reclamation, with priority given to the San Juan irrigation project. Max Drefkoff, a Department of Interior industrial consultant, wanted to use tribal funds for reimbursable loans to establish small industries for Navajo war veterans at a cost of $2 million. He also suggested that traders, Euro-American businesspeople residing on the reservation, pay the tribe rent based on the gross revenue from their trading stores. After the tribal council passed a resolution supporting the Drefkoff report, Krug asked the bureau to expand tribally owned business enterprises.[29]

Krug gave Assistant Secretary of the Interior William E. Warne overall responsibility for Navajo rehabilitation when Commissioner Brophy requested an extended sick leave to recover from tuberculosis. In October 1947, Warne traveled to Window Rock to testify at a hearing held by Ben F. Jenson, a Republican from Iowa and the chair of the House Appropriations Committee. He told Jenson the Navajos faced a crisis that required immediate attention. Over sixty-one thousand Indians lived in an arid environment where the range capacity provided an adequate standard of living for approximately thirty-five thousand people. It also was impossible to effectively treat health problems such as dysentery, tuberculosis, pneumonia, and infant mortality because the reservation did not have an all-weather road system.[30]

Warne estimated that Congress would have to spend $79 million to ensure Navajo economic independence. This represented almost 50 percent less than the $157 million recommended by the Indian Bureau and the Navajo Coordinating Committee. In order to get congressional support for his proposal, Warne decided to eliminate $60 million for the San Juan irrigation project and $18 million for Navajo education. Without consulting the tribal council, the assistant secretary estimated that schools would be required for only 13,500 students because 75 percent of the children would not attend school.[31]

Warne also submitted to Jenson's committee a separate report entitled "The Navajo Welfare Situation." It detailed the emergency aid needed by impoverished Navajos who were in the same predicament as hungry Irish peasants during the nineteenth century. Before Congress could act on this report, newspaper and radio accounts of impending starvation forced President Truman to intervene on behalf of the Navajos. In November 1947, he directed the Agriculture and Defense Departments, as well as the War Assets Administration, to provide the Navajos with surplus food, clothing, and equipment.[32]

The president also issued a press release to reassure the general public that he had taken decisive action. In this statement, he reviewed emergency efforts to prevent Navajo hunger and suffering. Truman concluded by promising to submit a long-range Navajo rehabilitation program before the next regular session of Congress.[33]

A short time later, Congress passed Public Law 39, which authorized $2 million to meet emergency relief needs and fund an off-reservation employment program. The Indian Bureau used $500,000 of this money to establish an Office of Employment and Placement that contacted state employment services, farm labor organizations, and traders to secure temporary off-reservation jobs for thirteen thousand Navajos.[34]

In the meantime, the Indian Bureau distributed emergency assistance from public and private agencies. The War Assets Administration sent over seventeen tons of food from decommissioned ships of the Maritime Commission, eight ambulances, and winter clothing. The Department of Agriculture supplied the Navajos with over one hundred tons of surplus potatoes. Gifts of food and clothing were received from forty-three states, Columbia, Venezuela, and France. Gallup businessmen organized Navajo, Inc., to handle the distribution of these commodities and $13,903 in cash contributions, while the Gallup Women's Club turned over 435 cartons from different areas of the United States. The Presbyterian Church, Latter-day Saints, and American Friends Service Committee also shipped staples, canned goods, shoes, and other items.[35]

In early December 1947, the National Congress of American Indians held its annual convention in Santa Fe. There, representatives from fifty tribes heard Sam Ahkeah blame the Indian Bureau for Navajo problems. Next, they listened to Ruth Kirk insist that standards for Navajo health, education, and welfare should be comparable to non-Indian communities. Napoleon Bonaparte Johnson, the NCAI president, also criticized Arizona and New Mexico for refusing to give Indians the franchise. More confrontational was James Curry, the NCAI legal counsel, who urged litigation and political pressure to secure social justice for Navajos. At the closing session, the delegates passed resolutions that requested a reorganization of the Indian Bureau, a Navajo relief and rehabilitation program, and the extension of voting rights.[36]

During the convention, Johnson and Ruth Muskrat Bronson met with Ahkeah at the LaFonda Hotel to discuss how to improve the Navajos' standard of living. After Ahkeah departed, Elizabeth Chief, an Indian social worker from Shiprock, took Johnson and Bronson to nearby hogans. There they observed firsthand how the federal government had neglected its responsibility as guardian (pl. 10).[37]

Chief, who worked for the Indian Bureau, was an outspoken critic of the New Mexico Department of Social Welfare. She questioned the integrity of state officials who did not provide assistance to aged, sick, and blind Navajos (pl. 11). Chief traveled on horseback over rough trails to assist mothers with malnourished small children and to investigate the condition of Indians who were drinking polluted water from irrigation ditches near the San Juan River. Chief's outspoken public statements against state officials and her use of photographs to document human misery brought a reprimand from Lucy Adams, the Indian Bureau's director of welfare and placement. Adams recommended Chief's transfer to the Pine Ridge Reservation in South Dakota.[38]

After the NCAI convention, Curry advised Alfred Miller, a Navajo veteran and theology student from Phoenix, to defy the Interior Department and run sheep on the reservation without a permit. Curry told Miller that in 1943 the tribal council had revoked its consent to grazing regulations that allowed an unequal allocation of permits to the owners of larger herds because under the Navajo Treaty of 1868 each Navajo was entitled to an equitable share of the range. Curry's legal action on behalf of Miller marked the end of stock reduction even though Secretary Krug had accomplished the same objective by turning over the enforcement of this program to the tribal council.[39]

Will Rogers Jr., the son of the world-famous cowboy political satirist from Oklahoma, participated in the NCAI effort to assist Navajos. After serving in General George Patton's army in World War II, Rogers carried on his father's humanitarian spirit by organizing the American Citizens League in Los Angeles to assist hundreds of urban Indians. He affiliated this pan-Indian group with the NCAI and became an outspoken critic of the Indian Bureau. Rogers believed that instead of championing self-determination, the bureau formulated policies without Indian consultation. For Rogers, the bureau should have a dual function: it should train Indians as top-level managers to assist less educated people and should gradually withdraw supervision over tribes that wanted to manage their own affairs (pl. 12).[40]

Rogers publicized the plight of Navajos in an article for *Look Magazine* entitled "Starvation without Representation." It noted that through government neglect the Navajo Reservation had become America's biggest slum. Rogers thought it was time to bring the Navajos into the nation's cultural and economic orbit and end the public scandal of sixty thousand citizens living "in a cultural zoo."[41]

He offered several recommendations to accomplish this objective, the most important of which included the complete reorganization of the Indian Bureau, approval by Congress of a ten-year Navajo rehabilitation plan, and the delivery of social services and medical care by the Federal Security Agency and Public Health Service. Rogers saw no reason why the Navajos should not have the same rights as other citizens. He also criticized both Arizona and New Mexico for discriminating against Indians by not letting them vote in state elections or participate in Social Security programs.[42]

Rogers's proposals to combat racial discrimination bore no resemblance to recommendations made by D'Arcy McNickle, in May 1947, before the President's Committee on Civil Rights. Speaking on behalf of the NCAI, McNickle asked President Truman to inform his official family that it was the policy of the United States to protect Indian customs and the civil right of tribal self-rule. McNickle also suggested that Truman should use his authority to prevent government officials from confiscating Indian timberland in Alaska and should guarantee tribes organized under the IRA the right to manage their own property without bureaucratic interference. The committee ignored this pointed criticism but did recommend that Arizona and New Mexico extend the suffrage to Indians and enforce the nondiscrimination sections of the 1936 Social Security Act.[43]

One year later, court rulings in Arizona and New Mexico upheld the Indians' right to vote. In July 1948, Justice Levi Udall of the Arizona Supreme Court, in response to litigation initiated by the National Congress of American Indians and other parties, held that the section of the Arizona Constitution that disqualified persons under guardianship from registering to vote did not apply to Indians as a class. He ruled that federal officials did not have custody over Indian plaintiffs except for holding title to their trust property. Udall emphasized that other citizens who were beneficiaries of trust estates did not become persons under guardianship.[44]

One month later, a three-judge federal constitutional court in Santa Fe ruled favorably on arguments presented by James Curry, Felix Cohen, and William Truswell on behalf of Miguel H. Trujillo, a Pueblo Indian plaintiff. The court held that the provision of the New Mexico Constitution denying the franchise to not-taxed Indians violated the Fifteenth Amendment to the United States Constitution. Solicitors from the Departments of Justice and Interior submitted *amicus curiae* briefs in both cases to support the Indians' legal position.[45]

The right of Navajos and other Indians to benefits under the Social Security Act, which provided old-age insurance, aid-to-dependent children, and assistance to blind people, took longer to resolve. In 1936, Solicitor Nathan Margold had ruled that Indians who remained wards of the government were entitled to share in Social Security benefits. Margold's opinion stated that Indians did not exist in a water-tight department impervious to state law. He also noted that the Social Security Board could stop payments if states refused to comply with this statute. Indians who failed to obtain relief through administrative channels could resort to judicial action.[46]

The states of Arizona and New Mexico, which had large Indian populations, disregarded Margold's ruling. They refused to authorize Social Security payments to Indians because it would drain their financial resources and reduce the level of benefits to other residents. More importantly, local officials did not want to set precedent for the transfer to their states of other expensive federal programs for Indians.[47]

The All Pueblo Council challenged this noncompliance with the provisions of the Social Security Act. It filed a lawsuit in the U.S. District Court of Columbia to block the expenditure of federal funds to operate racially discriminatory Social Security programs. The district court granted the Pueblo petition for equal treatment in June 1947. The Social Security Administration, however, refused to hold hearings in the summer of 1948 on this ruling or to withdraw $10 million in matching funds to compel Arizona and New Mexico to comply with the law.[48]

Secretary Krug and Oscar Ewing, the Social Security administrator, were determined not to air this controversy prior to the November 1948 presidential election. Consequently, they made an unusual agreement with state officials. Indians were allowed to apply for benefits, and the states forwarded their applications to the Indian Bureau. Secretary Krug used a portion of the $500,000 authorized by Congress in December 1947 for emergency Navajo relief to fund Social Security benefits. After this money was spent, Arizona and New Mexico continued to process applications and send them to the Indian Bureau.[49]

In September 1948, the NCAI filed a lawsuit in the U.S. District Court of Columbia to redress the deprivation of civil rights that occurred in Arizona and New Mexico when state authorities refused to process Indian Social Security applications. It indicated that the decision to exclude Indians had caused much suffering and eighty-two deaths from starvation or malnutrition. Krug and Ewing also were charged with a corrupt political conspiracy and misappropriation of public funds to disqualify Indians from the equal benefit of Social Security laws enjoyed by other citizens.[50]

Secretary Krug forwarded Navajo rehabilitation legislation to Congress during the prolonged controversy over Social Security benefits. It recommended $90 million in capital improvements to build roads and communications systems, set up a revolving credit fund, establish business enterprises, and provide adequate social services. The Navajo Tribal Council also was required to adopt an IRA constitution and participate in an off-reservation job placement program.[51]

Krug did not view this legislation as recognition of the Navajos' inherent right to self-rule. Instead, it represented the first step toward ending federal guardianship. The secretary was convinced that the large-scale resettlement of Navajos and construction of roads on the reservation would lead to rapid assimilation. He also thought a federally recognized tribal constitution would enable Navajo citizens to better understand American political ideology.[52]

Sam Ahkeah disliked the secretary of interior's paternalism. In March 1948, he wrote John Tabor, chair of the House Appropriations Committee, that Indian Bureau officials had spent two years preparing a rehabilitation plan and allowed the tribal council only four days to respond to this proposal. Ahkeah urged government officials to consult with the tribe on a regular basis, appoint a competent administrator with business experience to oversee Navajo economic development, fund the San Juan irrigation project to protect Navajo water rights, and appropriate more money for schools to honor the Navajo Treaty of 1868 (pl. 13).[53]

Ahkeah also objected to section 5 of H.R. 5392, which required the Navajos to draft a federally recognized constitution. He told Tabor the tribe had voted against the IRA to limit the authority of the secretary of interior. The Navajos preferred a form of government that could be easily amended to permit the fullest possible exercise of tribal powers and responsibilities.[54]

The tribal chair then asked for the resignation of Acting Commissioner William Zimmerman. Ahkeah resented Zimmerman's attempt in December 1947 to reappoint as superintendent E. Reesman Fryer, who was returning from other assignments at the end of World War II, and feared that Fryer might once again try to enforce unpopular grazing regulations. Ahkeah believed that the acting commissioner should have worked harder to help Indians assume their responsibilities as citizens instead of job hunting for favored personnel.[55]

Yet another confrontation with Zimmerman occurred when the Senate Interior and Insular Affairs Committee and the House Public Lands Committee met during March and April 1948 to consider Secretary Krug's Navajo-Hopi rehabilitation bills. At these hearings, Ahkeah asked Congress to double the $25 million targeted for education. Zimmerman, on the other hand, testified that the Interior Department's lower estimate of money would be sufficient for Navajo children who remained on the reservation. Because of this conflicting testimony, Navajo rehabilitation legislation did not pass the Eightieth Congress.[56]

In October 1948, the Navajo Advisory Committee, the executive arm of the tribal council, met with Zimmerman to express its continued dissatisfaction with the Indian Bureau. Joe Duncan asked the acting commissioner why the tribe's request for financial assistance to improve law and order remained on the shelf in a pile of dust. Howard Gorman also reminded Zimmerman that the fifteen Navajo police officers, who earned the pitiful sum of $1,080 a year, were responsible for the entire reservation of over sixty thousand people.[57]

The Advisory Committee wanted to hire twenty-five additional police at the district level and supplement their pay with tribal funds. Amos Singer thought these individuals would curb lawlessness by arresting drunks who insulted the tribal council. Howard Gorman and Zhealy Tso believed that an expanded police force would help families reclaim their grazing rights and prevent thugs from robbing off-reservation workers at the Gallup bus stop. Zimmerman told the committee that his request to double appropriations for law enforcement had been turned down because members of Congress thought states should assume responsibility for law and order in Indian country.[58]

After he returned to the nation's capital, Zimmerman received a letter from Ahkeah asking for clarification of the rights of Navajos who left the reservation to find jobs. The acting commissioner replied that Navajos employed outside the reservation would continue to have their property rights protected under the Navajo Treaty of 1868 and subsequent legislation. This did not apply, however, to individuals who relocated to the Colorado River Reservation in southern Arizona. There, settlers had to apply for an irrigation permit and tribal membership within three years or return to the Navajo Reservation.[59]

During the winter of 1948–49 the Navajos had to endure a series of blizzards, unprecedented snowfalls, and bitterly cold weather. Conditions were especially harsh for families and livestock on the western part of the reservation. There, Indians were marooned in drafty hogans and overcrowded government schools where snowdrifts reached eight feet. At the Teec Nos Pos school, a doctor reported cases of pneumonia, measles, and frostbite.[60]

Secretary Krug designated the Red Cross as the exclusive agency to administer emergency Navajo relief. This organization spent over $216,000 and worked closely with U.S. military and state authorities. More than ninety-five thousand pounds of food, as well as medicine, firewood, and hay for distressed livestock, were airlifted to Navajos in Operation Snowbound. The Red Cross also sent penicillin and blood plasma, recruited twenty nurses to work at Window Rock, and provided extended care to 565 families.[61]

This crisis put additional pressure on Congress to pass Navajo-Hopi rehabilitation legislation. Truman's presidential victory in November 1948 and the renewed Democratic control of Congress also produced positive results. During June 1949, bills were introduced and sent to the House Public Lands Committee and Senate Interior and Insular Affairs Committee that followed most of Secretary Krug's earlier recommendations. Furthermore, there were amendments to address issues raised by the Navajo Tribal Council that authorized the tribe to lease trust land for religious, educational, and other purposes. This legislation also created a bipartisan committee to study and administer reservation economic development.[62]

No one, however, listened seriously to the views of hereditary Hopi chieftains at the pueblos of Hotevilla, Shongopovi, and Mishongovi. They told President

Truman and members of Congress that the Hopi Nation had been self-governing long before the arrival of non-Indians. The Hopi opposed this legislation because it failed to recognize the boundaries of their homeland that the Great Spirit Masau'u had put on stone tablets. Government officials also had not consulted with them about economic assistance. The chieftains strongly objected to off-reservation employment and other programs that the government planned for their lives.[63]

The reluctance of Congress to accept the inherent power of tribes to run their own affairs became a public issue when Representative Antonio M. Fernandez of New Mexico inserted section 9 in the rehabilitation bill, an amendment that subjected Navajo and Hopi Indians to state jurisdiction. Nonetheless, Indian property remained tax-exempt, and federal laws were recognized that dealt with management, assignment, inheritance, and disposition of Indian land. Congress also maintained its responsibility for Navajo-Hopi education under revisions to this proposed legislation.[64]

The Fernandez amendment was part of the broader movement after the war to design a new framework for Indian affairs. By 1949, there was general agreement that the Navajos and other tribes should have equal citizenship. The problem was how to reconcile the actual circumstances of Indian life with the limited resources of state governments. It also was unclear how to make compatible the inherent power of tribes to self-rule, which often included special treaty rights, with equal protection under the federal and state constitutions.[65]

In June 1949, the Navajo Tribal Council met with John Nichols, the new Indian commissioner, to discuss the Fernandez amendment. Nichols had left his job as president of the New Mexico College of Agriculture and Mechanic Arts at Las Cruces to replace William Brophy, who had resigned the previous year due to bad health. Howard Gorman, a founding member of the NCAI, told Nichols that he opposed section 9 of the Navajo-Hopi Rehabilitation bill. Gorman believed that it would be a catastrophe for the Navajos to come under state jurisdiction because 85 percent of the tribe was illiterate. The commissioner indicated that he too opposed the Fernandez amendment because it created overlapping legal jurisdictions.[66]

Gorman then stated that Navajo judges and the tribal Court of Indian Offenses would best serve the needs of his people and that additional Navajo police were necessary to stop the activities of Mexican bootleggers. Nichols replied that the Indian Bureau had asked Congress to appropriate funds to employ more police and raise their salary to $1,800 a year. Instead of helping the tribal council deal with these complex issues, Nichols announced his early departure to Washington. The failure to provide leadership during this crisis undercut the commissioner's credibility with the Navajos and officials at the Interior Department.[67]

On 10 June, the tribal council held a lengthy discussion about the significance of section 9. Gorman emphasized that the Navajos had never requested state jurisdiction. He cited a 1948 NCAI report that reaffirmed the right of tribes to accept or reject state control over their courts and police. Gorman then announced that Napoleon Bonaparte Johnson, the NCAI president, would arrive soon to explain why some tribes welcomed state jurisdiction while others believed that it violated treaties, disrupted tribal administration of law and order, and abrogated their right to self-determination.[68]

The tribal council listened carefully to Gorman but followed the advice of Norman M. Littell, their attorney, who had withdrawn Justice Department support in 1939 for Felix Cohen's *Handbook of Federal Indian Law*, which upheld the principle of federal jurisdiction in Indian affairs. On numerous occasions, Littell had discussed the Navajo situation with Fernandez on the telephone. Both men believed that the tribe must come under state control to fully participate in the political life of the United States.[69]

Littell pointed out that Indian defendants did not have the right to a jury or a lawyer before tribal courts and that local businessmen would feel more confident in extending credit if state laws applied to the reservation. After further discussion, the tribal council approved the Fernandez amendment by a vote of 37 to 20. It also upheld the Navajo Treaty of 1868 and recommended that Navajo schools follow state educational policies.[70]

In early September 1949, the Navajo Advisory Committee conferred with Fernandez in Santa Fe. There, he admitted the only way Congress would approve state jurisdiction was to attach his amendment as a rider to the House bill. This convinced wary members of the committee to recommend that section 9 should be considered as separate legislation.[71]

Two weeks later, Ahkeah contacted members of a joint House-Senate conference committee and requested the removal of section 9. Senator Ernest W. McFarland of Arizona and Representative Toby Morris of Oklahoma ignored Ahkeah's advice because they were convinced that access to state courts would provide the Indians with the same opportunity as other citizens to redress wrongs and defend their rights. The joint conference committee's final report recommended $88,750,000 for Navajo and Hopi rehabilitation. The Senate conferees also added a provision that made Arizona, New Mexico, and Utah responsible for administering Indian Social Security benefits. These states had to pay 8 percent of the benefits, and the federal government paid the remaining 92 percent. Congress accepted this conference report by a voice vote and sent it to President Truman.[72]

In the meantime, Harold Ickes, John Collier, and Eleanor Roosevelt mounted a campaign to defeat this legislation. Ickes scheduled a conference with President Truman to criticize both Secretary Krug and Commissioner Nichols for not providing strong leadership to protect Indian rights. Collier met with Clark Clifford, a White House staff adviser, and requested a presidential veto. Roosevelt expressed similar views in a private letter to Truman.[73]

One of the most persuasive arguments for a veto came from Oliver LaFarge, president of the Association on American Indian Affairs, who told Truman that Congress had ignored the views of the Navajo Advisory Committee. LaFarge doubted the wisdom of substituting forced assimilation for the more reasonable policy of tribal self-determination. He warned that litigation and legal confusion would occur under concurrent tribal, federal, and state jurisdiction. LaFarge recommended that President Truman ask Congress to resubmit this legislation without section 9.[74]

Ahkeah responded to this crisis by calling an emergency meeting of the Navajo Tribal Council on 11 October 1949. He explained that the Navajo Advisory Committee on three occasions had asked Congress to consider the complex issue of state jurisdiction in a separate bill and was told that authority in this matter rested with the Navajo Tribal Council.[75]

After Ahkeah's introductory remarks, Littell tried to persuade the tribal council to once again support the Fernandez amendment. He indicated that Congress would not have approved this legislation without section 9, which gave the Navajos the right to participate in state government. Littell then played to the anti-Collier sentiment in the audience. He referred to a telegram that each councilman had received from the former commissioner stating that section 9 threatened Navajo water rights to the San Juan River.[76]

The Navajo attorney rejected as hysterical the idea that the tribe would relinquish its water rights. He warned the Navajos that Collier's credibility should be judged by past experience. He stated that the former commissioner had the greatest opportunity in the history of the Indian affairs to help the Navajos. Instead, he imposed draconian grazing regulations, vetoed money for roads between Tuba City and Kayenta to keep the Navajos as a national museum piece, built unusable day schools, and constructed a million-dollar capital at Window Rock known as Collier's folly. Littell argued that the Fernandez amendment provided a congressional alternative to that kind of administration.[77]

When the tribal council reconvened on 13 October, it heard the testimony of William Truswell, an attorney employed by the Indian Bureau at Window Rock. He was more effective than Collier in persuading the Navajos to question the wisdom of state jurisdiction. Truswell agreed with Littell that the amended bill did not pose a serious threat to Navajo water rights. The Navajos, however, would be liable for sales, inheritance, income, and other state taxes. Under concurrent jurisdiction, the Justice of Peace Courts in Arizona and New Mexico, which operated on a fee system, might run the underfunded tribal courts out of business. These two states also did not have adequate financial resources to provide law enforcement for such a large reservation.[78]

Gorman supported Truswell's testimony. He emphasized that the Navajos strongly favored the original rehabilitation bill. They mailed letters all over the United States, appeared before civic groups, and sent delegates to Congress to gain support for this measure. They did not, however, give tribal consent to section 9. Gorman noted that Indians from North Dakota, who were under state jurisdiction, had informed him that they still encountered racial discrimination. After Gorman concluded his remarks, the tribal council voted 26–19 against the amended bill and requested a presidential veto.[79]

The controversy over the Fernandez amendment divided officials in the Truman administration. Secretary Krug and Indian Commissioner Nichols recommended that Truman approve the bill because of the large amount of money authorized for reservation economic development. Those advocating a veto included Assistant Interior Secretary Oscar Chapman, as well as Charles Murphy and Philleo Nash from the White House Staff.[80]

On 17 October 1949, Truman vetoed the Navajo-Hopi bill. He confided to Ickes that the bill "was a shenanigan and not for the benefit of the Indians at all." The president was influenced by the vote of the Navajo Tribal Council. He believed that concurrent jurisdiction under section 9 would result in years of expensive litigation over Navajo land and water rights. Truman also thought that the imposition of state law conflicted with the recognized principle of self-determination in matters of local government. The president favored the complete merger of Indian groups into American society but saw no reason to prematurely compel tribal dissolution.[81]

In his veto message, Truman promised to support the Navajo-Hopi bill if Congress deleted section 9. Both the House and Senate complied with this request, and the president signed the $88.7 million Navajo-Hopi Rehabilitation Act on 19 April 1950. For Truman, this statute was milestone legislation because Congress, for the first time, had designed a long-range program that would hasten the day when federal assistance for Indians could be withdrawn.[82]

On 21 February 1951, Truman met with members of the Navajo Tribal Council in the White House Rose Garden and told them that Americans owed a debt to Indians that could never be repaid. The president then revealed that his interest in giving the Indians a fair deal came, in part, from reading books about great Indian leaders and the Iroquois League of Six Nations.[83]

During the Truman years, the Navajos made significant progress toward self-determination. They reaffirmed their government-to-government relationship with the United States by insisting that federal officials consult with them on all important matters. Another significant development was the more efficient operation of the seventy-four-member Navajo Tribal Council. It delegated considerable authority to an eleven-person advisory committee that successfully opposed the imposition of state jurisdiction. Furthermore, new election procedures were adopted that enabled Navajos off the reservation to vote for members of the tribal council without returning home. These changes laid the groundwork for a parliamentary system of government without the constraints of an IRA tribal constitution.[84]

The Navajos' greatest achievement was to persuade the federal government to design a comprehensive plan to develop reservation resources. Before President Truman left office, Congress had appropriated over $9 million for water development on range land, road construction, and irrigation facilities. In addition, a special revolving credit fund was used to build reservation boarding schools and enlarge the Tuba City hospital.[85]

Events on the Navajo Reservation had a dramatic impact on federal Indian policy. The effort to find off-reservation jobs for Navajos in America's prosperous postwar economy evolved into a comprehensive program to relocate Indians from all areas of the country to cities. National attention was drawn to the shortcomings of the reservation system, where Indians encountered poverty and heavy-handed federal paternalism. President Truman addressed this situation by including the Indian Bureau in his plans to reorganize the executive branch of government. In a parallel effort, Congress would attempt to emancipate Indians from wardship by identifying tribes that were ready to manage their own affairs under state jurisdiction.

5

EMANCIPATION FROM
FEDERAL WARDSHIP

Americanizing the Indian . . . is a regrettably patronizing phrase. After
all, we were Americans before you were. What you are interested in is
Europeanizing the original Americans. Many of us are willing to accept
European ideas about science and public health, but most reluctant to
accept European ideas about government. We think that we have made a
substantial contribution to the theory and practice of democracy, which we
taught to your ancestors. RUTH MUSKRAT BRONSON TO JOHN R. NICHOLS,
HOOVER COMMISSION TASK FORCE ON INDIAN AFFAIRS, FEBRUARY 1948

The movement to emancipate Indians from federal wardship, which began
during World War II, was neither temporary or superficial. The years 1945 to 1949
marked a turning point in Indian history comparable to the end of treaty making,
land allotment, and tribal organization under the Indian Reorganization Act.
Republicans in Congress took the lead, as they had after the Civil War, by
advocating a principled approach to politics that called for assimilation of
Indians, extension of citizenship rights, abolition of the Indian Bureau, and
the supremacy of national institutions.[1]

These sentiments, which reflected Cold War beliefs about the superiority
of Euro-American civilization and political ideology, had widespread support.
The Hoover Commission on the Reorganization of the Executive Branch of
Government and the Institute on American Indian Self-Government sponsored
by the Association on American Indian Affairs publicized the shortcomings of
the Indian Reorganization Act and made recommendations to integrate Indians
into the broader national society. In closely related endeavors, the National
Congress of American Indians established ARROW (American Restitution and
Righting of Old Wrongs). Furthermore, NCAI and other tribal leaders met with
the governors of states to end federal wardship.[2]

Secretary of Interior Julius Krug also took important steps to emancipate Indians. He cooperated with members of Congress to identify tribes in California and other states that were ready to manage their own affairs. Nonetheless, a tension remained between Krug and those individuals who identified with the New Deal tribal alternative to assimilation. Indian Bureau Commissioners William A. Brophy and John R. Nichols, Acting Commissioner William Zimmerman, and such Native American leaders as D'Arcy McNickle and Ruth Muskrat Bronson favored the full development of reservation resources during a gradual withdrawal under the Indian Reorganization Act and the continued federal recognition of tribal sovereignty.

In April 1945, one month after his appointment, Indian Commissioner William Brophy received a lengthy memo from Vernon D. Northrup, the director of the Division of Budget and Administrative Management of the Interior Department. In an unusual display of administrative candor, Northrup warned Brophy that Congress would never condone the waste of money and the inexcusable administrative expenses that occurred during the New Deal. Furthermore, Northrup advised the commissioner to address complex issues such as who was an Indian and under what circumstances wardship would end.[3]

Brophy responded to Northrup by making plans to close the Grande Ronde–Siletz, Great Lakes, New York, and Tomah agencies that served acculturated Indians. The commissioner dropped this initiative when Fred H. Daiker, the director of the Indian Bureau's Welfare Division, reminded him that tribes with IRA constitutions and bylaws had the legal right to self-rule under federal protection. Before the bureau liquidated these agencies, it would have to obtain tribal consent and make sure that trust property was protected under state jurisdiction.[4]

After considering the points raised by Daiker, Brophy decided that tribes should use their IRA charters to terminate the supervisory authority of the secretary of interior. Under this procedure, the Indian Bureau could begin an orderly withdrawal of federal supervision. Brophy asked D'Arcy McNickle, a field representative, and Assistant Interior Secretary G. Girard Davidson to discuss this idea with the Indians on the Flathead Reservation in Montana.[5]

In September 1946, McNickle and Davidson met with representatives of the Salish and Kootenai Tribes at agency headquarters in Dixon. McNickle, who was one-quarter Cree, had grown up on the reservation before attending the Indian boarding school at Chemewa, Oregon. He urged the tribal council to develop a plan under its IRA charter for self-determination because Congress might begin federal withdrawal without Indian consent. McNickle proposed that the Flatheads independently operate their municipal government by taxing tribal business enterprises and personal property.[6]

These ideas met with a cold reception. Tribal chair Eneas Granjo warned that administrative expenses would consume practically all of their income. Lester Dupuis, the council's vice-chair, feared that after federal withdrawal the government would ignore its moral and legal obligations under the Flathead Treaty of 1855. If this happened, they would lose important medical and educational services as well as unrestricted hunting and fishing rights. Dupuis also rejected McNickle's suggestion to hire a business manager because it gave one person too much authority. Other council members wanted to know if the government would continue to purchase additional land, build roads, make per capita payments, and provide adequate schools.[7]

The Flathead Tribal Council did appoint a special committee to study McNickle's recommendations. In June 1947, the tribal council informed Brophy that the Flatheads favored the status quo because they might lose control over valuable timber resources and rental income from the Kerr Dam. The council reaffirmed the U.S. government's responsibility to settle pending claims and honor treaty commitments.[8]

Because of poor health, Brophy was unable to coordinate a federal withdrawal under the IRA. In early 1946, the commissioner requested sick leave because of pneumonia. One year later, he requested more time off to recover from tuberculosis. This created problems at the Indian Bureau, where employees paid attention to administrative detail instead of broad policy perspectives.[9]

During Brophy's absence, the Senate Civil Service Committee took decisive action to emancipate Indians from federal wardship. William Langer of North Dakota, Zales N. Ecton of Montana, Dennis Chavez of New Mexico, and other senators on this committee were advocates of states rights and unrestrained economic development of the West. They disliked the Indian Reorganization Act, which imposed restrictions on the sale of property and encouraged a measured tribal separatism.

In January 1947, the Senate Civil Service Committee subpoenaed Acting Commissioner William Zimmerman to give sworn testimony. This heavy-handed procedure, which resembled tactics used during the Red Scare to intimidate witnesses, drove home the point that Congress would determine the direction of federal Indian policy. The senators demanded that Zimmerman provide them with a list of tribes ready for release from federal supervision. Assistant Secretary of the Interior Davidson encouraged this abrasive behavior when he testified that the Interior Department would assist the acting commissioner in completing this assignment.[10]

A short time later, Zimmerman submitted a list to the committee that closely resembled a document John Collier had presented in 1944 before the House Committee on Indian Affairs (see table 1).[11]

The standards Zimmerman established for determining federal withdrawal were similar to those mentioned by Collier. The acting commissioner used the amount of mixed blood, literacy, acceptance of white institutions, and local non-Indian support to determine levels of acculturation. Zimmerman also added three other criteria to make federal withdrawal more difficult: the ability of tribes to make a decent standard of living, tribal consent, and the willingness of states to assume responsibilities for their Indian citizens (see table 2).[12]

Acting Commissioner Zimmerman testified that Congress could terminate federal control at an early date for group 1 on his list. Included were 53,000 people who had requested the end of federal protection, the right to manage their own affairs, and the abolition of the Indian Bureau, or who had minimal contact with the federal government. This total was far less than the 151,000 predominately acculturated Indians Collier had identified in his group 1.

Zimmerman's group 2 included 75,000 semi-acculturated people, compared to Collier's 124,000. These tribes functioned with minimal supervision. Zimmerman felt that the government could release them from federal control in two to ten years, depending on the Indian Claims Commission awards.

Zimmerman's group 3 totaled over 250,000 Indians, compared to Collier's 94,000. These predominately Indian groups would remain under federal guardianship for an indefinite period. Zimmerman believed it would take at least fifty years for the Indians in this category to move into group 1 at the rate Congress had funded land purchase under the IRA.[13]

When Ruth Muskrat Bronson, the NCAI executive secretary, appeared before the Senate Civil Service Committee, she agreed that Congress should remove certain groups from federal supervision. This step was necessary for individuals who wanted to sever tribal ties and support themselves in urban areas. Bronson coupled this remark with the recommendation that Congress should provide those Indians who wanted to stay at home with more money to purchase land and build expanded irrigation facilities.[14]

The Eightieth Congress did not pass legislation to begin federal withdrawal. It did, however, continue to show a lively interest in Indian matters. In the first session of the Eightieth Congress, eighty-seven bills were introduced that required the secretary of interior to issue patents-in-fee to land allotments, whereas forty-six bills directed the government to sell individual pieces of submarginal land that had been purchased for Indians during the Great Depression. Other legislative proposals attempted to repeal the Indian Reorganization Act,

Table 1. John Collier's Withdrawal Recommendations

GROUP 1. PREDOMINANTLY ACCULTURATED POPULATION

California:

Hoopa Valley Agency and Reservation	1,602
Hoopa Valley Rancherias	373
Mission Indians	7,007
Sacramento Agency	10,825

Kansas:

Potawatomi Agency	2,186

Michigan:

Great Lakes Agency	1,454
Tomah Agency	3,700

Minnesota:

Consolidated Chippewa Agency	14,124
Pipestone School	950
Red Lake Chippewa Agency and Reservation	2,329

Nebraska:

Winnebago Agency	4,712

New York:

New York Agency	6,835

North Carolina:

Eastern Cherokee Agency and Reservation	3,622

Oklahoma:

Five Civilized Tribes Agency	57,000
Osage Agency and Reservation	4,331
Pawnee Agency	3,391
Quapaw Agency	3,711
Shawnee Agency	5,024

Oregon:

Grande Ronde–Siletz Agency and Reservation	485
Siletz Reservation	521
Fourth Section (All public domain)	789

Texas:

Alabama and Coushatta Reservation	351

Washington:

Taholah Agency, Unenrolled Indians	500
Tulalip Agency:	
Public domain (Clallam)	962
Public domain (Nooksak)	255
Public domain (Skagit)	230

Wisconsin:

Great Lakes Agency	5,338
Keshena Agency and Menominee Reservation	2,606
Tomah Agency	5,487

Total	**150,700**

GROUP 2. SEMI-ACCULTURATED POPULATION

California:

Carson Agency	1,580
Fort Independence Reservation	70

Idaho:

Fort Hall Agency and Reservation	1,894
Northern Idaho Agency	2,248

Iowa:

Sac and Fox Agency and Reservation	488

Mississippi:

Choctaw Agency: Chitimacha Reservation (Louisiana)	100
Mississippi Agency and Reservation	2,098

Montana:

Blackfeet Agency and Reservation	4,795
Crow Agency and Reservation	2,348
Flathead Agency and Reservation	3,305
Fort Belknap Agency and Reservation	1,697
Fort Peck Agency and Reservation	3,022
Rocky Boy's Agency and Reservation	829
Tongue River Agency and Reservation	1,661

Nevada:

Carson Agency	3,990
Western Shoshone Agency	1,434

North Dakota:

Fort Berthold Agency and Reservation	1,886
Fort Totten Agency and Devils Lake Reservation	1,095
Sisseton Agency and Reservation	59
Standing Rock Agency and Reservation	1,964
Turtle Mountain Agency and Reservation	7,215

Oklahoma:

Cheyenne and Arapaho Agency and Reservation	2,972
Five Civilized Tribes Agency	22,000
Kiowa Agency	
Kiowa Reservation	5,336
Wichita Reservation	1,672

Oregon:

Klamath Agency and Reservation	1,506
Umatilla Agency and Reservation	1,291
Warm Springs Agency and Reservation	815
Yakima Agency, The Dalles Allotments	51

South Dakota:

Cheyenne River Agency and Reservation	3,704
Crow Creek Agency	1,665
Flandreau School Jurisdiction	277
Pine Ridge Agency and Reservation	9,584
Rosebud Agency	9,162
Sisseton Agency and Reservation	3,007
Standing Rock Agency and Reservation	2,159

Washington:

Colville Agency	4,382
Northern Idaho Agency, Kalispel Reservation	103
Taholah Agency	2,532
Tulalip Agency	2,643
Yakima Agency and Reservation	3,092

Wyoming:

Wind River Agency and Reservation	2,534

Total **124,228**

GROUP 3. PREDOMINANTLY INDIAN POPULATION

Arizona:

Colorado River Agency	1,259
Fort Apache Agency and Reservation	3,023
Hopi Agency and Reservation	3,494
Navajo Agency and Reservation	25,243
Pima Agency	6,587
San Carlos Apache Agency and Reservation	3,244
Sells Agency	6,303
Truxton Canyon Agency	1,202
Uintah and Ouray Agency, Kaibab Paiute Reservation	83

California:

Colorado River Agency, Fort Yuma Reservation	930

Colorado:

Consolidated Ute Agency	808

Florida:

Seminole Agency and Reservation	619

Idaho:

Western Shoshone Agency and Reservation	209

New Mexico:

Jicarilla Apache Agency and Reservation	768
Mescalero Apache Agency and Reservation	823
Navajo Agency and Reservation	22,761
United Pueblos Agency	14,107

Utah:

Consolidated Ute Agency, Allen Canyon Subagency	36
Fort Hall Agency, Washakie Shoshone Subagency	131
Navajo Agency and Reservation	314
Uintah and Ouray Ute Agency	1,610
Western Shoshone Agency	250

Total **93,896**

Total Population of All Groups **368,819**

Source: U.S. Congress. House. Committee on Indian Affairs. *Hearings on H.R. 166: A Bill to Authorize and Direct and Conduct an Investigation to Determine Whether the Changed Status of the Indian Requires a Revision of the Laws and Regulations Affecting the American Indian*. Part 2: 78th Cong., 2nd sess., 1944.

Table 2. William Zimmerman's Withdrawal Recommendation

GROUP 1. PREDOMINANTLY ACCULTURATED POPULATION	GROUP 2. SEMI-ACCULTURATED POPULATION	GROUP 3. PREDOMINANTLY INDIAN POPULATION
Flathead	Blackfeet	Cheyenne and Arapaho
Hoopa	Cherokee	Choctaw
Potawatomi	Cheyenne River	Colorado River
Klamath	Colville	Consolidated Ute
Menominee	Consolidated Chippewa	Crow Creek
Mission	Crow	Five Tribes
New York	Fort Belknap	Fort Apache
Osage	Fort Peck	Fort Berthold
Sacramento	Fort Totten	Fort Hall
Turtle Mountain	Grande Ronde	Hopi
	Great Lakes	Jicarilla
53,000	Northern Idaho	Kiowa
	Quapaw (Wyandotte, Seneca)	Mescalero
	Taholah, Tulalip	Navajo
	Tomah	Pawnee
	Umatilla	Pima
	Warm Springs	Pine Ridge
	Wind River (Shoshone only)	Quapaw
	Winnebago (Omaha still predominantly full-blood)	Red Lake
		Rocky Boy
	75,000	Rosebud
		San Carlos
		Sells
		Seminole
		Shawnee
		Sisseton
		Standing Rock
		Tongue River
		Truxton Canyon
		Uintah and Ouray
		United Pueblos
		Western Shoshone
		Wind River (Arapaho only)
		Yakima
		250,000

Total Population of All Groups   378,000

Source: U.S. Congress. Senate. Committee on Civil Service. *Hearings on S.R. 41: Officers and Employees of the Federal Government*, 80th Cong., 1st sess., 1947; and John H. Province, The Withdrawal of Federal Supervision over the American Indian, 9 February 1949, Box 4, J. W. Wellington Papers.

abolish the Indian Bureau, and transfer the bureau's functions to other federal agencies.[15]

In April 1947, the House Subcommittee on Indian Affairs of the Public Lands Committee considered four bills introduced by Francis Case from South Dakota and Wesley A. D'Ewart from Montana. This legislation, which did not become law, would give veterans and other Indians emancipation certificates and would guarantee Indians the right of trial by jury in tribal courts, the right to appeal litigation to state or federal courts of appropriate jurisdiction, and the right to own allotted and heirship land that the government held in trust. Furthermore, if two-thirds of resident Indians voted yes, their reservations could be sold with a per capita distribution of tribal assets.[16]

Congress did not accept these proposals, but the House passed H.R. 1113 in July 1947. This bill gave Indians the same status as immigrant aliens before naturalization proceedings. Tribal officials were required to testify on the moral behavior and intellectual ability of Indians who applied before federal and state courts to become full-fledged citizens. Qualified individuals were exempt from Indian liquor laws, and the federal government had to relinquish supervision over their property, which could be mortgaged, taxed, and sold.[17]

In the Senate, Republicans Hugh Butler and Arthur V. Watkins joined forces to emancipate California Indians. They sponsored bills to give these Indians control over their property, an equitable share of tribal assets, and a per capita distribution of claims awards. For Butler and Watkins, this was a principled way to guarantee that all California Indians would become unrestricted and unsupervised citizens (pls. 14 and 15).[18]

Under S.R. 1685, a board of appraisal would, within one year, determine the fair market value of all Indian assets. The secretary of interior would purchase this property, except for agricultural land, which could be sold to enrolled adults under competitive bids. The proceeds from the sale of this and other real estate would be distributed to individual Indians, except minors and incompetent people with special money accounts. S.R. 1565 added nonresidents to the rolls of California Indians eligible for per capita payments from a Court of Claims award of $5 million.[19]

These bills did not pass Congress because of opposition from the Department of Interior. Secretary Krug wanted to amend S.R. 1565 and set aside $1 million in claims money to assist veterans and other needy Indians. He also made recommendations to help resolve a chaotic situation where three tribal groups, divided by deep-seated factionalism, had signed contracts with different attorneys to represent all California Indians before the Claims Commission.[20]

This did not mean that Krug disagreed with Senator Butler and Watkins about the need to give Indians control over their own resources. In February 1948, the secretary announced the appointment of Walter V. Woehlke to direct Indian affairs in California. Woehlke's assignment was to prepare a withdrawal plan and persuade the California state government to assume greater responsibility for its Indian citizens.[21]

The most important initiative by the Eightieth Congress concerning Indians was Public Law 162. It established the Commission on Organization of the Executive Branch of Government to make recommendations on how to promote economy, efficiency, and improved federal services. The twelve commissioners were appointed by President Truman, the Speaker of the House, and the president of the Senate. Former president Herbert Hoover chaired this commission, dominated its proceedings, took the initiative in choosing staff members, and selected topics for the commission's twenty-two task forces to study.[22]

Hoover targeted the administration of Indian affairs for review. Professor George Graham, from the Department of Political Science at Princeton University, chaired this task force. Other committee members were John R. Nichols, president of the New Mexico College of Agricultural and Mechanic Arts, Charles J. Rhoads, a Philadelphia banker and Hoover's former Indian commissioner, and the Reverend Dr. Gilbert Darlington, treasurer of the American Bible Society. Dr. Lewis Meriam, who had reviewed the problem of Indian administration in the 1920s, provided information on public welfare services for Indians.[23]

In December 1948, Graham submitted to the Hoover Commission a 160-page report. The rhetoric of this study mirrored the intolerant nationalism of the Cold War era by characterizing Indians as a conquered and primitive people. It noted that traditional tribal organization, the basis for historic Indian culture, had been dismantled for over a generation. Furthermore, the report indicated that most Indians wanted to benefit from modern civilization rather than being stereotyped as nineteenth-century storybook people. The only question for policymakers was what kind of assimilation and how fast.[24]

The task force indicated that the Indian Reorganization Act had correctly applied the principle of self-government to Indian administration. This statute also protected Indian land and encouraged respect for tribal culture. The task force praised the IRA credit fund and recommended that Congress provide technical assistance and appropriate significantly more money to meet the economic needs of qualified borrowers.[25]

Nonetheless, the task force noted that Indian support for the IRA had faded because it was a mistake to revive ancient institutions in the twentieth century. Tribal societies were dynamic, and most Indians did not want to return to an earlier stage of cultural evolution. The report indicated that the executive branch should regard self-rule under IRA not as a permanent recognition of tribal sovereignty but as a stage in the transition from federal tutelage to full Indian participation in state and local government.[26]

The Hoover report emphasized that Indians should actively participate in the formulation and execution of plans to end federal supervision. This joint effort would include specific target dates to transfer responsibility for Indian law and order, education, public health, and welfare to state governments. It also would involve the eventual abandonment of tax-exempt lands and the transfer of tribal property to Indian-owned corporations to prevent political meddling by tribal councils.[27]

The Hoover report recommended redesigning Indian chartered corporations to function under state law as capitalist rather than socialist business enterprises. Updated charters and financially accountable boards of directors would ensure the careful management of tribal loans and the inheritance of property on an individual rather than collective basis. Once these state corporations were established, the Indian Bureau could discontinue its supervision. Tribes residing on unallotted reservations would follow similar procedures except they would organize county governments.[28]

One of the most far-reaching recommendations concerned Indian removal. At least 30 percent of Indians did not own land. On the Navajo Reservation alone, a surplus population of twenty-five thousand people had to look elsewhere to make a living. The task force called for the creation of a relocation and placement program, with Congress providing financial support to Indians for three years to secure the cooperation of state and local governments.[29]

The task force report also called for the federal government and states to commit additional resources to Indian education. Ultimately, Congress should transfer all federal Indian schools to state jurisdiction. In the meantime, it must appropriate additional funds for education loans and scholarships, reorient curriculum to prepare students for off-reservation life, set up adult educational programs, and build expensive boarding schools for Navajo children.[30]

The task force challenged the concept of maintaining a separate tribal judiciary. Recent budget cuts by Congress for the salaries of Indian police and judges meant that it would be impossible to modernize an antiquated system of law and order on reservations. Therefore, it was critical for states to have legal jurisdiction over Indian country.[31]

Furthermore, a professional administrator should head the Indian Bureau to create an atmosphere of trust between Indians, the executive branch, and Congress. The commissioner should dismiss incompetent or disloyal public servants, organize field jurisdictions around geographic areas, give more authority to superintendents, and hold face-to-face discussions with Indians.[32]

The task force did not request the abolition of the Indian Bureau. Instead, it recommended that Congress transfer the bureau from the Department of Interior to the Federal Security Agency, which would bring officials at the bureau into closer contact with the Social Security Administration, the Public Health Service, the Office of Education, and state employment services.[33]

There were three dissenting opinions to this report. Dean Acheson, the vice-chair of the Hoover Commission, observed that the commission lacked jurisdiction to make recommendations that abolished functions of the executive branch and altered substantive legislative policy. Acheson's recollection of Supreme Court decisions in *Cherokee Nation v. Georgia* (1831) and *Worcester v. Georgia* (1832), as well as the painful history of Indian removal, made it impossible for him to endorse recommendations to put Indians under state jurisdiction.[34]

James H. Rowe Jr. and James Forrestal voted against the report for other reasons. Rowe believed it was unwise to transfer the bureau to the Federal Security Agency because of administrative problems associated with fifty million acres of Indian-owned land. Forrestal criticized the task force for adopting a controversial plan of forced assimilation without first considering the views of Indian people.[35]

This dissent and President Truman's surprising reelection provided Acting Commissioner Zimmerman with an opportunity to define an alternate program for Indians. In January 1949, at an address before the annual meeting of the Home Missions Council at Buck Hill Falls, Pennsylvania, Zimmerman warned that it would be a national scandal if Congress abolished the Indian Bureau prematurely. He believed that Truman's victory and Democratic control of the House and Senate made 1949 a year of opportunity. The acting commissioner was hopeful the Eighty-first Congress would ignore the Hoover report, increase Indian Bureau appropriations, and fund long-range reservation rehabilitation programs.[36]

Zimmerman believed that Indians stood at the threshold of a new era. They had come to a crossroads, and the path taken could lead to great achievement or catastrophe. He felt the correct course to follow was the gradual removal of federal supervision without casting aside sacred treaty commitments and obligations.[37]

At the beginning of his second term, Truman looked for a new Indian commissioner to replace Brophy, who had resigned in June 1948. The president wanted an administrator who would implement most of the recommendations made by the Hoover Commission. Only the personal intervention of Secretary Krug had prevented Truman from firing high-level officials at the Indian Bureau. Undersecretary of the Interior William Warne, who helped the president review

possible candidates, came up empty-handed because senators nominated political hacks. Truman responded to this dilemma by asking Dillon S. Myer, the
former director of the War Relocation Authority, to accept the job as Indian
commissioner.[38]

Myer had turned down a similar request in 1947 because of the bureau's tight
budget and the anti-administration views prevalent in the Eightieth Congress.
Myer once again declined the president's offer because he wanted to finish
drafting legislation that extended a charter for the Institute for Inter-American
Affairs. Myer later learned that Truman had personally approved a $5 million
budget for the institute to persuade him to eventually accept the "shittyass" job
of heading the Indian Bureau.[39]

In the meantime, Secretary Krug announced in January 1949 the appointment of an eleven-member National Advisory Committee on Indian Affairs to
consult with him on administrative matters. It unanimously recommended the
appointment of John R. Nichols as commissioner. Prior to serving on the Hoover
Commission task force, Nichols had advised the supreme allied commander in
Tokyo on educational reforms for Japan and served as president of the New
Mexico College of Agriculture and Mechanic Arts (pl. 16).[40]

The advisory committee endorsed Nichols after a private interview in which
Oliver LaFarge and Ruth Muskrat Bronson asked difficult questions about his
role on the Hoover Commission. Nichols confided to them that he was not
committed to the task force report. If a basic agreement could be reached on
a policy that recognized Indians as full-fledged citizens, the tempo of their
assimilation could be determined at a later date.[41]

President Truman nominated Nichols for the position of Indian commissioner at the request of Secretary Krug and Senator Clinton P. Anderson of New
Mexico. This decision was publicly challenged by William Langer, a Republican
from North Dakota. From the floor of the Senate, he asked why it was impossible
for the president to find a qualified Indian to head the bureau. In March 1949,
members of the Committee on Interior and Insular Affairs met briefly, ignored
Langer's criticism, and unanimously supported Nichols's nomination, which
subsequently received Senate approval.[42]

Once he became commissioner, Nichols surprised President Truman and
Secretary Krug by identifying with the Indian New Deal. In his annual report,
the commissioner indicated that the Indian Reorganization Act contained the
legislative authorization for the United States to withdraw from its historic role
as guardian. This statute permitted federal officials to relinquish authority to
a trained and responsible people, such as the Saginaw Chippewa Indians of
Michigan. Recently they had used provisions of their IRA charter to curtail the
supervisory role of the secretary of interior.[43]

Nichols also cited miscellaneous recommendations from the Hoover Commission report to argue against the desirability of rapid assimilation. He referred to sections of the report that asked Congress to respect Indian water rights, support education, and fund reservation economic development. He also indicated that treaties guaranteed Indians continuous possession of their lands and the right to self-determination. The mutual consent of Indians, the secretary of interior, and Congress was required to modify these legal arrangements.[44]

The commissioner pointed out that states had no jurisdiction over offenses committed by Indians on reservations or trust land, except where Congress had enacted special legislation in California, Iowa, Kansas, New York, and North Dakota. He opposed the additional transfer of Indian legal jurisdiction to states unless tribes voted in favor of this procedure at special referendums. Instead, he recommended increasing appropriations for tribal police and courts to create a modern law enforcement system for Indian communities.[45]

Nichols did cooperate with state authorities, employer groups, and church organizations to help Indians find jobs. In 1949 the bureau opened new placement offices in Aberdeen, Billings, Minneapolis, Muskogee, and Portland in addition to the Navajo-Hopi placement program. The commissioner also asked Indian children to attend state-run public schools if they were located within walking distance or accessible by bus.[46]

Nichols soon discovered that Congress was not committed to the Indian Reorganization Act. Instead, it appropriated an additional $7.8 million for Indian health, education, and welfare programs. Without adequate funds for bureau administrative services, tribal organization, and reservation economic development, Nichols was forced to reduce his central office staff from twenty-four to six people. More than one hundred employees who reported to his office were dismissed, and their duties were assumed by eleven area directors and ten superintendents.[47]

This budget reallocation gave Nichols little choice but to issue circular 3675 in May 1949. It asked tribal councils to submit updated long-range rehabilitation plans drafted during World War II.[48] Former commissioner John Collier had begun withdrawal programming in November 1943 and had requested data on the social and economic status of different Indian groups. Collier also reaffirmed the inherent power of tribes to organize corporations under IRA for modern community development. To discourage federal officials who ignored the reality of tribal existence, he noted that Indians were guaranteed the right to self-determination based on treaties, Supreme Court decisions, and federal Indian law.

Collier insisted that reservation planning should be democratic and participative, rather than authoritarian and directed. He reminded superintendents that the bureau's mission had changed from being a guardian to a consultant. This meant that Indians were to devise their own long-range plans to transfer federal authority to organized tribes.[49]

Nichols generally agreed with Collier's approach to federal withdrawal. He indicated in circular 3675 that by September 1950 all revised reservation plans should include recommendations on how to put Indians on an economic level comparable to other citizens, integrate them into the life of the nation, and end federal jurisdiction at an appropriate time in the future. Nichols insisted that Indians play a prominent role in designing withdrawal programs that set verifiable standards for the optimum development of reservation resources, adequate educational achievements comparable to other citizens, and health care that resulted in the reduction of mortality and morbidity rates.[50]

The commissioner requested that, whenever possible, these proposals provide for the progressive transfer to states of the responsibility for education, health, agricultural extension, public welfare, and other federal services. Tribal agricultural and business enterprises, on the other hand, would remain under the control of Indian federal corporations. This property would be subject to taxation only at the request of Indian owners and the approval of the interior secretary.[51]

The Association on American Indian Affairs supported Commissioner Nichols's approach to federal withdrawal at its annual meeting during May 1949. The AAIA adopted resolutions recommending that the government promptly, with Indian input, design rehabilitation plans to improve substandard economic and physical conditions on reservations throughout the United States. The AAIA believed it would be a major step toward self-determination if Indians had complete control of their tribal funds and the fullest democratic participation in reservation projects developed on their behalf.[52]

In 1949, bills to rehabilitate the Blackfeet, Chippewa-Cree, Fort Belknap Indians, Papago, Standing Rock Sioux, Sisseton-Wahpeton Sioux, and Turtle Mountain Indians were introduced in Congress. This legislation generally did not include the supporting documentation that accompanied the Navajo-Hopi long-range plan because of Indian Bureau budget cuts. Felix Cohen, the AAIA general counsel, found sections of these well-intentioned bills objectionable because they expanded bureau authority at the expense of Indian self-government, placed certain tribes under state jurisdiction, and subjected Indian land to taxation.[53]

More importantly, Elmer Staats, the acting director of President Truman's Budget Bureau, disliked approaching Indian self-determination through a series of expensive bills that gave priority to only a few Indian groups. Staats told

Senator Joseph O'Mahoney of Wyoming that it was more appropriate to increase the IRA revolving fund to meet the pressing needs of a much larger number of tribes. After the outbreak of the Korean War in June 1950, the Budget Bureau took the position that emergency military expenditures required the deferral of economic assistance to reservation communities.[54]

Commissioner Nichols created other problems. His extensive travel to Alaska, Oklahoma, and South America left Assistant Commissioner Zimmerman with the difficult task of defending rehabilitation bills before hostile committees chaired by Senators George Malone of Nevada and Hugh Butler of Nebraska. These two senators did not want to appropriate large sums of money for an overgrown federal bureaucracy that would operate for decades. Consequently, they refused to authorize additional funds for impoverished reservation communities where federal employees discouraged private enterprise by supervising tribal corporations.[55]

Many conservative members of Congress identified with the policies of the Interstate Association of Public Land Counties (IAPLC), which lobbied to protect eleven western states against the land acquisition programs of the Indian Bureau and other federal agencies. The IAPLC supported politicians who wanted to cut the bureau's budget, repeal legislation that permitted the government to acquire property and water rights for Indians, and dismantle tribal homelands such as the Klamath Reservation in Oregon.[56]

Indians shared some responsibility for this crisis. Theodore H. Haas, the chief counsel for the Indian Bureau, raised this issue in September 1949 at an address before the National Congress of American Indians in Rapid City. He noted that only 10 percent of the bureau's professional positions were filled by Indians. When the NCAI tried to correct this situation by compiling a list of qualified people, it discovered that no one was interested. Haas also wondered why more tribes did not request authority to manage their own affairs. The NCAI had passed resolutions calling for the gradual liquidation of the bureau, but only two small tribes in Michigan and Wisconsin voted to limit the supervision of the secretary of interior over their financial affairs.[57]

Haas's comments reflected a growing disillusionment with New Deal Indian reform. In April 1949, the AAIA sponsored an Institute on American Indian Self-Government at the Museum of Natural History in New York City. The purpose of this conference was to evaluate the Indian Reorganization Act and determine what changes were needed to encourage more self-determination. Distinguished guests included William Langer, Elmer Thomas, and Arthur Watkins from the Senate, as well as Philleo Nash, who represented the White House staff.[58]

Prominent speakers at this meeting were John Collier, Allan G. Harper, Felix S. Cohen, and John F. Embree. Collier told the delegates that the IRA gave tribes only limited powers of self-government. To remedy this situation, the Indian Bureau had circumvented Congress and drafted constitutions and charters to reaffirm inherent tribal powers. Collier also indicated that his attempt to use the extended family to strengthen Navajo self-government had failed when stock reduction resulted in a cumulative psychological tragedy.[59]

Cohen gave a somewhat different perspective of what happened, with pointed comments about Collier's unsatisfactory performance. Cohen vividly recalled that in 1934 he submitted a report to the Indian Bureau indicating that laws and court decisions clearly recognized that most tribes had all the governmental rights of states or municipalities. Solicitor Nathan Margold had used this study to write an opinion that upheld the inherent powers of tribes to manage their own affairs. Cohen found it very disturbing that officials at the Indian Bureau locked all copies of this important legal ruling in a cabinet because they feared adverse public reaction.[60]

Cohen disagreed with the Hoover Commission's contention that it was inappropriate to create a state within a state. This represented the whole premise of American federalism and tolerance. Indians and other people had the right to mix with their own friends. It was not the business of the Indian Bureau or other federal agencies to integrate Indians or other ethnic groups into the rest of the population. The duty of government was to respect the right of any group to be different as long as it did not violate criminal law.[61]

Cohen blamed officials at the Indian Bureau, who were committed to forms of colonialism, for the failure of tribal self-rule. They refused to acknowledge the basic truth that government was not about efficient scientific management but a matter of human purpose and justice. Administrative experts at the bureau had favored Indian self-determination except for the field over which they had jurisdiction. There was a long and bloody argument about this dilemma between unsophisticated bureaucrats and solicitors at the Interior Department. Commissioner Collier had finally upheld the principle written into most IRA charters that allowed Indians, at some point, to dispense with supervisory controls over their leases and contracts.[62]

Allan G. Harper, the Indian Bureau's assistant regional director at Billings, Montana, told conference guests that for years it had been evident that tribal councils on the Great Plains were inadequate vehicles for the initiation of economic activity. Only three tribes on the Great Plains had used the IRA to launch business ventures. The Flatheads built the Hot Springs Health Resort, Indian groups in Montana and Wyoming founded the Northern Plains Indian Arts and Crafts Association, and the Pine Ridge Sioux organized a tent-making project that failed because of the embezzlement of funds. This raised the question of whether tribal enterprises, which employed only a few people, were a realistic answer to Indian economic needs.[63]

Theodore H. Haas, the Indian Bureau's chief counsel, noted that almost twenty years had passed since the gospel of self-government had been preached as the primary objective of Indian affairs. In reality, Indians did not exert much influence over important issues that affected their lives. They were conspicuously absent from the bureau's central office, the Indian Claims Commission, and the Interior Department's National Advisory Committee on Indian Affairs. Furthermore, the last four Indian commissioners had been selected in a miasma of secrecy without Indian consultation.[64]

Haas emphasized that administrative inertia, a reluctance to give up power, and a hiding of knowledge and intentions from criticism had hampered Indian self-determination. Promise and performance, plans and achievements, tended to be different. The Indian Bureau, which suffered from hardening of the arteries, exercised virtually absolute power over Indians in places remote from public surveillance. Even when Indians had been asked to participate in policy matters such as reservation long-range plans or the Tongass Timber bill, they acted merely as rubber stamps for ideas that had already been formulated by government officials.[65]

John Embree, an anthropologist in the Foreign Area Studies Department at Yale University, delivered the most influential paper at the Institute on American Indian Self-Government. He challenged the applied anthropologists at the University of Chicago who used an Indian Personality Study to make recommendations for improving the effectiveness of public administration. Embree warned that many anthropologists suffered a cultural lag by thinking that Indians should be preserved *in situ* for future generations of scholars. They overlooked the basic fact that modern Indians bore little resemblance to their independent pre-Columbian ancestors.[66]

Embree disliked the Indian Reorganization Act because it gave a dependent people the illusion of governing their own affairs. He remarked that it was a common trait of colonial administrators to impose social systems unacceptable to free citizens. Indirect rule did not encourage democratic self-reliance, private ownership of property, or universal education. Instead, it perpetuated wardship and made Indians paupers in the midst of the richest nation on earth. Indians who objected to being treated as helpless people were viewed as troublemakers, which forced them to take their grievances to Congress.[67]

Embree recommended that the government follow the example of the War Relocation Authority (WRA) to curtail the autocratic power of the Indian Bureau. Japanese-Americans relocated to detention camps during World War II had been treated as wards for several years. First-generation Japanese, like older Indians, developed habits of dependency. Fortunately, Dillon S. Myer, who directed the WRA, set a time schedule to abolish this undesirable government agency. Embree proposed using a similar approach to liquidate the Indian Bureau during the next fifteen years.[68]

After this conference adjourned, Oliver LaFarge, the president of the AAIA, sent a letter to board members that mirrored some of Embree's views. LaFarge expressed discontent that under Commissioner Nichols the bureau had become hopelessly entangled in past errors and bad precedents. LaFarge was convinced that Indians should join the general population because a minority of four hundred thousand could not retain its identity forever among a different culture of 150 million people. It was time to decide what functions performed by the federal government should be turned over to tribes, under what conditions and safeguards, and press for those changes.[69]

Alexander Lesser, the executive director of the AAIA, agreed with LaFarge that present Indian policy was outdated—it resembled a wandering minstrel, a thing of threads and patches. Hangovers from the nineteenth century had been dealt with by wishful thinking, a dash of idealism, and heavy doses of paternalism. The central flaw of current policy was that it treated Indians in a vacuum, as if the rest of the United States, which engulfed the Indians, did not exist. The rehabilitation bills before Congress, which encouraged Indians to live only in rural communities, reflected this mentality. This legislation resonated with the sentimental attempt to preserve Indianism that was a hallmark of the New Deal.[70]

Lesser told LaFarge that many Indians disliked farming and that no other Americans faced this occupational restriction. He was convinced the Indians' greatest need was not more land but additional cash income. During the Great Depression, myopic officials at the Indian Bureau had invented tribal cooperatives and other enterprises as a way for Indians to earn wages. This no longer made sense in postwar America, where there existed a bewildering array of jobs and careers. Indians required assistance finding jobs in the private sector rather than invented forms of employment. Once the government better understood the potential for Indian employment off the reservations, it could develop intelligent plans for Indians who preferred to remain on reservations.[71]

Three months after the conference on American Indian self-government, Will Rogers Jr., in cooperation with Napoleon Bonaparte Johnson, the NCAI president, established ARROW (American Restitution and Righting of Old Wrongs), with headquarters in New York City, Los Angeles, and Washington DC. Appointed to the board of trustees were Robert L. Bennett, Oneida; Louis R. Bruce,

Mohawk; Ben Dwight, Choctaw; Yeffe Kimball, Osage; and John C. Rainer, Taos Pueblo. The purpose of ARROW was to raise money and initiate a national campaign to liberate impoverished Indians from second-class citizenship.[72]

In October 1949, Rogers issued a press release from his Beverly Hills home stating that Indians did not want to live as wards on government handouts. He called for the withdrawal of federal guardianship as soon as possible so Indians would no longer live as curios on public bounty at reservation museums. Rogers received support from a bipartisan sponsoring committee that worked to provide Indians with equality of opportunity. Well-known members of this committee were Patrick Hurley, Eddie Cantor, Senator Paul H. Douglas, Oscar Hammerstein, Senator Hubert Humphrey, Lewis Mumford, Walter P. Reuther, and Franklin D. Roosevelt Jr. This committee helped ARROW raise money to fund Indian scholarships and assist impoverished Navajos. It also underwrote three national broadcasts where Roy Rogers, Gregory Peck, and other Hollywood stars put Indian problems in historical perspective.[73]

Furthermore, Governor Luther W. Youngdal of Minnesota called a governors conference at which fourteen states with large Indian populations began joint planning to implement the recommendations of the Hoover Commission report. The governors met on 14 March 1950 at the University of Minnesota with Commissioner Nichols and seventy-five Indian delegates. Indian leaders at this meeting were Steve DeMers, Flathead Reservation; Four Souls, Rocky Boy Reservation; William C. Knorr, Fort Peck Reservation; and J. H. Dussome, a spokesman for Montana's landless Indians.[74]

At the Minneapolis meeting, it was clear that Commissioner Nichols no longer set the agenda for Indian affairs. State officials and Indians sharply criticized the bureau for failing to develop a national plan to assimilate Indians. A consensus emerged at this conference that the solution to the Indian problem rested on the abolition of the reservation system. There also was common agreement that once Indians received appropriate educational training and economic assistance, they should come under state control.[75]

President Truman dealt with this public discontent at his vacation headquarters in Key West, Florida. There, he consulted with Oscar L. Chapman, his new secretary of interior, Philleo Nash, a special assistant on minority affairs, and other staff members. One week after the governors' conference, President Truman, in a surprise announcement, told the press that Dillon S. Myer would replace Nichols as Indian commissioner.[76]

Myer undertook bold new reforms based on his experience at the War Relocation Authority. He developed plans to encourage tribes to manage their own affairs under state jurisdiction, relocate unemployed Indians to urban centers, and provide tribal people with greater access to public education. The commissioner, however, encountered resistance from Indians when he used bureaucratic coercion to implement these policies and refused to consult with them about government plans for their future. The Mescalero Apaches, Pyramid Lake Paiutes, and other tribes surprised Myer and almost everyone else in the federal government by insisting not only on first-class citizenship but also the right to self-determination based on a separate tribal sovereignty.

6

FROM FEDERAL PATERNALISM
TO FULL INDEPENDENCE

Under the old way of running things, the superintendent was in the driver's seat, and the Indians were in the wagon behind. Since 1936, under the Indian Reorganization Act, we thought Indians were supposed to be in the driver's seat, holding the reins, with the superintendent out in front guiding us. But when we try to act on that understanding, and put our hands on the reins, we get kicked off the wagon. RUFUS SAGO, MESCALERO APACHE LEADER, TO COMMISSIONER DILLON S. MYER, 4 OCTOBER 1950

Dillon S. Myer seemed a promising choice for the position of Indian commissioner. He was a self-confident, honest, and experienced public servant. A specialist in agronomy, Myer had worked as a county extension agent to bring efficiency and centralized planning to agriculture. In 1934, he joined the staff of the Agricultural Adjustment Administration in Washington DC. During the New Deal, Myer held a series of government-related jobs because of his reputation as a practical, hard-headed bureaucratic infighter who dealt effectively with complex issues (pl. 17).[1]

His most difficult assignment was to direct the War Relocation Authority (WRA) during World War II. Myer supervised the evacuation of 120,000 people of Japanese descent from the Pacific Coast and managed ten detention camps in the Western United States. His record at the WRA was controversial. Myer worked to close these undesirable internment camps, but he also created separate colonies for troublemakers, used informers, and required loyalty oaths from individuals who relocated to midwestern and eastern cities.[2]

After his appointment to head the Indian Bureau, Myer followed many recommendations of the Hoover Commission report and the Governors' Interstate Indian Council and cooperated with Congress to liberate Indians from federal wardship, poverty, and second-class citizenship. Nonetheless, his autocratic style of governance and limited appreciation of Indian rights created numerous problems. Especially troublesome was his inability to work with Ruth Muskrat Bronson and other NCAI leaders; Rufus Sago, the president of the Mescalero Apache Business Committee; and Avery Winnemucca, chair of the Paiute Pyramid Lake Tribal Council. This eventually triggered a bitter conflict and growing divergences between Indians and federal officials over the meaning of self-determination.

In early 1950, Myer set preconditions of employment before accepting President Truman's offer to become Indian commissioner. Oscar Chapman, the new secretary of interior, gave Myer authority to remove undesirable Indian Bureau employees and begin a staged federal withdrawal from tribal communities. There also was an understanding that Myer would report directly to Chapman. This enabled Myer to bypass Assistant Secretary William E. Warne, who had publicly defended the bureau for its experimental work with tribal self-government.[3]

On 5 May 1950, Myer began his duties at the Indian Bureau. He believed that the 1924 Indian Citizenship Act, which guaranteed all Indians political freedom under the Bill of Rights, was one of the most important milestones in the history of Indian affairs. By contrast, he felt that the Indian Reorganization Act, which encouraged a tribal alternative to assimilation, was a serious mistake. This unrealistic legislation had initiated a "glass case policy" that tried to preserve Indians "as museum specimens for future generations to study and enjoy." In Myer's eyes, the IRA was flawed because only twenty-five tribes had adequate natural resources to justify charters of incorporation. The commissioner concluded that IRA tribal constitutions also made little sense in light of a federal court ruling in 1949 that Indians had the constitutional right to vote in state elections.[4]

In Myer's judgment, it would be necessary for the federal government to redefine its trust responsibilities, which had evolved from treaties and statutes since the earliest days of the American Republic, before Indians could achieve meaningful self-determination. For Myer, federal supervision of Indian property was inconsistent with the basic concepts of freedom that most Americans cherished. Thus, the notion of trusteeship, which many tribes passionately favored, contained a paradox: it protected Indian property but also continued a deeply ingrained dependence on federal paternalism.[5]

Myer emphasized that the continuation of day-to-day administration of Indian affairs would never resolve this dilemma, but he did not favor the wholesale liquidation of federal responsibilities toward Indians. Instead, he proposed to develop a series of withdrawal programs, in consultation with tribal groups, that would make it possible for him to lead Indian people "in the mass out of the shadow of federal paternalism into the sunlight of full independence."[6]

These steps were far-reaching but not a surprise. They followed earlier recommendations by Congress, Indian rights groups, the NCAI, the Hoover Commission, and the Institute on American Indian Self-Government that were designed to help Indians manage their own affairs. Myer called for careful administrative planning to ensure Indian independence. This involved the productive use or sale of heirship lands, the voluntary relocation of unemployed Indians to cities, the renegotiation of treaty provisions and statutes in light of present-day realities, and the gradual transfer of bureau functions to Indians themselves or to state government. In order to counter anticipated criticism of his policies, Myer indicated that no compulsion would be used to break up reservations or force people to move against their will.[7]

Shortly after he took office, Myer dramatized his commitment to helping Indians become less dependent on the federal government by replacing personnel. Resignations or transfers to other agencies were required from Associate Commissioner William Zimmerman, Theodore H. Haas, the bureau's chief counsel, and Don C. Foster, the director of Alaska's Native Service. During the next few months, other administrators associated with Indian New Deal reform voluntarily left: Willard Beatty, director of Indian education; Joseph C. McCaskill, assistant commissioner and manager of the Indian Arts and Crafts Board; and Assistant Secretary of the Interior William Warne.[8]

Myer replaced these individuals with people who had worked with him at the War Relocation Authority. H. Rex Lee was appointed associate commissioner, Ervin J. Utz, assistant commissioner, Edwin E. Ferguson, the bureau's chief counsel, and Lewis A. Sigler, associate chief counsel. Myer also picked Hugh Wade, who worked in Alaska with the Federal Bureau of Investigation, as the new director of the Juneau area office.[9]

Myer enjoyed support from the House Public Lands Committee in his first efforts to redesign federal Indian policy. In July 1950, Reva Beck Bosone, a Democrat from Utah, introduced House Joint Resolution 490 after listening to Indians from all over the country testify at committee hearings about how they wanted to manage their own affairs. Convinced that, more than anything else, Indians wanted to "live as the white man," she set in motion a procedure to end Indian wardship. The Bosone Resolution required Secretary Chapman to report by January 1951 which tribes were ready for the end of federal control. It established a firm target date for beginning the withdrawal programs recommended by Commissioner John Collier during World War II and presented more comprehensively in 1947 by Acting Commissioner William Zimmerman before the Senate Civil Service Committee.[10]

Myer saw the Bosone Resolution as an opportunity to obtain financial assistance from Congress to implement withdrawal plans for New York and

California Indians and update information that former commissioner Nichols had requested in circular 3675. Therefore, he asked Associate Commissioner Lee to tell Bosone the Interior Department agreed with the intent of her resolution. More time, however, was needed to prepare a staged withdrawal for diverse tribal groups. This would prevent a chaotic situation from developing that would put the Indian Bureau, Congress, and everyone else on the defensive for the next five or ten years. After meeting with Lee, Bosone approved a revised resolution that extended the time period for reporting on tribes to January 1952. Myer also was authorized to spend $250,000 from current Indian Bureau appropriations to hire programming specialists.[11]

In June 1950, Interior Secretary Chapman told Congress the Bosone Resolution was necessary because postwar globalism had brought nations closer together. He noted that recent improvements in transportation and communications had created an interdependence between once-isolated tribes and the rest of the country. Chapman predicted that federally sponsored programs for Indians would eventually disappear in this new environment but warned that it would be a disaster to end federal guardianship without Indian consent or before states provided tribes with adequate social services (pl. 18).[12]

The Bosone bill encountered little opposition. An editorial in the *Saturday Evening Post* titled "Indians Might Do Better with Less Protection" agreed with Congresswoman Bosone that Indians had the same inherent intelligence and capacity for performance as other Americans. The United States should treat them like other citizens, instead of "giving the country back" to tribes.[13]

The Bosone Resolution was endorsed by pan-Indian groups. Frank Tom-Pee-Saw, a Cherokee and legal officer of the League of Nations, saw it as an opportunity to end the practice of using tribal trust funds to pay for Indian Bureau programs. F. G. Collett, who represented the Indians of California, Inc., favored the resolution because Indians had clamored for years to have complete freedom from federal management and control. The NCAI also wanted to transfer control from the bureau to tribal councils.[14]

Nonetheless, the NCAI objected to the short deadline for preparing withdrawal programs and to taking money from the bureau's budget for this purpose. Ruth Muskrat Bronson warned that Indians could not suddenly "have the blanket lifted from their hot house and expect any vigorous life to withstand the sudden glare that would flood in." Tribes needed "repeated exposure to the strong sunlight of experience in various forms of self-government" before complete independence.[15]

William Fire Thunder, former president of the Oglala Sioux Tribal Council and first vice-president of the NCAI, was even more critical of the Bosone

Resolution. He thought it breached contracts, terminated legal protections and services guaranteed by treaties, and nullified the Indian Reorganization Act. Fire Thunder could not understand why local Indian leaders had made speeches "in support of the final expropriation of the Sioux."[16]

The only significant opposition to the Bosone Resolution came from two former New Deal administrators. In July 1950, John Collier informed Harold Ickes that a harmful resolution had passed the House. Upset by this news, Ickes requested a meeting with President Harry Truman to discuss a veto if the Senate approved this resolution. Truman coyly replied that he did not know anything about the Bosone Resolution but would "never let anything affecting Indians go by without a complete investigation."[17]

The Bosone Resolution did not pass because of objections raised by Senator Arthur V. Watkins on the consent calendar. He doubted the wisdom of diverting Indian Bureau appropriations for administrative expenses and questioned the need for additional field studies. Watkins noted that in 1947 Acting Commissioner Zimmerman had filed a report with the Senate that listed tribes ready to manage their own affairs. For Watkins, action on recommendations already made was long overdue.[18]

While Congress considered the Bosone Resolution, Commissioner Myer left Washington DC to advance his program of Indian self-determination. Beginning in August 1950, he spent four months traveling to different agencies throughout the West to get acquainted with Indians and bureau employees. Myer was well received when he promised to allow all Indians to live independently from the federal government. The commissioner, however, encountered a less favorable reception when he spoke to Indians in a condescending way and rejected their proposals to hold tribal referendums on future withdrawal legislation.[19]

During this trip, Myer delivered an important address, on 29 August 1950, to the National Congress of American Indians at Bellingham, Washington. There, he promised that the guiding principle of his administration would be self-determination for Indians. Myer told the NCAI delegates that he intended to operate the bureau in accordance with the Bill of Rights because their aspirations, like those of other citizens, were truly in the American tradition. Since 1934, Indians had increasingly shaped their own destiny by ratifying civic documents, including 180 constitutions and 167 corporate charters. The Bosone Resolution would help him determine which tribes were ready to manage their affairs without federal supervision.[20]

Nowhere was it more apparent than in Myer's Bellingham speech that he identified with the political ideologies that had crystallized nationally during and after the successful conclusion to World War II. Most Americans, like Myer, believed that their country was blessed with superior principles and democratic institutions that all people should adopt. This conservative Cold War ideology contributed to a view among policymakers that Indian culture was deficient and an unwanted part of American life.

At Bellingham, Myer did not ask delegates for their assistance in defining what self-determination meant. In a question-and-answer session at the conclusion of the commissioner's talk, Joseph Garry, a Coeur d'Alene from Idaho, pointed out that Indian Bureau area offices were remote bookkeeping centers that no longer solved human problems. Garry recommended the abolition of these offices and the reassignment of administrators to work directly with Indian communities. The commissioner replied defensively that organizational questions were his responsibility.[21]

It would be wrong to conclude, however, that Myer's initial effort to lead Indians "into the sunlight of full independence" did not have significant grass-roots support. The experience of self-rule under the IRA had disillusioned many individuals. Furthermore, the increased contact that Indian veterans and war workers had with the outside world resulted in a deeper awareness of how government paternalism had affected their lives. They wanted freedom, along with other Indians, from the twenty-two hundred federal regulations and restricted property rights that, in practice, made them wards.[22]

The National Congress of American Indians was the most important tribal group to advocate a fundamental change in federal Indian policy. Will Rogers Jr., the head of the NCAI office in Los Angeles, backed Myer's appointment as commissioner because the former WRA director would know how to curb the power of the Indian Bureau. Avery Winnemucca, the chair of the Paiute Pyramid Lake Tribal Council, and other Indians also endorsed Myer's candidacy at the 1949 NCAI Denver convention to push for more autonomy under the Indian Reorganization Act.[23]

Rogers and Winnemucca, however, still adhered to the NCAI's definition of Indian self-determination, which differed in important respects from Myer's use of that term. The NCAI did not advocate an end to all supervision over Indian affairs. It emphasized that federal trusteeship, tax-free land, and Indian self-government were vested legal rights. The NCAI also reaffirmed the federal responsibility for economic development on reservations and insisted that Congress secure tribal approval before passing legislation that affected Indian life and property.[24]

The NCAI did not oppose individual Indians or tribes that wanted to use their right of self-determination to remove federal guardianship. As noted earlier, the NCAI affiliate, ARROW (American Restitution and Righting of Old Wrongs), endorsed federal withdrawal and increased state responsibility in California.

Louis R. Bruce Jr., a Mohawk and member of the NCAI business committee, also publicly discussed his own family background in *Reader's Digest* to demonstrate how the Protestant work ethic helped him avoid second-class citizenship. Bruce resented Felix Cohen's romantic stereotyping of Indians. In April 1950, he asked Interior Department officials to stop circulating books and pamphlets written by this former government official. Bruce, like other New York Iroquois, strongly disliked the paternalism associated with the Indian Reorganization Act.[25]

Another way that individual members of the NCAI brought about change was to work closely with the Governors' Interstate Indian Council (GIIC), which was organized in March 1950 to conduct open discussions of problems in states with large numbers of Indians. Most of the governors who belonged to the GIIC supported Myer. They demanded a timetable for ending federal wardship and turning the management of tribal property over to state-chartered corporations.[26]

The GIIC reflected two important trends in postwar American society: a renewed emphasis on state's rights and the economic development of the West. The council adopted a comprehensive reform program that included an early settlement of Indian claims, the transfer of bureau services to states and other federal agencies, and uniform law enforcement in Indian communities. In addition, it recommended programs to rehabilitate dispossessed and landless Indians, with emphasis on individual self-reliance, adequate housing, permanent jobs away from reservations, expanded educational opportunity, and the repeal of discriminatory liquor laws.[27]

Indians from the NCAI actively participated at GIIC meetings. Edwin Rogers, a Chippewa attorney from Minnesota and NCAI vice-president, introduced the resolution that gave the GIIC its name. Frank George, a Nez Percé and NCAI officer from the Colville Reservation in Washington, was elected vice-president of the GIIC. Napoleon Bonaparte Johnson, the NCAI president, served on the GIIC Law and Order Committee. He spoke frequently at council meetings, echoing Myer's policies by proposing the Indian Bureau's gradual liquidation.[28]

Myer addressed many of the concerns of the Governors' Interstate Indian Council. The commissioner encouraged individual self-reliance when he allowed Indians more control over their personal property, asked states to provide Indians with educational and health services, and created a pilot relocation program to help people find off-reservation employment. Myer's reforms met the expectations of those Indians who most desired personal freedom and economic opportunity.

In June 1951, the commissioner issued new regulations governing individual money accounts to enable Indians to spend their income from restricted property without supervision. Under the old rules, this money could not be used without the approval of agency personnel, superintendents, and officials at the Indian Bureau. Myer's order affected eighty thousand individual money accounts with an average balance of $800. Indians had the option of leaving this money at agency headquarters but were encouraged to use private banking facilities.[29]

In much the same spirit, Myer permitted the mortgaging of restricted Indian real estate. This enabled Indians to borrow money from banks and credit unions for housing facilities and business enterprises. The commissioner, however, did not permit the mortgaging of forest and grazing land because foreclosure on this property could interfere with federal management of timber and grazing units. Myer also made special arrangements with the Farmers Home Administration and Veterans Administration to ensure that Indians qualified for the benefits of their lending programs. The commissioner reported in 1951 that Indians had access to loans worth more than $20 million from sources other than the IRA revolving credit fund.[30]

In another initiative, Myer gave area directors more authority to issue fee patents and remove restrictions on the sale of Indian real estate. This pleased many unemployed veterans and those who had moved to urban areas as early as the 1920s; both groups were anxious to get private loans and put their land up for sale. As a result, the Indian Bureau was swamped with several thousand applications from Indians who wanted to sell their restricted allotments to profit from inflated land prices that accompanied the demand for foodstuffs during World War II.[31]

Myer also forced Indians to stop looking at the bureau's IRA loan program as a source of cheap credit and to rely instead on commercial lenders that served other citizens. The commissioner took this step because he agreed with Congress that this federal fund had been mismanaged between 1936 and 1946, with Indian Bureau officials spending over $1 million for administrative expenses. During the next five years, the Interior Department loaned Indians an additional $7 million after Congress appropriated money to cover administrative overhead. When Myer ended this arrangement in 1951, the only source of future IRA loans was repayments and interest income.[32]

Furthermore, Myer used educational reform to encourage individual self-reliance. He firmly believed that Indian children were entitled to a free universal public education because their parents were citizens of states under the Fourteenth Amendment to the U.S. Constitution. To underscore this point, the commissioner closed Indian Bureau schools in Idaho, Michigan, Washington, and Wisconsin and then transferred twenty-five Indian Bureau schools to state departments of education.[33]

Myer spent more than $2 million annually under the Johnson-O'Malley Act to subsidize local school districts that provided public education for twenty-two thousand Indian students. Myer believed this program would accelerate integration, make states more responsible for Indian children, and encourage adults to participate on local school boards and parent-teacher associations. Many Indian groups, however, insisted on their legal right to a federal education, and states with large Indian populations were reluctant to impose additional financial burdens on their school districts.[34]

Myer's educational policies resembled those of former commissioner Thomas Jefferson Morgan, who worked to assimilate Indians at the end of the nineteenth century. Both men epitomized the assertive Americanism of their time and strongly believed in the superiority of public schools. Morgan asked Congress to create a national educational system to prepare Indians for the duties of patriotic citizenship. By 1895 there were over two hundred Indian schools, with an enrollment of eighteen thousand students. As one historian has noted, this segregated federal school system lost its mission during the first part of the twentieth century and degenerated into a system of education for dependent people.[35]

To his credit, Myer found this situation unacceptable. He appointed Hildegard Thompson, who fought for universal education on the Navajo Reservation, as director of the bureau's educational program. She restructured the curriculum at federal Indian schools to improve Indian literacy in English, promote citizenship, and provide vocational skills for off-reservation employment. Thompson also worked with Congress to make more classrooms available for eighteen thousand Indian children who did not attend school.[36]

An important part of Myer's educational reform was a boarding-home placement program for Indian children. It resembled the outing system at the Carlisle Institute, where students lived with non-Indian families to better appreciate Christian civilization. Secretary Chapman was especially interested in this initiative. During the 1920s, he worked as a probation officer and handled the cases of over ten thousand children for Judge Ben Lindsey's Juvenile Court in Denver, Colorado. There Chapman concluded, along with Lindsey, that the environment decisively influenced childhood development.[37]

In 1951, Chapman persuaded President Truman to approve a budget request to fund foster care for Indians. During the next two years, a monthly average of 409 children were placed in the homes of strangers. Most of these children resided in Alaska, where their parents had entered sanatoriums for the treatment of tuberculosis. This well-intentioned program, which nonetheless violated Indian cultural freedom and family rights, became a featured government policy in subsequent years.[38]

The commissioner further diminished the bureau's role by transferring some of its health services to states. Hospitals at Hayward, Wisconsin, and Bernalillo County, New Mexico, were turned over to local control, with the provision of priority services for Indians. Myer also closed hospitals at Fort Berthold, Fort Totten, and the Uintah and Ouray jurisdictions, where health-care services were available in surrounding communities.[39] The commissioner, however, remained evasive about transferring all Indian medical care to the Public Health Service because tribes would remain under federal jurisdiction for an extended period.[40]

Myer believed that an outmoded reservation system was largely responsible for problems such as illiteracy and poor health. Treaties and other legal agreements had caused past policymakers to mistakenly view all Indians as farmers or stockmen. This trust relationship served a useful purpose, but it also led to segregation and encouraged people to live in rural slums surrounded by an atmosphere of paternalism. For the commissioner, the severity of this problem was revealed in a 1951 study of sixteen reservations indicating that resources were available to support only 46 percent of their resident populations with a subsistence standard of living.[41]

Another harsh reality was that Congress had stopped funding the IRA land purchase programs and abandoned rehabilitation plans drafted by the Indian Bureau for sixty-seven reservations. In 1951, Congress prohibited Indians residing in Nevada, Oregon, Washington, and Wyoming from using public or tribal trust funds to purchase land or water rights inside or outside of reservation boundaries.[42] Johnson, the NCAI president, responded to this threat by asking President Truman to issue a public statement critical of this unjust and discriminatory legislation. The president declined this invitation but did express an interest in "extending the control of Indian tribes over their own funds and in enlarging the sphere of self-government."[43]

In December 1951, Commissioner Myer unveiled a far-reaching plan to break the cycle of poverty, paternalism, and despair on Indian reservations. In an address before the National Council of Churches of Christ at Buck Hill Falls, Pennsylvania, he recommended that Congress establish a relocation program with sponsorship arrangements similar to those established for Japanese-American evacuees and refugees from Europe during World War II. Myer pointed out that resettlement would enable the government to remove surplus Indian populations to more prosperous urban areas, free up resources for those that stayed behind, and provide more space at overcrowded boarding schools.[44]

At Buck Hill Falls, the commissioner asked church groups to once again play a dynamic role in Indian affairs. Relocation of Indians would give Christian families an opportunity to adopt over eight thousand Indian orphans, help relocatees find jobs, and combat racial discrimination. In this context, Myer showed little sympathy for Indians or an understanding of their cultures. He was confident that once Indians had established residence in Euro-American communities, they would become self-reliant and civic-minded people.[45]

To encourage relocation, the commissioner established job placement centers at Indian Bureau area offices and in large cities such as Chicago, Los Angeles, and Salt Lake City. He also created a separate Branch of Relocation at the bureau's central headquarters. In 1951, he asked Congress to appropriate over $8 million to relocate Indians but received only enough money to begin a pilot program where eighteen hundred people received financial assistance for transportation to cities and up to three weeks subsistence expenses while they looked for jobs.[46]

Many Indian veterans, landless tribal members, returned war workers, and young families were anxious to take advantage of this opportunity even though it meant living in an urban environment. Relocation offered these people an alternative to Indian Bureau paternalism, economic insecurity, and second-class citizenship. Throughout the decade of the 1950s, the bureau received more applications for relocation than it could process.

Myer was unable to make further progress toward self-determination because of a credibility gap between his rhetoric and the reality of his performance. Publicly he continued to recognize the principle of self-determination, yet at the same time he increased the power of the Indian Bureau over Indian life. This was evident in his response to events surrounding the removal of Superintendent John Crow from the Mescalero Apache Reservation in New Mexico and the transfer of E. Reesman Fryer from the Paiute Pyramid Lake Reservation in Nevada. In both instances, Myer turned down opportunities to work with attorneys, government officials, tribal leaders, and the NCAI to help Indians move beyond the shadow of federal paternalism.

Controversy on the 460,000-acre Mescalero Apache Reservation, where 950 Chiricahua and Mescalero Indians resided, began soon after Congress passed the Indian Claims Commission Act. In September 1947, Ruth Muskrat Bronson wrote the tribe a letter on behalf of the NCAI to solicit a claims and general counsel contract for James Curry. One month later, Curry visited the reservation and persuaded the ten-member Mescalero Business Committee to allow him to represent their case before the Indian Claims Commission. Curry subsequently made arrangements with Roy T. Mobley, a local attorney from Alamogordo, to help with both claims and general counsel services. These two attorneys quickly became involved in bitter disputes over sharing retainer fees, work assignments, and other matters.[47]

For example, on 16 September 1949, Curry attended a meeting of the Mescalero Business Committee to discredit Mobley. He told Rufus Sago, the committee's president, and other tribal leaders that Mobley was disqualified by law from serving as their claims attorney because he worked as a federal employee at a nearby airbase. After listening to Curry's comments, the committee approved a resolution that terminated Mobley's contract.[48]

At this meeting, Curry also encouraged Mescalero Apaches to amend their 1936 IRA constitution to gain more independence from the federal government. This constitution gave the business committee the following enumerated powers of government, subject to approval by the secretary of the interior: the right to borrow money, employ legal counsel, pass law enforcement ordinances, negotiate with federal, state, and local governments, review Indian Bureau appropriation requests, veto the sale or leasing of tribal lands, and remove nonmembers whose presence was injurious to the tribe.[49]

Curry believed that the Indian Reorganization Act was a delusion and snare for tribes because of the way it was administered. He told the business committee that not only did the IRA give tribal councils specified authority, but it also recognized other Indian rights vested in law. Instead of protecting these prerogatives, the Indian Bureau persuaded tribes to accept enumerated powers that could be altered only by constitutional amendments approved by the secretary of interior. To redress this problem, Curry recommended that the Mescalero Apache tribe rewrite its IRA constitution to reaffirm inherent powers that did not require government approval. According to Curry, the business committee would then resemble a state legislature, with much more authority to manage its own affairs.[50]

Committee members agreed to discuss possible constitutional amendments with Charles M. Wright, a NCAI attorney who lived in Tucson. Their more immediate but related concern was to air grievances against Superintendent John Crow, a Cherokee who closely identified with the policies of former Indian commissioner Collier. Complaints were raised about substandard schools, the misuse of tribal funds, undeveloped farmlands, inadequate health care, and the superintendent's refusal to abide by decisions of the tribal loan committee. At the end of this discussion, the business committee voted in favor of removing Crow and two of his subordinates from the reservation.[51]

Three days later, Superintendent Crow retaliated by discharging four members of the Mescalero Business Committee from their jobs because funds were unavailable for road work on the reservation. He then called a general tribal meeting in early October 1949 that was attended by two hundred people. There, Salone Sombrero, the chair of the assembly, and John Tahnito, the chief judge of the tribal court, criticized Rufus Sago and the business committee for acting without sufficient knowledge and support. It was clear from this event that the tribe was divided. Younger people and veterans, who favored more self-determination, supported Sago, while more conservative Apaches and those interested in a claims settlement looked to the federal government for guidance.[52]

Sago tried to overcome this division by working with Curry and NCAI leaders on a campaign to make the Crow episode a cause célèbre on behalf of self-determination. Sago sent letters from Curry's Washington address to members of Congress, asking them to support full self-government for the tribe and to contact officials at the Interior Department about the need to remove or transfer Superintendent Crow. This campaign turned into a public relations disaster. Rather than projecting a positive image of Indians, the incident led to the perception that Mescalero Apaches, even with an experienced Indian administrator, were unable to manage their own affairs.[53]

This did not prevent Sago's reelection as president of the Mescalero Business Committee. Nevertheless, his grass-roots support gradually diminished after Superintendent Crow rehired four dissident members of the business committee. Sago also found it difficult to attract a wider following because of a drinking problem. Upset that Crow still remained in office, he persuaded a small number of his followers to boycott the business committee. A rump committee led by Bernard Little continued to hold meetings without a quorum. It passed nonbinding resolutions that rescinded the vote to remove Crow and asked the Indian Bureau to investigate whether Curry and Mobley were satisfactorily performing their duties of prosecuting tribal claims.[54]

In May 1950, after being arrested on drunk and disorderly charges and convicted in a Tularosa municipal court, Rufus Sago, Perry Via, and John Allard were forced to resign from the business committee. They were replaced with new committee members who supported Crow's decision to transfer $48,000 to the government-run tribal store, with a $50 credit given to each Apache to save the cooperative from bankruptcy. Over three hundred people protested this per capita payment because it denied them the right to individually manage their tribal funds. They asked Commissioner Myer to intervene and reverse this decision.[55]

The endless quarreling on the Mescalero Apache Reservation confirmed Myer's view that most Indians were a primitive and indigent people incapable of running their own affairs. For Myer, the Apaches exemplified this problem because they still lived in tepees on the northern part of the reservation and depended on public welfare to survive. The commissioner thought the control of Indians by other Indians was a serious problem because Indian politicos, presumably like Rufus Sago and John Crow, exploited their neighbors.[56]

These perceptions, and this distrust of Curry, who seemed more interested in public controversy than defending Indian claims, prevented Commissioner Myer from establishing a close working relationship with the NCAI. Strained relations surfaced in August 1950 when President Napoleon Bonaparte Johnson appointed a special NCAI committee to determine how to prevent interference with tribal democracy on Indian reservations. Members of this committee were Ruth Muskrat Bronson, chair, Lawrence E. Lindley, general secretary of the Indian Rights Association, and Ben Dwight, a NCAI official.[57]

In September 1950, Myer broke the promise made at the NCAI Bellingham convention that self-determination would be the guiding principle of Indian policy. He told Area Director Eric T. Hagberg that the defacto business committee was illegally constituted. The Mescalero Apache tribe had only those powers conferred by its constitution, bylaws, and charter. Myer observed that the Mescalero constitution did not confer on the Business Committee the authority to dismiss Sago, Via, and Allard or to operate in the absence of a quorum. Furthermore, this legislative body did not have the inherent power to remove constitutional officers elected for a fixed term.[58]

The commissioner then indicated that a duly elected business committee would have to reach an independent conclusion on whether Curry and Mobley had done satisfactory legal work for the tribe. But Myer was willing, on request, to terminate the general counsel part of their contract because these two individuals could not cooperate with each other. Their long and unpleasant controversy also interfered with the presentation of claims. Therefore, if asked, Myer would cancel their claims contract once the tribe hired a new attorney to appear before the Indian Claims Commission.[59]

In early October 1950, after all major decisions were made, Myer met with a delegation of Mescalero Apaches at the Albuquerque Indian Sanitarium. This group represented all members of the Mescalero Business Committee, including individuals who had been removed and the persons put in their place. The entire discussion centered around the legitimacy of the old business committee versus the new. Myer reiterated the position taken in his letter to Hagberg that the current committee was illegally constituted. He also disapproved of a memo circulated by Superintendent Crow that appeared at odds with this decision.[60]

The commissioner, however, did not announce the removal of Superintendent Crow. This evasive behavior upset John C. Rainer, a Taos Indian and the new NCAI executive secretary. Consequently, he sent copies of Bronson's *Report on the Findings of a Special Subcommittee to Investigate the Status of Tribal Self-*

Government at the Mescalero Apache Reservation to tribal officials throughout the United States. In this report, Bronson cited numerous examples of how Superintendent Crow had interfered with self-determination. She emphasized that what happened on the Mescalero Apache Reservation was of universal importance. It would set a precedent on the right of all tribes to govern themselves.[61]

Bronson's NCAI report recommended that Commissioner Myer remove Crow to allow Apaches freedom of choice in upcoming tribal elections. She rejected the notion that Curry had stirred up the Indians to revolt. Bronson considered it a sign of maturity that Sago and other business committee members were sophisticated enough to use Anglo-Saxon methods of public protest. She concluded that publicity was the only weapon that Indians had against despotism, and she censured Commissioner Myer for not immediately taking steps to right a wrong.[62]

Abel Paisano, a former chair of the All Pueblo Council, had a different perspective. He told Napoleon Bonaparte Johnson that special interest groups, more interested in attacking the Indian Bureau than learning the truth, had used the NCAI. Paisano pointed out that the great majority of Mescalero Apaches opposed Sago. He criticized Bronson for presenting only one side of a complex political controversy. For Paisano, Crow was "an all American hero" to people who believed that Indians were able to take care of themselves.[63]

In February 1951, Commissioner Myer demoted Crow to assistant superintendent and transferred him to the Colorado River Reservation in Arizona. This was an opportunity to diminish the influence of an employee who identified with New Deal policies that encouraged a tribal alternative to assimilation. Crow's departure and Myer's autocratic administrative style also made the business committee, under the direction of Wheeler Tissnolthtos, more compliant. On 10 February, it passed Resolution 365, which stated that Mescalero self-government should be directed from within rather than through outside pressure. To move in this direction, the committee terminated Curry and Mobley's attorney contracts. Subsequently, Commissioner Myer notified these two lawyers that they had sixty days to show cause why he should not discontinue their legal services.[64]

The Mescalero Apaches were not the only tribe that Myer did not lead from "the shadow of federal paternalism to the sunlight of full independence." Myer refused to cooperate with Superintendent E. Reesman Fryer, who wanted to protect the water rights and tribal autonomy of the Pyramid Lake Paiutes in Nevada. Instead, Myer followed the advice of Senator Patrick McCarran and transferred Fryer to another reservation. The commissioner also used this controversy to develop political ties with ethnocentric members of Congress who used Cold War anti-communist rhetoric to discredit the NCAI and tribal self-rule under the Indian Reorganization Act.

In June 1950, Senator McCarran met with Myer to discuss the activities of Superintendent Fryer and Curry, the Paiute's attorney (pl. 19). McCarran was upset because these two individuals had orchestrated a publicity campaign to help the tribe recover land from Euro-American settlers. Pete Peterson, the senator's political assistant, also had reported that Fryer and Curry were helping organize all of Nevada's Indians to defeat him in the upcoming November election.[65]

The commissioner learned firsthand about Fryer's plans for the Paiutes when the superintendent wrote him that it would be possible to end federal supervision over these Indians within three to five years. Fryer recommended that the Indian Bureau work closely with the Bureau of Reclamation to restore the trout fishery at Pyramid Lake to rehabilitate the tribe's economy. He told the commissioner that, under their IRA constitution, the Paiutes could negotiate directly with the state of Nevada to charge fees for fishing licenses and the operation of boats on the lake.[66]

Myer disapproved of this withdrawal plan because it allowed the tribe to operate outside of state jurisdiction. Consequently, he listened with great interest when Senator McCarran contacted him a second time about Superintendent Fryer's intention to remove water from the Truckee River that was set aside for white settlers. To protect Paiute rights, Fryer had fenced off Indian land. He also encouraged the Paiutes to organize committees to police the fences and made plans to siphon water from the Truckee River for use by 142 Indian families. Nearby ranchers, who were McCarran's political allies, had retaliated by cutting off water to irrigation ditches serving Paiute land.[67]

Superintendent Fryer aggressively defended Paiute rights because the Supreme Court in *Depaoli v. United States* (1944) had reaffirmed the Indians' ownership of this contested property. After this favorable ruling, the tribal council leased land to the Depaoli and Garaventa Land Company until Paiute veterans returned from World War II. Euro-American ranchers, however, remained on Indian property after their leases expired. They also refused to cooperate on the joint use of irrigation ditches. Consequently, the Department of Justice filed a lawsuit in May 1950 to evict the settlers.[68]

Encouraged by this development, Superintendent Fryer began field surveys on the Pyramid Lake Reservation to construct a canal and distribution system. This initiative was abruptly ended when Myer announced that funds were unavailable to continue the surveys. Even more surprising was a phone call Fryer received while conferring with an attorney in Los Angeles over the pending lawsuit. In this conversation, the commissioner told Fryer that he was being transferred, effective 15 October, to the Colville Reservation in Washington.[69]

When Avery Winnemucca, the Paiute tribal chair, learned about Superintendent Fryer's transfer, he contacted Curry and asked the National Congress of American Indians for assistance. Curry and other NCAI officials were extremely worried about Myer's intentions. In 1949, Ruth Bronson had received a disturbing letter from McCarran in response to her criticism of his constitutional amendment (S.R. 120) to terminate federal authority over tribes by eliminating the power of Congress to regulate trade with Indians.[70]

The senator told Bronson that only Western civilization had a history and dynamics. He praised the "specimens of American manhood" that had acquired land from Indians by purchase or conquest. McCarran emphasized that these energetic European homesteaders had turned "wild wastelands" into "productive, wealth-creating, revenue-producing property." Furthermore, the entire edifice of the Indian Bureau was built on "the fiction of tribal political organization and the constitutional delegation to the federal government of power to deal with Indian tribes." McCarran informed Bronson that "real American Indians" did not want to live forever under the supervision of the secretary of the interior or attend Indian educational facilities that were "the psychological equivalent of a school for mental defectives or other backward students."[71]

The senator did not view Paiute Indians as an independent and self-reliant people. Instead, they were supporters of an alien political ideology. He was certain that John Collier had established the NCAI in 1944 to destroy the more patriotic American Indian Federation. Fortunately, the House Un-American Activities Committee had uncovered this conspiracy and shown that the NCAI was a "communist front organization" that received funds from the Robert Marshall Trust.[72]

The NCAI leaders were concerned that Myer's removal of Fryer meant that he supported not only McCarran but also other Western members of Congress who disregarded Indian rights. In recent years, Senator Hugh Butler of Nebraska had worked closely with Albert Grorud, a clerk on the Senate Indian Subcommittee, to discredit Indian self-determination in Alaska and elsewhere. Grorud mocked Indians by referring to himself as Sitting Bull and circulated a document from Butler's office entitled "The National Congress of American Indians: An Indian Bureau Organization and How It Was Formed," which stated that the NCAI was a "link in the chain" to keep Indians under the "communist" Indian Reorganization Act.[73]

McCarran's and Butler's stereotyping of Indians as disloyal aliens during the second Red Scare put the NCAI on the defensive at a critical time in the struggle for self-determination. For example, in California, Leta Smart, who was of Omaha ancestry and instrumental in organizing the Los Angeles branch of the NCAI, resigned after receiving material from Butler's office. Thomas Largo, a Cahuilla Indian and sachem for the California Indian Rights Association in Pasadena, also disaffiliated from the NCAI for fear of being labeled "disloyal."[74]

On 28 September 1950, Bronson and Rainer, the new NCAI executive secretary, met with Commissioner Myer to determine whether he had forged an alliance with members of Congress who wanted to discredit their organization. They urged Myer to uphold Paiute rights and warned that Fryer's transfer would greatly discourage Indians all over the United States who faced similar pressures. The commissioner replied that McCarran was not responsible for the transfer and gave the impression that Fryer had initiated this decision. At a follow-up meeting with Bronson, Myer implied that he removed the superintendent because of their rivalry while Fryer was regional director of the branch of the War Relocation Authority in San Francisco.[75]

The commissioner's refusal to reconsider Fryer's removal caused a firestorm of protest. Friends of the Paiutes appealed their case directly to the White House. During early October, President Truman received telegrams critical of Myer's decision from the NCAI, AAIA, Indian Rights Association, Institute of Ethnic Affairs, and General Federation of Women's Clubs. Harold Ickes also contacted government officials and wrote an editorial in the *Washington Post* critical of McCarran. More importantly, Curry, in his capacity as legal counsel for the NCAI, arranged for Bronson to see President Truman on 10 October 1950 to discuss the Pyramid Lake controversy.[76]

Two days later, just before flying to a meeting with General Douglas Mac-Arthur at Wake Island in the Pacific, Truman blocked Fryer's transfer to give McCarran's political opponents an issue prior to the November election. After McCarran was reelected, officials at the White House lost interest in the Paiutes. They dealt with the Pyramid Lake controversy by offering Fryer a two-grade promotion to become director for a Point 4 program at the State Department as a way to get rid of him and thus support Myer.[77]

Emboldened by this decision, Commissioner Myer pushed ahead with plans to carefully regulate the activities of tribal attorneys. Myer was especially interested in diminishing the influence of James Curry and Felix Cohen, two socialist lawyers who fought for self-determination based on tribal sovereignty and federal protection under the Indian Reorganization Act. With these two opponents out of the way, Myer could move boldly forward to dismantle the reservation system.

On 9 November 1950, Myer issued a detailed set of regulations concerning contracts between tribes and their attorneys. These regulations went beyond the intent of an 1872 statute that gave the commissioner authority to prevent abuse on the part of unethical lawyers in the prosecution of tribal claims. By taking this action, the commissioner set the stage for a prolonged and bitter debate between claims attorneys, Indians, federal officials, and the general public over the Indians' constitutional right to independent counsel.[78]

7

THE RIGHT TO EMPLOY LEGAL COUNSEL

These [attorney contract] rules violate and disregard the principles of self-determination. There can be no real solution to the so-called Indian problem unless the Interior Department embraces the principle of self-determination of Indian people by actual practice. . . . The time has arrived when this well-intentioned paternalism on the part of the Indian Bureau must be abandoned. STATEMENT OF DOLLY AKERS, ASSINIBOINE, FORT PECK RESERVATION, DEPARTMENT OF INTERIOR HEARINGS ON ATTORNEY CONTRACT REGULATIONS, JANUARY 1952

In May 1950, almost before his feet were squarely under the desk, Commissioner Dillon S. Myer learned from Secretary of the Interior Oscar L. Chapman that contracts between tribes and their attorneys posed serious problems. Chapman was especially concerned about the activities of James Curry, who specialized in general counsel contracts, and the relationship of Felix Cohen with the Joint Efforts Group of law firms. Curry's militant defense of Indian rights challenged federal authority, while Cohen's claims work gave the impression that the Interior Department approved an arrangement that violated federal law.[1]

Curry had used his position as NCAI legal counsel on several occasions to encourage Indian self-determination and attract clients to his private law practice. As noted earlier, Ruth Muskrat Bronson solicited contracts for Curry to help tribes prepare their claims and to increase NCAI membership. By October 1950, Curry held general counsel contracts with twenty-six tribes and thirty claims contracts. Overextended by these commitments, he assigned numerous contracts to other lawyers and kept a portion of the retainer fee. Curry told Napoleon Bonaparte Johnson, the NCAI president, that his motives for representing so many tribes were "a mixture of public service and personal gain."[2]

Curry's general counsel contracts often distracted him from claims litigation. For instance, he opposed Indian Bureau plans to use property on the Colorado River Reservation in Arizona for Navajo colonization, helped Laguna Pueblo acquire one hundred thousand acres of submarginal land, and fought in court against the imposition of taxes on Omaha trust land. Furthermore, Curry defended the Salt River Pima Maricopas, Pine Ridge Sioux, and Mescalero Apaches when they disagreed with their superintendents and other government employees.[3]

A bitter feud with Cohen was another reason Curry found it difficult to prosecute claims. Before he resigned from the Interior Department in December 1947, Cohen made a gentleman's agreement to join the law firm of Curry, Bingham, and Cohen. Part of this arrangement was an offer by his cousin Henry Cohen to continue subsidizing Curry's claims business. In return, Felix Cohen had the option of becoming a partner. There also was an understanding that Cohen would not engage in claims work because he had played a key role in creating the Indian Claims Commission. This would placate Interior Department officials who worried about being charged with "complicity in a lawyers' racket."[4]

Another aspect of this agreement was an understanding that Cohen would eventually replace Curry as the NCAI general counsel. At Curry's request, Johnson sent Cohen a telegram inviting him to accept a joint appointment as associate general counsel. Cohen turned down this offer because he wanted Curry to resign before he left the Interior Department. In early December 1947, Curry telephoned Cohen and expressed a willingness to step down as general counsel after meeting with the NCAI Executive Committee. In the meantime, Cohen left his job at the Solicitor's Office without mentioning his intention to work for the NCAI.[5]

In January 1948, Curry refused to quit as NCAI general counsel after learning that both he and Bronson were targets of a Senate investigation for soliciting claims contracts. Once again, Curry failed to persuade Cohen to accept a joint NCAI appointment. Nonetheless, they cooperated as members of separate law firms on four general counsel contracts and defended the right of Indians to vote and receive Social Security benefits.[6]

In the meantime, Curry met with Alexander Lesser of the Association on American Indian Affairs. They discussed plans by Montgomery Arkusch and other New York attorneys to form a syndicate for lawyers holding claims contracts and hire a separate law firm to coordinate their research. After listening to Lesser's proposal, Curry drafted an alternate plan and invited either Felix or

Henry Cohen to submit it to interested parties. Curry recommended that the NCAI establish a research office in Washington DC to assist claims attorneys. The NCAI would borrow money from philanthropic organizations to finance an annual budget of $100,000 for claims research and use 2 or 3 percent of future claims awards to pay back these loans.[7]

Felix Cohen rejected this proposal and in the summer of 1948 terminated his professional ties with Curry. His cousin, Henry Cohen, also withdrew $4,000 a month in financial support for Curry and closed the law firm of Curry, Bingham, and Cohen. Curry continued to operate on his own but lacked the financial resources to successfully prosecute the Mescalero Apache, Paiute, and other claims cases.[8]

Cohen, on the other hand, became a consultant for the New York law firm of Riegelman, Strasser, Schwarz, and Spiegelberg, which belonged to the Joint Efforts Group. Under this arrangement, a pool of money was set aside to finance Cohen's salary and claims research from an office in Washington DC. Cohen's compensation remained the same whether claims were won or lost.[9]

In February 1949, Curry received a phone call from Cohen and a letter from Riegelman's law firm inviting him to utilize their research facilities to prepare claims cases in return for a percentage of fees from future claims awards. Curry rejected these offers because of "the malicious way" Cohen had treated him. His associate Charles M. Wright had also lost a claims contract with Yuma Indians after Cohen contacted this tribe on behalf of the Joint Efforts Group. Upset with unwanted claims competition, Curry decided it was time to burst Cohen's "great big bubble" and expose him for violating section 284A of the Federal Criminal Code, which prohibited federal employees from participating in claims cases for two years after they left government service.[10]

During July 1949, two events occurred that put Cohen on the defensive and embarrassed officials at the Interior Department. Charles M. Wright, who represented the NCAI in Tucson, filed a complaint with Secretary of Interior Julius Krug about Cohen's alleged illegal activities. Curry also contacted the publicity division of the Republican National Committee to confirm that Iowa congressman Ben F. Jenson had written Krug about Cohen's work for the Joint Efforts Group. Curry was told that the Interior Secretary had asked the Criminal Division of the Justice Department to review these charges.[11]

In September 1949, Curry put additional pressure on Krug. He persuaded the NCAI to adopt a resolution that called for an investigation by the attorney general to determine whether Cohen had broken the law by engaging in claims work. This resolution indicated that a syndicate of twenty law firms had banded together, on 17 December 1948, with the approval of Acting Commissioner

William Zimmerman, to set aside a pool of money to finance research and share information common to all claims cases. It also alleged that Cohen and other attorneys were involved in a "lawyers' racket" to collect $6 billion for a few tribes.[12]

One month later, Curry met with officials at the Justice Department to discuss NCAI charges against Cohen. There he learned that evidence in the Cohen file did not justify an indictment for a felony, but that the FBI would continue its investigation. Disappointed by this response, Curry contacted Congressman Jenson for more information. Jenson told him that "people with more authority . . . had indicated that he should not proceed with this matter."[13]

This news intensified Curry's concern that his attack on Cohen might rebound. In March 1950, he asked Secretary Chapman to stop efforts by officials at the Indian Bureau to ruin his law practice. Curry complained that they had refused to approve five of his pending attorney contracts, with fees totaling more than $12,000, and had demanded a detailed accounting of his legal work.[14]

In the spring of 1950, Commissioner Myer began a comprehensive review of the attorney contract problem. He discovered that current policy was based on "Regulations Governing Negotiation and Execution of Attorney Contracts" written in 1938 by Associate Solicitor Cohen and approved by Assistant Secretary of the Interior Chapman. These guidelines established different rules for organized and unorganized tribes.[15]

Myer found Cohen's regulations unsatisfactory. Primarily procedural in nature, they dealt with issues such as selection of counsel, qualifications of attorneys, completing alternative forms of contract, reports by superintendents, and the determination of fees and expenses. In this review, the commissioner did not consult with Indians or their attorneys. He also glossed over important sections of the regulations that dealt with Indian self-rule under the IRA.[16]

The fees for attorney contracts with organized tribes were subject to approval by the secretary of interior under the department's 1938 regulations. Nonetheless, these contracts had to comply with the provisions of IRA constitutions and charters. The Interior Department recognized these enumerated powers by refusing to approve payment for attorneys' fees and expenses without tribal consent.[17]

Myer would not acknowledge the clearly defined legal authority that tribes possessed under IRA because he intended to withdraw federal authority in Indian affairs. Instead, he formulated a general policy statement based on criteria used by the bureau in recent years. Under these guidelines, the commissioner turned down Curry's contracts with the Fort Peck Assiniboine and Sioux, Omaha Indians, and the Alaskan native villages of Kake, Angoon, and Unalakleet.[18]

In October 1950, Edwin E. Ferguson, the Indian Bureau's chief counsel, publicly announced new policies to govern attorney contracts with tribes. He stated that the bureau would determine attorney fees and not approve monthly retainer contracts, that tribes must employ local attorneys except for claims and legislative work with Congress, and that the bureau would decide whether tribes needed legal assistance and if they could afford lawyers. Furthermore, attorneys could accept only a limited number of Indian contracts, and tribes could not make advance payments to claims attorneys, who were to work on a contingency-fee basis.[19]

Ferguson's announcement upset John C. Rainer, the NCAI executive secretary, who warned in a press release that Indian civil rights were in extreme peril (pl. 20). Rainer believed that Myer's new regulations tied Indians closer to "the bureau's apron strings," when what they wanted was to "become increasingly self-reliant and independent." He also pointed out that Indians had employed attorneys on monthly retainer contracts to obtain a variety of legal services at a fixed cost. Many tribes disliked local attorneys because they rarely understood the political situation in Washington or the need for greater Indian self-determination. Rainer noted that in Alaska the residents of Kake paid three times the appraised value of a salmon cannery when the Indian Bureau insisted on hiring its own attorney for this transaction.[20]

Myer refused to listen to the NCAI. Instead, he issued thirty-six regulations that governed contracts between attorneys and Indian tribes. These regulations gave the commissioner authority to carefully monitor the activities of Curry, Cohen, and other lawyers. They were designed to discourage Indian political activism and restrict awards by the Indian Claims Commission.[21]

Myer limited claims contracts to ten years unless there were extenuating circumstances. He prohibited multiple claims contracts if they impaired an attorney's performance. Only contingency fees were permitted, and either the Indian Claims Commission or Indian commissioner would determine equitable fees for attorneys. With tribal consent, Myer could terminate the contracts of claims attorneys without cause. The assignment of contracts was prohibited in most instances, and claims attorneys were required to complete detailed reports about their work.[22]

The commissioner restricted three-year general counsel contracts to specific legal services. The only exceptions were representation before government agencies or Congress. Myer also required tribes to consider local attorneys to resolve problems related to "state affairs and personalities." With tribal authorization, the commissioner could terminate attorney contracts without cause to preclude "hasty and ill-considered action."[23]

1. John Collier watches William A. Brophy being sworn in as Indian commissioner. Brophy was absent from his job for extended periods due to illness between 1945 and 1948. Nonetheless, he worked to reorganize the Indian Bureau, improve Navajo education, and encourage more tribal autonomy under the Indian Reorganization Act. (Courtesy of the Harry S. Truman Library)

2. Nathan R. Margold, solicitor at the Department
of the Interior between 1933 and 1942. His rulings
upheld the inherent power of tribes to govern
themselves. Margold also tried to protect the rights of
Alaskan Natives to salmon, timber, and other natural
resources. (Courtesy of the National Archives)

3. Felix S. Cohen, solicitor at the Department of
the Interior between 1933 and 1947. Cohen drafted
the 1934 Wheeler-Howard Bill to create utopian
socialist democracies. He helped establish the Indian
Claims Commission and later, as a private attorney,
upheld the right of Blackfeet and other tribes to
self-determination. (Courtesy of Yale Collection
of Western Americana, Beinecke Rare Book and
Manuscript Library)

4. Ruth Muskrat Bronson, executive secretary
of the NCAI between 1945 and 1950. Bronson
defended the possessory rights of Haida and Tlingit
Indians in Alaska. She also assisted the Mescalero
Apaches and Pyramid Lake Paiutes in their fight
for self-determination under IRA. (Courtesy of the
National Anthropological Archives, Smithsonian
Institution)

5. Napoleon Bonaparte Johnson, the first president
of the NCAI, lobbied before Congress to establish the
Indian Claims Commission and protect the rights
of Alaskan Indians. He also joined the Governors'
Interstate Indian Council, which encouraged state
governments to provide Indians with social services.
(Courtesy of the National Anthropological Archives,
Smithsonian Institution)

6. Harold L. Ickes, secretary of the Interior between
1933 and 1946, supported the Indian Reorganization
Act, the creation of the Indian Claims Commission,
and departmental hearings to determine the
possessory rights of Indians in southeastern Alaska.
As a private citizen, Ickes upheld the right of tribes
to hire independent legal counsel. (Courtesy of the
National Archives)

7. President Harry S. Truman shakes hands
with Utah Indians at the White House after
signing into law a bill creating the Indian
Claims Commission on 13 August 1946. Left
to right: Reginald Curry, Uncompahgre Ute;
Lawrence Appah, White River Ute; and Julius
Murray, Uintah Ute. (Courtesy of AP/Wide
World Photos)

8. Ruth Kirk at her Gallup, New Mexico,
home admiring Native American pottery.
Kirk was shocked by deplorable conditions
on the Navajo Reservation. She played an
important role in the national campaign
to reform federal Indian policy. (Courtesy
of the National Anthropological Archives,
Smithsonian Institution)

9. Secretary of the Interior Julius A. Krug in the middle of the Navajo Reservation between Ganado and Window Rock on 16 September 1946. Krug met with Chee Dodge, chair of the Navajo Tribal Council, while visiting Hunter's Point Day School. Krug was accompanied by his son and William H. Zeh, an Indian Bureau employee. (Courtesy of the National Archives)

10. The home of Bessie Manygoats and her two children on the Navajo Reservation. This family, like most Navajos in the 1940s, lived in extreme poverty. The hogan of Manygoats lacked modern conveniences such as central heat and running water. (Courtesy of Yale Collection of Western Americana, Beinecke Rare Book and Manuscript Library)

11. Esan Begay was an eighty-year-old Navajo woman from Huerfano. Crippled and partially blind, she lived alone and wove crude rugs to obtain money for food. Her plight demonstrated why the Navajos desperately needed Social Security benefits. (Courtesy of Yale Collection of Western Americana, Beinecke Rare Book and Manuscript Library)

12. Will Rogers Jr. exemplified the growing sense of Indianness among different tribes in postwar America. He joined the NCAI, worked on behalf of urban Indians in Southern California, and publicized the plight of Navajos. (Courtesy of the National Anthropological Archives, Smithsonian Institution)

13. Sam Ahkeah chaired the Navajo Tribal Council from 1947 to 1954. He fought for the universal education of Navajo children, the right to vote in state elections, access to Social Security benefits, and the economic rehabilitation of the reservation. Ahkeah insisted that government officials consult with the Navajos on all important matters. (Courtesy of the National Archives)

14. Senator Hugh Butler of Nebraska upheld the supremacy of national institutions and rejected the idea that tribes had inherent powers of self-government. Butler worked to repeal the IRA and Alaska Reorganization Act, discredit the NCAI, liberate California Indians from wardship, and impose state jurisdiction throughout Indian country. (Courtesy of the Nebraska State Historical Society)

15. Senator Arthur V. Watkins at his desk, 5 April 1947. Watkins took the lead in the Eightieth Congress to emancipate Indians from federal wardship in Alaska, California, Oregon, and Utah. (Courtesy of Brigham Young University)

16. John R. Nichols, commissioner of Indian
Affairs for less than a year between 1949 and
1950. Nichols surprised almost everyone by
endorsing tribal self-determination under
IRA because he had served on the Hoover
Commission task force that recommended
state jurisdiction in Indian affairs. (Courtesy
of the National Archives)

17. Dillon S. Myer, commissioner of Indian
Affairs between 1950 and 1953. He followed
the recommendations of the Hoover
Commission task force that called for the
rapid assimilation of Indians and dismantling
of the reservation system. Myer's coercive
administrative style and all-or-nothing
approach to self-determination made him
unpopular throughout Indian country.
(Courtesy of the National Anthropological
Archives, Smithsonian Institution)

18. During Secretary of the Interior Oscar
L. Chapman's tenure, federal Indian policy
moved away from tribal organization under
IRA toward a staged federal withdrawal to
encourage full independence for Indian
people. This was a tumultuous transition
because Indians insisted on determining
their own destiny between 1949 and 1953.
(Courtesy of the Harry S. Truman Library)

19. Senator Patrick McCarran of Nevada opposed self-determination for the Pyramid Lake Paiutes, called the NCAI a communist-front organization, and proposed a constitutional amendment to terminate federal jurisdiction over Indian Affairs. (Courtesy of the Nevada Historical Society)

20. As NCAI executive secretary, John C. Rainer criticized Commissioner Dillon S. Myer's attorney contract regulations, joined ARROW to solicit nationwide support for Indian civil rights, and encouraged self-determination on the Mescalero Apache Reservation. (Courtesy of the National Anthropological Archives, Smithsonian Institution)

21. Avery Winnemucca, chair of the Pyramid
Lake Paiute Tribal Council, played a leading
role in the movement toward more Indian
self-determination. (Courtesy of the National
Anthropological Archives, Smithsonian
Institution)

22. Nevada Indians protest in Washington. In
October 1951, Paiute leaders affirmed their
right to rehire James E. Curry as their lawyer
to protect water rights, evict Euro-American
settlers from Indian land, and maintain
self-rule under the Indian Reorganization
Act. Left to right are Elisabeth Roe Cloud,
field secretary of the National Congress of
American Indians; Ruth Muskrat Bronson,
NCAI executive director; Warren Toby, a
Paiute council member; Avery Winnemucca,
tribal chair; James E. Curry, attorney; and
Albert Aleck, secretary-treasurer of the tribe.
(Courtesy NYT Pictures)

23. Blackfeet lockout, 14 April 1951. Tribal chair George Pambrun, Cora Irgens of the Blackfeet Business Council, and attorney Felix S. Cohen watch a worker post a "no trespassing" sign to assert Blackfeet jurisdiction over buildings at agency headquarters in Browning, Montana. These political activists were engaged in a calculated act of civil disobedience to publicize and defend the Blackfeet right to self-determination. (Courtesy of AP Wide World Photos)

24. Frank George followed in the footsteps of Chief Joseph. In 1952, this Nez Percé leader became executive director of the NCAI. He disapproved of state jurisdiction over Indians without the consent of tribal governments. George resisted Commissioner Dillon S. Myer's plans to begin a unilateral federal withdrawal from Indian affairs. (Courtesy of the National Anthropological Archives, Smithsonian Institution)

25. Oscar L. Chapman meets with Indian
consultants in 1952. (Courtesy of the Bancroft
Library, University of California at Berkeley)

On 12 November 1950, the National Civil Liberties Clearing House asked Secretary Chapman to hold a conference regarding Myer's regulations. This umbrella organization represented the NCAI, American Civil Liberties Union (ACLU), National Association for the Advancement of Colored People, National Jewish Congress, Americans for Democratic Action, American Friends Service Committee, Association on American Indian Affairs, and other groups. Chapman refused to meet with these civil rights organizations because of pressing departmental and defense-related business. He did, however, confer with several tribal attorneys.[24]

One month later, the secretary of interior received a legal brief entitled "Memorandum on the Right of Indian Tribes to Counsel" from attorneys representing fifteen law firms that belonged to the Joint Efforts Group. Two of the signers, Charles L. Black and Felix S. Cohen, represented the views of the AAIA, while Theodore Haas spoke for the ACLU. This document condemned Myer's authoritarian administrative style, upheld Indian legal rights, and defended the inherent power of tribal self-rule under federal protection. It was widely distributed to members of Congress, civil rights groups, and Indian welfare organizations. It marked the beginning of a coordinated effort to derail Myer's plans to withdraw federal supervision over Indian affairs.[25]

This legal brief argued that Myer's regulations violated a basic constitutional principle that separated the judicial from the executive branch of government. These rules were also based on an obsolete 1872 statute restricted to "Indians — not citizens." They deprived modern Indians of the constitutional right to an attorney guaranteed by the Fifth Amendment to the U.S. Constitution.[26]

It also was inappropriate for an executive officer to control the choice of legal counsel and set the fees for lawyers who filed lawsuits before the Indian Claims Commission. Sixteen law firms representing over two hundred attorneys were affected by this decision because they refused to accept contingency fees for less than 10 percent. Furthermore, many Indians could not effectively present their claims if prohibited from using tribal funds to pay for retainer fees to help cover litigation costs.[27]

Another fundamental issue concerned the legal right of tribes under the Indian Reorganization Act. Section 16 of this law gave them the power to employ attorneys and fix their fees subject to the secretary of interior's approval. The IRA constitutions and charters also confirmed the legal authority of tribes to sue and be sued, conduct corporate business, and sign contracts.[28]

The circulation of this legal brief led to a nationwide protest. In January 1951, Secretary Chapman received correspondence critical of Commissioner

Myer's regulations from the Churches of Christ, General Federation of Women's Clubs, Indian Rights Association, Institute on Ethnic Affairs, and New Mexico Association on Indian Affairs. The All Pueblo Council and Clarence Wesley, chair of the San Carlos Apache tribe, also condemned Myer for violating the rights of Indian citizens.[29]

These public statements did not clearly identify the hidden agenda behind the attorney contract controversy: how to prevent Curry and the NCAI from using Cohen's claims research to embarrass the Truman administration, to limit the ability of both Cohen and Curry to defend Indian self-determination under federal protection, and to make it more difficult for the Joint Efforts Group to prosecute costly tribal claims. Secretary Chapman and Commissioner Myer disagreed on how to handle this complex situation. Consequently, they remained on the defensive and never fully disclosed their motives.

Isolated by these events, Curry turned to the NCAI, Pyramid Lake Paiute Indians, and President Truman to protect his law practice. In February 1951, President Truman received a telegram from the NCAI that criticized Commissioner Myer for not renewing Curry's attorney contract with the Paiutes. The NCAI pointed out that these Indians urgently needed a lawyer to block a bill introduced by Senator Patrick McCarran that threatened their property rights.[30]

A short time later, Myer approved Curry's contract subject to four conditions that reaffirmed his authority to supervise tribal attorneys. The commissioner insisted that the contract continue for two instead of ten years, allow for its termination with tribal consent on sixty days' notice, require Curry to reach an understanding with the Paiutes to employ local counsel and pay for work that he assigned other lawyers, and make Curry submit semi-annual reports detailing services performed by the contract. David K. Niles, the president's administrative assistant, endorsed this decision. He notified the NCAI that Myer's stipulations were designed to safeguard Indian interests.[31]

Commissioner Myer, encouraged by President Truman's support, announced that three Indian groups wanted to sever their legal relationship with Curry. The Mescalero and Jicarilla Apaches were upset because he failed to prosecute their claims with diligence and competence, whereas Alaskan natives at Klawock found his services imposed unacceptable financial burdens. Myer gave Curry sixty days to submit written or oral arguments why the Indian Bureau should not terminate these attorney contracts.[32]

In March 1951, Myer released a formal reply to the earlier legal brief written on behalf of law firms belonging to the Joint Efforts Group. The commissioner insisted that his attorney contract regulations closely resembled previous guidelines used at the Interior Department. Myer also dismissed the argument that the

1872 statute regulating tribal attorneys applied only to noncitizen Indians. He noted that in the revised law codes, someone had inadvertently scored a comma between the phrase "Indians, not citizens." This represented a departure from the original punctuation found in the 1871 Appropriation Act, which prevented attorneys from signing contracts with "any tribe of Indians, or individual Indians not a citizen," without departmental approval.[33]

Myer dismissed the idea that he was part of a sinister plot to defeat Indian claims. Recently, he had asked area office field directors to ascertain if any tribes experienced difficulty in finding a claims attorney. The commissioner also doubted whether his ban on retainer fees was a serious problem because 90 percent of the claims litigation was based on contingency contracts. Furthermore, the American Bar Association in 1946 had ruled that its cannon 42, which prohibited lawyers from paying for litigation expenses without reimbursement, did not apply to Indian claims.[34]

Myer believed that the legislative history of the IRA provided three compelling reasons to maintain control over attorney contracts: the federal responsibility of safeguarding tribal assets, the feeling among members of the House and Senate that supervision should continue until Congress turned tribes loose, and the concern about lawyers who were involved in a racket to solicit Indian business. Myer, who relied on political support from conservative members of Congress during the attorney contract controversy, was endorsing the views of Senator Patrick McCarran, who wanted to destroy Curry's "legal monopoly" to prevent "trouble among the Indian tribes."[35]

Ruth Muskrat Bronson believed that the commissioner's attempt to deny Indians independent legal counsel represented a grave threat. In April 1951, she told Harold Ickes, Curry's personal attorney, that the NCAI had received reports from tribes all over the United States that revealed resentment, bitterness, and a sense of frustration. One month later, Ickes wrote an article for *New Republic* that characterized Myer as a "Hitler and Mussolini rolled into one."[36]

In June 1951, Secretary Chapman responded to this adverse public criticism. He asked Solicitor Mastin G. White to rule on his authority to issue revised attorney contract regulations. White had an opportunity to endorse Nathan Margold's earlier opinion that the most basic principle of Indian law was that tribes did not have powers delegated by Congress but rather inherent powers of a limited sovereignty. Instead, he chose to uphold the immense authority of the secretary of interior over Indian life. This decision cast a long shadow over the movement for self-determination by treating Indians as a dependent people.[37]

In this ruling, White ignored the question of whether the 1872 statute applied only to Indians, not citizens, by inserting three asterisks in his summary of the provisions of this law. The solicitor decided that Chapman had broad discretionary power over both IRA and unorganized tribes. It was his opinion that under the plenary power of Congress, the secretary of interior could grant or withhold approval of an IRA or other tribal attorney contract for any reason.[38]

One month after White's decision, Secretary Chapman drafted new attorney contract regulations that encompassed minor changes. In August 1951, they appeared in the *Federal Register* as "Notice of Proposed Rule-Making." Chapman reduced the number of regulations from thirty-six to twenty-six and required attorneys to negotiate contracts in accordance with IRA constitutions and charters, or at general council meetings for unorganized tribes. The secretary prohibited the solicitation of contracts, used performance factors to limit the total number of Indian clients, and outlawed contract assignment without the prior consent of the tribe and commissioner. Furthermore, the commissioner could terminate contracts on sixty days' notice, require the employment of local counsel in most circumstances, and make exceptions to the requirement that all claims contracts contain a contingency fee clause.[39]

Chapman invited critics to comment on his revisions, but this effort at compromise only led to more public protest. Charles L. Black, the chair of the Association on American Indian Affairs legal committee and a professor at Columbia Law School, informed Chapman that the solicitor had neglected to carefully examine the manifest intent of Congress to change federal law and expand tribal self-rule under the 1934 Indian Reorganization Act. Alexander Lesser, the executive director of the AAIA, warned that the rules published in the *Federal Register* violated the ethics of the legal profession.[40]

Two prominent Indians also wrote Secretary Chapman. Elizabeth Roe-Cloud, the chair of the General Federation of Women's Clubs, told the secretary of interior that he had violated the constitutional right of Indians to legal counsel and hindered their struggle to become more independent. Napoleon Bonaparte Johnson, the NCAI president, complained that Interior Department regulations extended rather than removed federal paternalism.[41]

This ongoing controversy was closely related to a separate initiative undertaken by Chapman to destroy Curry's legal practice. In July 1951, he asked Solicitor White to review Curry's contract with the Pyramid Lake Paiute Indians. White ruled that Chapman had the authority to limit this contract to two years and terminate it after sixty days' notice even though the Paiutes had adopted an IRA constitution and charter. Armed with this legal opinion, the secretary of interior turned down the Paiute's request to rehire Curry.[42]

On 20 September 1951, Avery Winnemucca, the chair of the Paiute Tribal

Council, sent Chapman a letter that criticized Solicitor White's preference for administrative stability over tribal self-rule. Winnemucca reminded the secretary of interior that he should resolve all difficult issues in favor of tribal democracy and against the Indian Bureau. Winnemucca pointed out that by law appellants were entitled to a public hearing before the secretary of interior to challenge questionable decisions. If Chapman refused to grant this request, tribal leaders would insist on meeting with President Truman (pl. 21).[43]

The Paiute Tribal Council then authorized the expenditure of $700 from tribal funds to send a delegation to the nation's capital to meet with either Chapman or Truman. Nonetheless, Myer's approval was needed to spend this money. In March 1951, the commissioner had issued an executive order on "The Conduct of Tribal Government," which required tribal councils to initially discuss problems with area directors before traveling to Washington DC. Under these regulations, Indians had to select small delegations, make brief trips, and submit certified resolutions that authorized delegates to speak on an approved agenda. If unauthorized Indians found themselves stranded without funds, Myer referred them to the District of Columbia's travelers' aid society and assumed no responsibility for their transportation home.[44]

On 26 September, the commissioner told Burton A. Ladd, the superintendent of the Carson Agency, that he would authorize the expenditure of money for two Paiute delegates to visit the nation's capital. When Myer broke this promise by delaying the release of tribal funds, the Paiutes raised travel money from friends in Reno and elsewhere. On 17 October, a delegation that included Winnemucca, Albert Aleck, and Warren Tobey arrived in Washington after riding a bus for three days and nights. It was their intent to squat in the nation's capital, just as white settlers had squatted on their land, until the government approved Curry's attorney contract.[45]

During the next few weeks, Winnemucca, Aleck, and Tobey, with assistance from Curry and the Association on American Indian Affairs, wrote letters to people all over the United States asking for help. The Paiutes received favorable coverage in Nevada newspapers, the *New York Times*, and the Kiplinger newsletter. John Collier's Institute on Ethnic Affairs also provided the delegates with public relations advice and scheduled meetings with students in nearby colleges. The Paiutes also met with journalists from *Time* and *Life*, visited representatives from the Daughters of the American Revolution, held interviews with radio stations, and made arrangements with the NCAI to appear before the National Press Club.[46]

On Saturday, 20 October, the Paiute delegation met with Secretary Chapman. Winnemucca said very little about the tribe's attorney contract with Curry because he intended to discuss this subject at a subsequent public hearing. Instead, Winnemucca asked Chapman to evict squatters from the Olinghouse irrigation ditch. The interior secretary replied that he had already instructed the Justice Department to file a lawsuit to protect Paiute water rights.[47]

Four days later, Winnemucca, Aleck, and Tobey, accompanied by Curry, met with Commissioner Myer at the Indian Bureau. There they held inconclusive discussions on the eviction of squatters and contested property rights. This meeting ended on a low note when Myer personally informed Curry that he would not renew his attorney contract with the tribe (pl. 22).[48]

On 3 November 1951, Governor John W. Bonner of Montana intervened on behalf of the Paiute tribe. He sent President Truman a telegram that expressed concern over Interior Department regulations that interfered with the Indians' freedom to pick their own attorneys. The president replied that Secretary Chapman was aware of the gravity and importance of this problem and would take no action that jeopardized "the right of Indian tribes to be represented . . . by counsel of their own choice."[49]

Five days later, the American Bar Association (ABA) added fuel to the fire by issuing a report prepared by a special committee that for seven months had studied the question of contracts with Indian tribes. Written by Rufus G. Poole, John Pratt, and Isadore Alk, it concluded that Chapman's authority under section 16 of the IRA did not go beyond reviewing a tribe's choice of counsel and the fixing of fees. This report also cited a 1938 ruling by Acting Solicitor Frederic Kirgus that directed superintendents to inform attorneys that all other contract provisions were "alterable at the pleasure of the tribe."[50]

The ABA recommended that Chapman hold public hearings because the department's proposed regulations adversely affected a fundamental right of all Americans—the freedom to choose a lawyer of one's own choice. With regard to the activities of Curry, the report stated that the solicitation of contracts was grounds for disqualifying an attorney, but a proper administrative tribunal rather than the Indian commissioner should make this determination. The ABA also recommended that Chapman transfer authority over tribal contracts from the Indian Bureau to the Solicitor's Office, where government attorneys would be more objective.[51]

On the same day that the ABA issued its report, Secretary Chapman unveiled a Machiavellian plan to end the attorney contract crisis and quell public criticism. He announced departmental hearings early in January 1952 to discuss the grievances of Indians and their attorneys. Prior to this decision, Chapman and Myer met with Senator Clinton P. Anderson of New Mexico and persuaded him to simultaneously hold congressional hearings to investigate frauds committed by tribal attorneys.[52]

Both Chapman and Myer were eager to silence Curry. The secretary of interior disliked Curry's public criticism of Cohen's claims research intended to discredit and embarrass officials at the Interior Department. Myer viewed Curry as a "thorn in the flesh" because he used the NCAI to solicit attorney contracts, orchestrate intratribal conflict on the Mescalero Apache Reservation, and encourage the Paiutes as well as other Indians to mistrust the federal government. Senator Anderson shared these views and also wanted to discourage tribal claims that drained millions of dollars from the U.S. Treasury.[53]

On 3 January 1952, more than two hundred people crowded into room 5160 at the Interior Department building to attend a two-day hearing on Chapman's proposed attorney contract regulations. They listened to the testimony of forty-four people. Twenty-four of these individuals, including brightly clad Pueblo delegates with their hair in braids, were from fifteen tribes that represented over two hundred thousand Indians.[54]

Secretary Chapman presided at this hearing. Commissioner Myer sat in silence as all the witnesses upheld the right of tribes to choose independent legal counsel. The proceedings began with a written statement from Harold Ickes, who was confined to a hospital bed because of a painful disease that soon claimed his life. For Ickes, the attorney contract controversy was about the future of tribal self-government. He called on Indians and their friends to prevent the IRA from being "murdered in its youth."[55]

Frank George, vice-president of the NCAI and secretary of the Affiliated Tribes of Northwest Indians, agreed with Ickes. George believed that the proposed regulations contradicted the promise of more self-determination that Myer had made in 1950 before the NCAI convention at Bellingham, Washington. The NCAI leader favored an early end to federal wardship, but not at the expense of threatening and destabilizing tribal governments that represented the Indians' "last remaining link with the pageantry of a glorious past."[56]

Avery Winnemucca, chair of the Paiute Pyramid Lake Tribal Council, made an even more dramatic presentation. Speaking on behalf of all Indians, he told the audience that President Franklin D. Roosevelt had endorsed the Indian Reorganization Act in 1934 to extend to tribes "the fundamental rights of political liberty and local self-government." Winnemucca then asked Chapman, the "last direct political descendant of Roosevelt," if the president's words "were just a sham." Winnemucca stressed that the commissioner's effort to prevent Indians from selecting their own attorneys was "an attempt to destroy what Franklin Roosevelt said we should have."[57]

William V. Creager testified that Indians from Laguna Pueblo had made significant progress toward self-determination prior to the attorney contract controversy. They had acquired title to one hundred thousand acres of sub-marginal land, gained access to Social Security benefits, and won the right to vote in state elections. In September 1950, Laguna Pueblo had drafted an IRA charter to manage oil, gas, uranium, and other natural resources. Myer refused to approve these bylaws because he viewed Felix Cohen, their attorney, as a troublemaker and stereotyped Indians as backward people who were unable to handle "financial transactions over two dollars."[58]

Ben Chief, who spoke for eleven thousand Oglala Sioux, also complained that Myer had disapproved his tribe's attorney contract with Cohen for political reasons. At a recent council meeting, the Sioux had passed a resolution that criticized the commissioner's budget priorities and the employment of useless personnel at area offices. The Sioux felt that instead of respecting the Bill of Rights, Myer had treated them "as savages" and had tried to persuade them to hire another attorney. They also felt he tried to silence protest by freezing $140,000 in their IRA credit fund.[59]

Rufus Wallowing, chair of the Northern Cheyenne Tribal Council, saw a direct relationship between Myer's regulations, self-rule, and the development of reservation resources. The tribal council had asked Myer, without success, for permission to hire an attorney to update the Northern Cheyenne IRA constitution and charter. Wallowing was convinced that with proper legal advice, the tribal council could better develop grazing and farming land, as well as timber and coal deposits.[60]

Dolly Akers, an Assiniboine and member of the Fort Peck Business Committee, stressed that the time had come for federal officials to allow Indians to practice the principle of self-determination. This meant abandoning Indian Bureau paternalism. Only through trial and error could tribes learn more about freedom and democracy.[61]

William C. Knorr, the chair of the Fort Peck Tribal Council, then criticized Commissioner Myer for telling Indians that $3,000 was too much to spend on an attorney because the tribe had only $13,000 deposited in the U.S. Treasury. This was a phony figure. The Fort Peck Indians had received $72,000 from just one of their oil leases. Knorr emphasized that a tribal lawyer would help them defend subsurface mineral rights, restore surplus land that remained after allotment, remove squatters from the towns of Wolf Point and Poplar, and control tribal funds.[62]

Tom Main, a Gros Ventre, spoke on behalf of the Fort Belknap Indian community and as chair of the Montana Inter-Tribal Policy Board, a federation of tribes representing more than twenty thousand people. Main testified that Montana's Indians were unanimously against Myer's regulations. They insisted on the right to hire attorneys to stop the leasing of land without their consent and to prevent government officials from meddling in tribal elections.[63]

Main used "$40 cowboy language" to explain how Indians had made real progress toward self-determination prior to 1950. But after Myer became commissioner, employees at the Billings Area Office purposely lost two attorney contracts and treated Indians "like prisoners in a concentration camp." Consequently, the Fort Belknap Tribal Council decided to hire Cohen as general counsel under the authority of their IRA charter without the commissioner's approval. If the Indian Bureau overruled this decision, the tribe would challenge the government in any U.S. court.[64]

Sam Ahkeah, chair of the Navajo Tribal Council, suggested that the relations between a lawyer and tribe were as delicate and confidential as the relationship between husband and wife. The Navajos were an unorganized tribe and bound by the requirements set forth in the 1872 statute. Nevertheless, once the tribe signed its attorney contract with Norman M. Littell, the commissioner had "no further business with it."[65]

Rufus Poole, who represented the American Bar Association's Administrative Law Section, supported these Indian leaders. He indicated that Myer's regulations shocked the bar associations of the country. ABA members were gravely alarmed at the extent to which the commissioner proposed to intrude into the relationship between attorneys and their Indian clients. Poole emphasized that tribes would never have political or economic freedom unless the federal government respected their right to select lawyers of their own choice.[66]

Felix Cohen, who testified on behalf of the Association on American Indian Affairs, indicated that the movement of the 1930s and 1940s to encourage self-rule had been challenged by Myer, who wanted to control tribal activities. Cohen asked Chapman to disapprove of the commissioner's autocratic rules and follow the department's 1938 guidelines. He then criticized the Indian Bureau for using an 1872 law, which represented an ugly period in American history, to expand its authority over unorganized tribes. Cohen compared Myer to President Ulysses S. Grant. Indian history after the Civil War and World War II demonstrated that acts of oppression were unjust even when inspired by the highest patriotic motives.[67]

Fundamental issues of the attorney contract dispute were raised by James Curry, who noted that both the 1872 law and the 1934 Indian Reorganization Act permitted but did not require government interference with the right of Indians to pick their own attorneys. The real question was why Chapman and

Myer did not show restraint instead of imposing restrictive regulations. The answer for Curry was their interest in preventing certain tribes from retaining particular lawyers.[68]

Curry believed that the commissioner had drafted attorney contract regulations as a smoke screen to hide a vendetta against himself and a few other attorneys. A problem arose when Myer's "smoke got in other people's eyes." This caused irritated lawyers from all over the United States who had an interest in claims to defend the legal rights of Indians. It also was important to realize that the obstructionist tactics of government officials went far beyond the disapproval of contracts. Curry indicated that he had gone through a "chamber of horrors" that included slander, libel, refusal of access to public documents, and interference with the hiring of associate attorneys. He stated that this unethical behavior made it more difficult for him to defend the rights of Alaska's natives, prosecute numerous tribal claims, and help Indians collect damages after the government built a Japanese-American concentration camp on the Colorado River Reservation without prior approval.[69]

Curry concluded his statement by encouraging everyone to recognize that they lived during a transitional period in Indian affairs. After the passage of the Indian Claims Commission Act, an avalanche of lawyers had fallen on the Indian Bureau. This upset many people but meant the Indians had begun to control their own destiny.[70]

After these hearings ended, Chapman carefully examined the testimony of Indians, tribal attorneys, and representatives of the American Bar Association. On 14 January 1952, he sent Myer a draft memorandum that rejected departmental attorney contract regulations and established a review committee to make future policy recommendations. Its membership included individuals who identified with the ABA and two attorneys retained by Indian tribes. This proposal shocked Myer. He was especially upset that the secretary wanted to name Cohen, an old friend of Chapman's, as one of the attorneys on the committee.[71]

One week later, Myer made a dramatic appearance before the Senate Subcommittee on Interior and Insular Affairs. There, he testified that "fomenters of trouble" had misled people through factual distortion, irrelevant argument, and personal abuse. Myer emphasized that the Senate should consider the question of attorney contracts not in a vacuum but in the context of federal legislation dealing with Indian property.[72]

Myer warned Clinton Anderson and other senators that Curry and Cohen had encouraged tribes to request self-determination without providing adequate safeguards. Myer said this was unacceptable because he knew of instances where tribal officials had mismanaged Indian property. He felt it also was important to allow all Indians to benefit from the recent discovery of oil and mineral deposits on their reservations.[73]

Secretary Chapman disapproved of the regulations published in the *Federal Register* four days after the commissioner's appearance before the Senate subcommittee. The interior secretary then appointed a committee that did not include Cohen to study the adequacy of the department's 1938 guidelines. More importantly, Chapman requested a congressional review of his authority to regulate attorney contracts.[74]

During the summer of 1952, Commissioner Myer took additional steps to destroy Curry's effectiveness as a champion of Indian self-determination. He used existing Interior Department regulations to turn down Curry's contracts with the Paiutes, Northern Cheyennes, and other tribes.[75] Myer also sent Chapman a seventy-page memorandum detailing charges against Curry to lay the groundwork for possible disbarment proceedings. This memo, along with pressure from Anderson's Senate subcommittee, forced Napoleon Bonaparte Johnson to notify Curry in July that his employment as NCAI legal counsel would terminate within six months.[76]

In January 1953, after gathering more than twenty-six hundred pages of testimony, the Anderson subcommittee published its findings in a report that concluded it did not have authority to determine whether Secretary Chapman should relax or abandon federal supervision over Indians. Until Congress decided otherwise, the Interior Department had a trust responsibility to regulate attorney contracts because of the questionable activities of Curry and other lawyers.[77]

The Anderson report resembled a government inquisition. Nowhere did it present the opposing viewpoint of Indians or their lawyers. Its objective was to defend government officials and discredit people who favored more tribal self-determination under federal protection. To accomplish this end, the report cited testimony critical of the activities of Bronson, Curry, Cohen, and the NCAI. Particular attention was devoted to Alaska to explain why Senators Anderson and Watkins voted for the Tongass Timber Act.[78]

The subcommittee report reprimanded Curry for soliciting contracts. Two examples of how he violated the cannons of professional ethics were Bronson's typing of Curry's name on contracts during a 1947 trip to Alaska and Cohen's gentlemen's agreement with Curry to resign from the Interior Department to help him assign a pool of claims contracts to law firms. The Senate report also stated that Curry had brokered claims contracts to the Indians' detriment, interfered with the employment of other attorneys such as Roy Mobley, and relegated Indians to the role of pawns.[79]

The Anderson report discredited an outspoken proponent of Indian self-determination. On the other hand, tribal leaders and their friends destroyed Myer's credibility as an opponent of federal paternalism. They also made it more difficult for the commissioner and Congress to concentrate on withdrawal programming. The critics of Myer and Chapman, however, unwittingly weakened the principle of federal guardianship, which posed a barrier to tribal dissolution, by insisting that Indians had the right to select their own attorneys without federal oversight. Even more damaging was the bitter conflict between Cohen and Curry, which tarnished the reputation of the NCAI and shattered the solidarity between two attorneys committed to defending tribal political autonomy.

Despite these internal problems, the legal profession in the early 1950s had a significant impact on Indian history. The American Bar Association played a pivotal role in defeating regulations that limited the ability of lawyers to prosecute claims. During the attorney contract controversy, major law firms throughout the United States also became aware of the Indian demand for more self-determination. Their ongoing interest in grievances of Indian clients provides a historical context to better understand Supreme Court decisions, beginning in 1959 with *Williams v. Lee*, that reaffirmed the permanency of tribal governments in the federal system.[80]

The history of the Pyramid Lake Paiute Indians provides an example of how tribes benefited from their right to employ independent legal counsel. Even though Commissioner Myer refused to renew Curry's contract, the Paiutes evicted squatters from their homeland. In 1952, William Ceresola and other settlers finally agreed to sell adjacent ranching property and valuable water rights to the tribe for $383,344. The Paiutes also used their IRA government to hire lawyers who negotiated with state and federal authorities. Forty years after the attorney contract dispute, the tribe fulfilled Avery Winnemucca's expectations of self-determination by participating as equal partners in the management of the Truckee River Basin.[81]

In yet another unexpected development, Felix Cohen strengthened his position within the American Bar Association. Support from other attorneys allowed Cohen to more effectively represent Indians who opposed Commissioner Myer's policies. This was especially true on the Blackfeet Reservation, where tribal leaders aggressively defended their right to self-determination under the Indian Reorganization Act.

8

BLACKFEET DECLARE
THEIR INDEPENDENCE

It soon will be 176 years since the United States began with a Declaration of Independence that says all men are created equal. My people want to be part of that Spirit of 1776. . . . We want the right to handle our own affairs. We even want the right to make mistakes. STATEMENT OF GEORGE PAMBRUN, BLACKFEET LEADER, BEFORE THE SENATE INTERIOR AND INSULAR AFFAIRS COMMITTEE, 15 APRIL 1952

On 14 April 1951, George Pambrun, the chair of the Blackfeet Business Council, accompanied by Felix Cohen, the tribal attorney, directed Indian police to issue eviction notices to federal employees who worked at the agency headquarters in Browning, Montana. Pambrun took this action to confirm Blackfeet ownership of a warehouse and other buildings. He was responding to a settlement where the Court of Claims had deducted $4 million in offsets for capital improvements on the reservation from a recent claims award.[1]

This act of civil disobedience was part of an ongoing campaign by Blackfeet political activists to sever their colonial relationship with the U.S. government. Pambrun and other tribal leaders fought for self-determination by upholding the authority of the IRA Business Council to independently manage reservation resources and conduct free elections. They also collaborated with the National Congress of American Indians and the pan-Indian Montana Inter-Tribal Policy Board to discredit policies that threatened their political autonomy, separate ethnic identity, and livelihood.

At stake was a fundamental principle of democratic government: whether the Indian Bureau or the elected tribal government would determine the circumstances of Blackfeet life. Nonetheless, this movement for self-determination took place against the backdrop of financial problems that confirmed Commissioner Dillon Myer's belief that Indian politicos had used the IRA to take advantage of less fortunate people. This scandal deeply offended six hundred full-bloods who looked to President Harry S. Truman to safeguard their interests.

The business council adamantly opposed federal wardship because Blackfeet leaders served in the Montana legislature, in county government, and on local school boards. The tribe had over 120 college and 700 high school graduates. Proud of these achievements, members of the Blackfeet council could not understand why federal officials had repeatedly turned down their requests for more autonomy.[2]

To overcome this dilemma, the business council hired Cohen as legal counsel. He codified all treaties, laws, and executive orders that applied to the reservation. Cohen also worked behind the scenes with Sister Providencia, a Roman Catholic nun who taught at the College of Great Falls, and Tom Main, a Gros Ventre leader on the Fort Belknap Reservation. It was their expectation that three semireligious ceremonies scheduled for the summer of 1950 would cement tribal unity in Montana prior to the Indians' "last great stand for self-determination."[3]

In the meantime, Henry Magee, chair of the Blackfeet Business Council, contacted Secretary of Interior Oscar Chapman. Magee told him the tribe wanted to hold a referendum on whether to terminate the supervisory authority of the secretary of interior under the Blackfeet Constitution and Charter. A favorable vote would enable the business council to lease tribal property, deposit IRA corporate funds in local banks, and manage other assets without federal oversight.[4]

Chapman turned down Magee's request because of recent complaints concerning the eligibility of Blackfeet voters. To ensure that future referendums were legitimate, Chapman ruled, in what later became a troublesome issue, that only permanent residents on the reservation were eligible to vote. The secretary also instructed the tribe to set up polling places in each district, appoint an election board, and make sure that election judges certified the accuracy of votes by returning ballots in sealed and locked boxes to the superintendent's office.[5]

In April 1950, Chapman gave Magee other compelling reasons why the Interior Department should continue its supervision over tribal affairs. The results of a recent audit by the accounting firm of Douglas, Wilson, Ferris and Company of Great Falls, which covered the previous eight years, contained disturbing information about how the business council had failed to properly administer Blackfeet finances. The council had loaned $209,000 from tribal funds to nine hundred destitute people with no security and little chance of repayment. Furthermore, the $110,000 expense to operate the tribal government exceeded current income by $16,000. The secretary warned Magee that these problems jeopardized the future of self-government, which rested on the integrity of persons elected to office.[6]

Soon after he took office, Commissioner Myer met with Superintendent Rex D. Kidlow and Paul L. Fickinger, director of the Billings Area Office, to review the Blackfeet financial crisis. Fickinger requested an FBI investigation because he believed that certain individuals on the business council belonged in a penitentiary. Myer supported Fickinger, but the Department of Justice would not proceed further unless the Indian Bureau presented concrete evidence of wrongdoing.[7]

The Blackfeet scandal provided the commissioner with an opportunity to publicly discredit an IRA tribal government that stood in the way of his plans to dismantle the reservation system. In May 1950, Myer instructed Fickinger to inform the business council about its record of maladministration. One month later, the area director sent the tribe a letter that sharply criticized the council for depositing $76,000 in tribal funds at the First National Bank of Browning without legal authorization. These deposits clearly exceeded the $5,000 limit written in the tribe's IRA charter and the amount insured by the Federal Deposit Insurance Corporation.[8]

Fickinger conceded that small bank accounts were not the best way to handle the recent growth of revenues from oil leases. He recommended that the tribe amend its IRA charter to provide a legal means to deposit large sums of money in local banks. In the meantime, the area director ordered the tribe to withdraw all deposits not insured by the FDIC and put this money in the agency's Individual Money Account. If the business council did not follow these instructions, the federal government would compel compliance with the Blackfeet charter.[9]

Fickinger also notified the Blackfeet Business Council that it had failed to submit annual budgets and maintain proper records for the tribal store. Other problems were check overdrafts, unsecured loans, purchase of merchandise without provision for repayment, and a 35 percent delinquency rate for IRA loans. The area director warned that the Indian Bureau would take appropriate legal action if the council refused to end these irregularities.[10]

There were serious consequences to the mishandling of Blackfeet funds. In August 1950, the Interior Department informed Senator Joseph O'Mahoney of Wyoming that it disapproved of proposed legislation to rehabilitate the Blackfeet because of the tribe's troublesome record of self-government under IRA. The senator also learned that the business council had mismanaged oil income of over $2 million, owed $55,000 in delinquent loans, and authorized twelve unpaid loans that exceeded $8,000 to current or former tribal officers and employees.[11]

In their zeal to hold the tribal government financially accountable, government officials overlooked the plight of impoverished people on the reservation. During the harsh winter of 1950, destitute tribesmen had organized a committee at Browning to investigate malnutrition and other health-related problems. This citizen's group was especially interested in verifying reports by a local newspaper and radio station that hungry Blackfeet were eating skunk and porcupine to avoid starvation.[12]

Fickinger responded to this crisis by interfering in the June 1950 tribal election. In a radio broadcast, he described wrongdoing by members of the Blackfeet Business Council. The area director took this step because he wanted the Blackfeet to vote against incumbent council members and disapprove a proposed referendum to end the supervisory power of the secretary of interior. Fickinger also ordered employees at the Billings Area Office to mimeograph several hundred copies of his letters to the business council that detailed financial mismanagement. Irate Blackfeet leaders refused to distribute this material when it was delivered by mistake to tribal headquarters.[13]

This turmoil led to the resignation of Superintendent Kidlow. One month later, George Pambrun, the newly elected tribal chair, met with Myer. He asked the commissioner to consult with the tribe before naming a new superintendent. The Blackfeet wanted Myer to appoint a kind and considerate person with experience in stock raising and financial management, as well as an individual familiar with Montana winters. Pambrun recommended the names of four Indians and two former superintendents with these qualifications.[14]

The Blackfeet tribal attorney also reminded the commissioner that it was important to find a constructive way to address administrative problems. Cohen told Myer that it was customary to consult in advance with the officials of the nation to whom the United States sent diplomatic representatives. For many years the reservation had been a battleground between Indians who bitterly resented paternalism and superintendents who treated them as young children or a primitive people. This insulted the Blackfeet, who wanted, more than anything else, responsibility for managing their own affairs.[15]

In November 1950, Myer unexpectedly picked Guy Robertson as the new superintendent. Prior to his appointment, Robertson had directed the War Relocation Authority detention center at Heart Mountain, Wyoming, where eleven thousand Japanese-Americans were incarcerated. After World War II, he managed Rockefeller trust lands at Jackson Hole and the Nobel Hotel at Lander.[16]

Pambrun bitterly resented the commissioner's selection of Robertson. He thought the new superintendent's only qualifications were his personal friendship with Myer and their common experience in supervising inmates at concentration camps. The tribal chair expressed his dissatisfaction by asking the commissioner to promptly allow the tribe to manage its own affairs. Myer turned down this request because the Blackfeet had not prepared a comprehensive withdrawal program.[17]

Nonetheless, the business council had taken important steps to address problems on the reservation. It distributed a flyer that acknowledged financial irregularities, such as incomplete minutes and the lack of proper records for land purchases, exchanges, and assignments. The council also disclosed that the tribe owed thousands of dollars for medical bills, grocery orders, and other debts. During the next few months, Pambrun and other Blackfeet leaders worked diligently to correct past mistakes. They improved collection procedures, investigated borrowers, and drafted mortgage security forms. Impressed by these financial reforms, officials at the Indian Bureau sent the tribe a letter of congratulations for promptly collecting old debts.[18]

In yet another initiative, Pambrun established a special loan board staffed by individuals experienced in business affairs. This eliminated bureaucratic delays and political pressure on people who handled loan applications. Myer objected to this procedure because it did not follow regulations in the Indian Bureau Credit Manual. Defiant tribal officials then proceeded without government supervision to collect delinquent debts, process mortgages, and review new loan applications.[19]

Pambrun also asked for full control over the tribe's cattle repayment program. In 1934, the federal government had purchased dying cattle from drought-stricken farmers. Some of this livestock was shipped by the Federal Relief Surplus Corporation to Indian reservations for food or to establish foundation herds. The Blackfeet received 5,792 cattle and reimbursed the government for this livestock. Nevertheless, Superintendent Robertson continued to dispose of cattle that were used as security for unpaid IRA loans.[20]

The Blackfeet Business Council sent a delegation to Washington DC after Myer turned down this request to control the cattle repayment program. In February 1951, Joseph Brown, a council member, testified before the House Appropriations Subcommittee that Blackfeet were ready to assume more responsibility under the IRA. He also observed that $450,000 was appropriated annually for useless jobs on the reservation. Rather than maintaining this elaborate administrative system, Congress should redirect funds to provide beneficial social services.[21]

Brown then criticized the way Myer handled grazing leases. Under a power of attorney agreement, the commissioner had set aside enough restricted allotted land for Indians to graze their livestock but made no provision for them to increase the size of their herds. The business council also had leased tribal lands at 15 cents an acre to assist Blackfeet who were raising cattle. Myer doubled the rental price, which threatened to drive these ranchers out of business. Brown emphasized the tribe's legal right to manage this property under the Indian Reorganization Act.[22]

While Brown testified before Congress, Pambrun ran a publicity campaign from the Roger Smith Hotel. He persuaded the *Washington-Herald American* news bureau and the *New York Times* to run feature columns that criticized the Indian Bureau for starting an old-fashioned cowboy and Indian war by issuing grazing permits to white ranchers without tribal consent. To stop this practice, the business council placed advertisements in Montana newspapers that warned outsiders to keep their sheep and cattle off the reservation.[23]

In these articles, Pambrun argued that Myer had used the methods of "a communist dictatorship" to deny the Blackfeet the right to manage their private property. He also complained that Indian veterans, who operated cattle herds, were being liquidated because of a 100 percent increase in grazing fees. The tribal chair concluded that "Stalin could learn a lot about how to run a dictatorship" by watching the Indian Bureau.[24]

The commissioner responded to these charges when he appeared in February and March before the House Appropriations Subcommittee. There, Myer complained that Blackfeet leaders, and Felix Cohen as their lawyer, constantly worked at cross-purposes with the bureau. Especially troublesome were business council resolutions that requested the discontinuance of certain federal programs while simultaneously asking Congress to appropriate money for health, education, and other costly services. The commissioner rejected this piecemeal approach to self-determination and called on the Blackfeet to harmoniously work with him to draft a comprehensive federal withdrawal plan.[25]

After these hearings ended, Pambrun notified Superintendent Robertson that the tribe owned the warehouse and other government buildings at the agency headquarters in Browning. It paid for these capital improvements in 1935 when the Court of Claims deducted offsets against their claims award in *Blackfeet Nation v. the United States.* Pambrun told Robertson that the business council intended to collect rent from the government as long as federal employees used these buildings.[26]

The superintendent forwarded Pambrun's confrontational letter to the Billings Area Office. Nothing happened until 14 April 1951, when Robertson, after learning about unusual activity on the reservation, went to an unoccupied warehouse located on the agency circle road. There, he encountered Cohen, Pambrun, Cora Irgens, and a tribal police officer. The superintendent ordered these individuals to remove a "no trespassing" sign they had posted next to the warehouse door.[27]

After a brief investigation, Robertson discovered that someone had forced open a basement window to get inside the building. According to a historian who carefully studied this act of civil disobedience, the superintendent told Pambrun that it was unlawful to break and enter government property. Cohen responded that the tribe owned the warehouse and welcomed a government lawsuit on this issue. Robertson replied that he was responsible for the property. He then threatened to arrest the Indians and their attorney and even to kill a tribal employee if they did not stop this protest (pl. 23).[28]

Five days later, Commissioner Myer corresponded with Pambrun about this incident. It was Myer's opinion that the decision by the Court of Claims gave the Blackfeet, at most, only equitable interest in the title to this property. The commissioner insisted that the buildings remained under federal jurisdiction because Congress still required the Indian Bureau to administer their affairs. Myer also told Pambrun that he followed closely Blackfeet proposals to transfer certain Indian Bureau programs to the tribal government. The commissioner emphasized once again that the Blackfeet must develop an orderly withdrawal plan before the federal government relinquished its guardianship responsibility.[29]

Myer provided Pambrun with a road map of how to achieve complete Indian self-determination. The commissioner reiterated his policy of gradually transferring the bureau's responsibilities to Indians or to local, state, and federal agencies. Myer stressed that past experience had demonstrated conclusively that a partial or piecemeal approach to Indian self-government led to unsatisfactory results. This was especially true on the Blackfeet Reservation, where tribal lands intermingled with individual trust allotments and created exceedingly complex problems.[30]

The commissioner encouraged the Blackfeet to become less dependent on the U.S. government. He volunteered to send consultants to Browning to help tribal representatives draft a withdrawal program that would contain mutually satisfactory arrangements on how to manage trust land, provide extension services, and meet the financial needs of both individuals and tribal enterprises.[31]

Myer's approach to self-determination reflected the conservative nationalistic, and sometimes intolerant mood of the postwar era. Felix Cohen commented on this trend at an address before the Yale Philosophy Club. There, he asked students and all citizens to reject the fear, hatred, and hysteria that accompanied McCarthyism and the Cold War. The Blackfeet attorney noted that, instead of trying to police the world, the people of the United States should proclaim the moral truths of the Judaic-Christian tradition and the Declaration of Independence to fight for racial tolerance, human equality, and the rights of underprivileged groups.[32]

Cohen shared his beliefs with Indian clients. In June 1951, he attended a two-day conference at Helena, Montana, called by Governor John W. Bonner to hasten the day when Indians controlled their own destiny. At this meeting, Cohen told 115 delegates they had "God's blessing" in their struggle to end federal paternalism.[33]

The next speaker was Napoleon Bonaparte Johnson. He first learned about the plight of Montana Indians in October 1945 when the Blackfeet tribe hosted the second annual NCAI Convention at Browning. Johnson praised Governor Bonner and other state officials for taking an active interest in the future of Indian people. The NCAI president cited Oklahoma as a state where Indian citizens were not treated as a segregated minority. He encouraged Montana Indians to vote and request that the state provide them with health care and other services.[34]

At afternoon sessions, representatives from each reservation in Montana discussed the importance of being self-reliant individuals. For instance, Joseph Brown emphasized that Blackfeet should have the right to independently manage business enterprises. Tom Main, from Harlem on the Fort Belknap Reservation, added that all educated Indians in Montana were ready, if given a chance, to run their own affairs without interference from federal officials at the Billings Area Office.[35]

Main urged all Montana Indians to unite behind the slogan "Tethered to Federal Law, Not Turned Loose and Not Choked Down." For Main, each letter in the word *tether* represented a positive platform to advance self-determination:

T   was for the time each tribe needed to figure out its program of change.
E   was for the education of young people who would have to live a new way.
T   was for tribal council rights guaranteed by federal law.
H   was for home base—a guarantee that Indians would always have reservation homes.
E   was for Indian economic planning to guarantee tribal assets and self-government.
R   was for needed reform by both Indians and whites based on mutual responsibility to God and His laws.[36]

The delegates at the first Montana Indian Affairs Conference, held in Helena, followed Main's advice. They adopted resolutions recommending that Montana's tribes control their own income, have the right to lease lands without signing powers of attorney to superintendents, and receive the money saved by abolishing the Billings Area Office. The delegates also reminded the federal government of its duty to reopen the hospital at Lame Deer on the Northern Cheyenne Reservation, provide housing for elderly people, and find jobs for landless Indians.[37]

Five months after the Helena conference, Main circulated "An Indian Declaration of Independence" at a meeting of the pan-Indian Montana Inter-Tribal Policy Board. It used words written by Thomas Jefferson in 1776 to declare a state of rebellion against Commissioner Myer for establishing an absolute tyranny over Indian people through repeated injuries and usurpations. Main's declaration listed twenty-three examples of despotic colonial rule where the commissioner had extended an unwarrantable jurisdiction over tribes. In this document, Montana Indians resolved to maintain their legal and constitutional rights as free and independent citizens of the United States. They pledged their lives, fortunes, and sacred honor to resist Myer's efforts to tell them how to vote, where to travel, and who to employ as legal counsel.[38]

Main's "Indian Declaration of Independence" provided the theoretical backdrop for yet another Blackfeet confrontation with the federal government. On 15 April 1952, George Pambrun appeared before the Senate Committee on Interior and Insular Affairs to testify in favor of legislation that gave the tribe more autonomy. Pambrun told Senators James E. Murray and Zales Ecton of Montana that the Fourth of July was a great holiday on the reservation because the Blackfeet believed in the Declaration of Independence. He emphasized that Indians, too, wanted to be part of the revolutionary spirit of 1776. As one member of the tribe had observed, he would rather sing "his own death song, than sing a song that the Indian Bureau put in his mouth."[39]

Pambrun asked the Senate committee to endorse six bills. This legislation would enable the Blackfeet to make long-term leases to develop a resort on the shore of St. Mary's Lake and commercial property along the highway, secure firm title to submarginal land purchased for the tribe, repeal discriminatory laws that prevented Indians from selling their personal property, and transfer medical services to the Public Health Service. It would also give the Blackfeet Business Council complete control over tribal funds and the right to handle IRA loans without cumbersome Indian Bureau regulations.[40]

Pambrun then criticized Myer's approach to self-determination, which allowed expert policymakers to determine the Indians' future. He noted that during the last ninety-seven years, the Blackfeet had endured a series of programs for their civilization and improvement that had resulted in the tribe's retaining only 2 percent of the land it once owned while per capita wealth had declined by 67 percent. Pambrun stressed that the Blackfeet could not afford to lose any of their remaining land to please Indian Bureau officials.[41]

He concluded his remarks by asking the Senate for assistance to guarantee the right of all Blackfeet citizens to vote in upcoming tribal elections. Pambrun was referring to the fact that Superintendent Robertson had disqualified nonresident Indians from voting so that he could authorize a referendum to amend the tribe's IRA constitution to protect the interests of full-bloods. The business council protested this decision by scheduling a separate referendum that included all Blackfeet voters. The major issue in this conflict was the control and distribution of oil revenues in an equitable manner.[42]

Full-bloods disliked the IRA constitution because it created a tribal government based on proportional representation from four reservation districts. This gerrymandered elections and left full-bloods with only two out of thirteen positions on the business council. The underrepresentation of full-bloods also gave mixed-bloods permanent control of the IRA credit fund. Even more troubling was a constitutional provision that empowered council members to supervise oil leases on trust land and distribute royalties. It allowed the business council to loan money from oil revenues to purchase real estate for landless mixed-bloods.[43]

These policies angered Louis Plenty Treaty. In March 1951, he sent a letter to Montana Senator James E. Murray in which he asked Congress to revoke the Blackfeet Constitution and Charter. Plenty Treaty complained that the tribal government had made loans based on political favoritism, held excessive meetings to inflate per diem and mileage reimbursement, and invested in business enterprises that benefited only a few people.[44]

Plenty Treaty, Charles Reevis, and other full-bloods resented the patronizing attitude of well-educated Indians. In his testimony before the Senate Interior and Insular Affairs Committee, Pambrun had publicly criticized full-bloods for not accepting written ballots, loans, and other modern ways. He also created irreconcilable differences by excluding full-bloods from the tribe's legislative plans for more self-determination.[45]

Senator Murray replied to Plenty Treaty in May 1951, after consulting with Commissioner Myer about how to amend the Blackfeet Constitution. He told Plenty Treaty that it would be a backward step to rely on the federal government to run tribal affairs. Murray recommended two alternatives to abandoning their IRA form of self-government. Full-blood petitioners could employ legal counsel and present their grievances to the tribal council for resolution, and they also had the right to propose an amendment to the constitution that permitted the recall of council members who were unresponsive to the needs of all tribal members.[46]

Commissioner Myer did not encourage dissident Blackfeet to follow Senator Murray's advice. Instead, he asked them to consult with Superintendent Robertson about how to undercut the authority of the business council. The superintendent helped the full-bloods draft a petition that requested an election to vote on Amendment 3 to the tribal constitution. This revision increased the superintendent's financial control over the Blackfeet, limited the power of the business council, and provided Myer with an opportunity to muzzle Indians who disagreed with his policies.[47]

Amendment 3 required the Blackfeet Business Council to deposit tribal funds outside the U.S. Treasury in a special account controlled by the superintendent. Of these funds, 50 percent could be used for per capita payments twice a year, 20 percent for health, welfare, and funeral expenses, and 30 percent for the administration of tribal government, educational loans, and taxes. Unspent deposits automatically reverted to the U.S. Treasury. The business council could not spend this money without authorization from the secretary of interior or a majority of Blackfeet voters at a special referendum.[48]

In November 1951, Plenty Treaty and other full-blood leaders sent the Indian Bureau a petition with over six hundred signatures that asked Secretary Chapman to call a tribal election on Amendment 3. Under the tribe's IRA constitution, amendments could be proposed by one-third of the tribe or a majority vote of the business council. Myer reviewed this petition and forwarded it to Robertson with the tacit understanding that Article 8 of the constitution stipulated that only Indians who resided within four reservation districts were eligible to vote. By disqualifying approximately a thousand nonresident adult members, Robertson could verify that a third of the Blackfeet voters had signed the petition.[49]

Walter S. Wetzel, the newly elected chair of the Blackfeet Business Council, and Cedor B. Aronow, a local attorney, challenged Robertson's authority to call this tribal election. In April 1952, the council passed a resolution that upheld its exclusive constitutional mandate to supervise Blackfeet voting. To demonstrate this empowerment, the business council scheduled a simultaneous IRA election on 9 May to consider an amendment to allocate 50 percent of tribal income for per capita payments and the remaining 50 percent for social services. The council, rather than the superintendent, would control the expenditure of this money.[50]

One week later, Felix Cohen addressed more than one hundred Indians at a meeting on the reservation. He warned that Amendment 3 threatened Blackfeet autonomy by giving the superintendent complete control over tribal funds. Robertson responded to this provocation by refusing to serve on the election board for the referendum sponsored by the business council without the required minimum of twenty days' notice. The superintendent also reminded Wetzel that under the Blackfeet Constitution the secretary of interior had to approve the calling of an election.[51]

A short time later, Robertson sent an open letter "To Members of the Blackfeet Tribe" in which he objected to what he felt was selfish and misleading information circulated by Cohen and Wetzel to defeat Amendment 3. The superintendent stressed that the referendum called by Plenty Treaty was an honest and straightforward effort to earmark tribal funds.[52]

Wetzel was upset by what he felt was interference in Blackfeet internal affairs and asked Secretary Chapman why the Interior Department did not have the common courtesy to inform the business council about the decision to call an election on 9 May. Wetzel criticized the superintendent for campaigning at government expense for Amendment 3 while threatening to charge the tribe for the cost of running an illegal election. This unacceptable behavior resembled the tactics Robertson and Myer had used to administer Japanese-American concentration camps during World War II.[53]

Wetzel demanded that Chapman take disciplinary action to stop this type of conduct. He reminded the secretary of interior that the Blackfeet's sense of propriety, knowledge of constitutional government, and love of freedom equaled that of other American citizens. They had proven their loyalty to the government on numerous occasions and would not tolerate interference in local elections.[54]

Wetzel emphasized that Governor John W. Bonner was aware of the seriousness of the situation. Bonner had promised the Blackfeet Business Council that he would contact President Truman after learning about the shameful way federal officials treated the tribal government. The governor had also indicated that he would intervene to restore law and order if violence occurred because two elections were scheduled on the same day.[55]

In the meantime, President Truman received letters and telegrams that protested the Indian Bureau's interference with tribal self-government. For instance, Representative Mike Mansfield of Montana sent the White House copies of correspondence from Wetzel that was highly critical of Superintendent Robertson. Alarmed by these events, President Truman asked Philleo Nash, his special assistant on minority affairs, to manage the Blackfeet crisis.[56]

On 9 May, the day of the elections, Nash received phone calls from two apprehensive government officials. Secretary Chapman reported that departmental solicitors believed the election held by Superintendent Robertson was legal. Nonetheless, they were willing, if necessary, to set aside the results at a later date. Commissioner Myer reassured Nash that one-third of the eligible voters had signed a petition to amend the Blackfeet Constitution. In addition, he indicated that no attempt was made to close down the alternate polling places used by the IRA tribal government.[57]

The simultaneous voting at two locations created a confusing situation. In the Indian Bureau election, the vote was 460 to 146 in favor of Amendment 3. The vote in the IRA election was 154 to 373 against the alternate amendment. This left Secretary Chapman with no alternative but to rule on the official outcome.[58]

On the day after the election, Plenty Treaty thanked Secretary Chapman for calling the election on Amendment 3 to give all Blackfeet equal access to tribal income. Plenty Treaty reiterated his complaint that the IRA had transferred power from traditional leaders to an irresponsible mixed-blood majority. These "half-breeds" had spent millions of dollars to "emancipate themselves" from the Blackfeet tribe. He asked the Interior Department to more carefully supervise the activities of the tribal government to prevent future problems.[59]

Secretary Chapman had to consider this request along with other issues before reaching a final decision. On 26 May, Cohen reminded Chapman that the Indian Bureau election was invalid because one-third of the adult members had not requested Amendment 3 as required by law in the Blackfeet Constitution. Furthermore, Amendment 3 violated President Truman's policy of protecting Indian civil rights.[60]

Two days later, Chapman received a sharply worded letter from Senator Murray that asked why an election was held to give a superintendent control of tribal funds already handled by Indians themselves. Murray believed this policy reversed Blackfeet progress toward self-determination. To discredit the Indian Bureau, he requested an analysis of conflicting claims concerning the number of adult Blackfeet eligible to vote.[61]

Upset by this criticism, the secretary of interior ordered Myer to prepare a summary of events that led to the rival elections. Chapman told the commissioner that he intended to personally hand this memorandum to President Truman. After further deliberation, it was decided that Solicitor Mastin G. White would declare both elections invalid.[62]

On 18 July 1952, White issued an opinion on Amendment 3. He noted that the question had been raised whether 30 percent of the eligible voters actually participated in the election. The answer to this query turned on the proper construction of Article 8 in the Blackfeet Constitution. It stated that any member of the tribe twenty-one years or older could vote at a polling place within his or her voting district. When Superintendent Robertson certified Amendment 3, he interpreted this to mean that voters must live in one of four districts on the reservation. More than one thousand Indians had been disqualified under the superintendent's theory that only residents were qualified to vote.[63]

White concluded that Robertson's imposition of a residency requirement gave the tribal constitution a meaning its framers could hardly have intended. It was self-evident from the language of Article 8 that the constitution regulated the voting process, rather than disqualifying nonresident Indians. White ruled that election laws must be construed liberally in favor of the right to vote.[64]

White also reaffirmed the Blackfeet right to self-government under the Indian Reorganization Act. He indicated that IRA constitutions had been carefully prepared under departmental supervision. The question of whether residence on a reservation should be a prerequisite for voting was determined in accordance with the wishes of different tribes. The Blackfeet had decided not to disqualify nonresident members. This meant that twenty-eight hundred Blackfeet were eligible to vote. Nonetheless, both Amendment 3 and the IRA election were invalid because less than 30 percent of the tribe participated in each of these elections. Furthermore, it was impossible to combine the ballots because the secretary of the interior had not authorized the IRA election.[65]

Commissioner Myer refused to recognize the legitimacy of White's ruling. In August 1952, he wrote Chapman that nothing contained in the Blackfeet Constitution, or the IRA, required the secretary of interior to obtain a petition signed by one-third of the eligible voters before calling an election. In a total disregard of Indian rights, Myer cynically recommended that Chapman ignore White's opinion, count the total votes, and approve Amendment 3. If this was unacceptable, Myer suggested that Chapman arrange for yet another election on Amendment 3. These two recommendations were met with stony silence.[66]

Solicitor White's opinion was an unexpected setback for Myer. This ruling acknowledged the importance of consent in Indian affairs, as well as the legitimacy, measured separatism, and permanence of IRA tribal governments. It slowed the commissioner's frontal assault to dismantle the reservation system.

During a period in American history that witnessed the erosion of civil liberties, the Blackfeet Business Council reaffirmed the political ideology found in its IRA constitution and the Declaration of Independence. Inspired by this revolutionary heritage, courageous council members stood up to Indian Bureau policies that resembled colonial rule. They confronted an authoritarian superintendent, held unsupervised tribal elections, occupied agency buildings, and proposed creative legislative alternatives to Commissioner Myer's all or nothing approach to self-determination.

Brown, Pambrun, Wetzel, and other Blackfeet leaders also used the concurrent constitutional powers of the tribe and the state of Montana to counterbalance the overextended authority of the federal government. At the first Montana Indian Affairs Conference at Helena, Blackfeet delegates defended their citizenship rights and the authority of the tribe to contract for state services. At the same time, both state and tribal officials questioned the basic premise of federal withdrawal by asking Congress to continue funding expensive social and economic programs for Blackfeet people.

In this effort, the mixed-blood majority consistently overlooked the rights of the full-blood minority. Louis Plenty Treaty and his followers clearly did not want a tribal council patterned after the U.S. government. Their vision of self-determination included respect for the role of traditional leaders, consensual decision making, and a vigilant stewardship over reservation resources. They also reminded President Truman of this duty to respect treaty rights and protect their trust property.

Commissioner Myer found himself in an administrative cul-de-sac during his confrontation with the Blackfeet. The mixed-bloods successfully defended their IRA government while full-bloods received his tacit support in their demand for continued federal guardianship. With nowhere to turn, Myer would have to alter his policies or impose them on Indian America.

He chose the second option. The commissioner continued to make life unpleasant for the Blackfeet and other Indians so they would be more willing to accept his long-range plans to transfer tribal authority over law and order to states. Among other things, Myer sponsored legislation that authorized Indian Bureau employees to make searches and arrests for violating federal regulations. This further alienated Indians and made it much more difficult for either the commissioner or Congress to impose state jurisdiction throughout Indian country.

9

STATE JURISDICTION IN INDIAN COUNTRY

Some tribes welcome the aid of state enforcement officers on their reservations and some prefer to control their own problems. . . . If Congress passes this law repealing the right to administer law and order on reservations, which has been written into Indian constitutions and charters for the past 15 years, all other rights of self-government may later be similarly lost. RUTH MUSKRAT BRONSON, MEMORANDUM TO MEMBERS OF THE NCAI, 3 APRIL 1948

In February 1952, the House Subcommittee on Indian Affairs met to consider whether to give states jurisdiction over crimes committed by or against Indians within Indian country. Members of the subcommittee had to examine treaty rights, study the constitutional empowerment of tribal courts under the Indian Reorganization Act, and determine if Indian consent was required to confer state authority over a "legal no-man's land" to regulate crime, bootlegging, and the illegal consumption of alcohol on reservations. Without a satisfactory resolution of these questions, and with the controversial law enforcement legislation sponsored by Commissioner Myer, it would be extremely difficult for the federal government to completely withdraw from Indian affairs.[1]

The U.S. government initially treated tribes as distinct independent political communities that held from time immemorial the natural right to maintain law and order and administer justice. The creation of new states, removal, the intrusion of non-Indian settlers, and land allotment altered this policy. Congress ended treaty making in 1871 and extended federal and state law over Indians. This created a complex and confusing situation with concurrent federal, state, and tribal jurisdiction.[2]

In 1883, Congress established Courts of Indian Offenses under the supervision of the secretary of interior to maintain law and order in Indian communities.

These administrative tribunals operated under the Code of Federal Regulations, which gave tribal courts jurisdiction over misdemeanors, civil disputes, and moral offenses such as gambling, the sun dance, and polygamy. Indian judges generally handed out lenient sentences, and reservation jails were used as places of temporary confinement.[3]

Congress also created an Indian police force at seventy-six agencies. Tribal officers maintained law and order and prevented the introduction of liquor into Indian country. They also served as couriers, truant officers, and interpreters. In some instances, superintendents rewarded compliant or acculturated Indians with police appointments to curtail the authority of traditional leaders.[4]

As noted earlier, federal officials redesigned the tribal judicial system during the New Deal. Solicitor Nathan Margold ruled that one of the inherent powers of self-government was the right of Indians to establish their own tribunals and administer justice. This led to an independent court system for some tribes that organized under the IRA and for others a revised law code to govern Courts of Indian Offenses.[5]

This form of jurisprudence did not function properly. Only 16 percent of the 258 tribes that voted on the IRA operated either IRA tribal courts or Courts of Indian Offenses. Congress discouraged the expansion of this rudimentary judicial system by refusing to appropriate enough money for the Indian Bureau's law and order budget, which ranged from $207,000 in 1936 to $290,000 in 1946. It also shut down the Emergency Conservation Work program that trained Navajo mounted police.[6]

The parsimony of Congress created severe law and order problems. An understaffed Indian Bureau force of thirty-four police and one assistant could not effectively patrol tribal communities in sixteen states. For instance, only two police officers were in charge of liquor traffic among the New Mexico Pueblo Indians. They were overwhelmed by incidents of drunken driving, public brawls, bodily injury, and the selling of farm equipment and household items to purchase wine. On one occasion, a Mexican bootlegger escaped when an angry mob surrounded the police and asked them to leave the pueblo because of the Indians' right to self-government.[7]

These undesirable circumstances raised the question of whether Congress should further extend state jurisdiction in Indian country. In 1943, the Association on American Indian Affairs commissioned Robert Solenberger from the University of Pennsylvania to undertake an impartial study of law and order on New York Iroquois reservations. Solenberger learned on his field trip that Indians adamantly opposed state control. In 1939, the Tonawanda Council had sent the governor of New York a "Declaration of Independence" indicating that the Seneca no longer wanted the state to handle minor criminal offenses because this diminished their tribal sovereignty.[8]

For the Seneca and other New York Indians, tax-free reservations were places where bands survived as social units. These homelands also were used for vacations, as areas of refuge during periods of unemployment, and as safe havens during retirement. More importantly, reservations were cultural centers for the Longhouse religion and Christian churches that utilized the Iroquois language in their services.[9]

In his report to the AAIA, Solenberger recommended that Congress obtain Indian consent before imposing state jurisdiction. He also cautioned that except for California, New York, Minnesota, and Wisconsin, most states were unwilling to provide costly law enforcement services for Indian communities. Solenberger emphasized that tribal courts were an important part of self-government. Nonetheless, Indians would have to adopt state legal codes to overcome gaps in federal enforcement, giving precedence to tribal laws in areas of concurrent jurisdiction.[10]

Solenberger's report was part of a broader reexamination of Indian policy. In 1948, the Hoover Commission recommended that the federal government develop plans for the progressive transfer to state governments of the Indian responsibility for maintaining law and order. It found tribal courts deficient because Indian judges handed out lenient sentences that failed to maintain social discipline. Furthermore, Indian police could not apprehend culprits once they left the reservation.[11]

More vitriolic was an article entitled "Indian Treaty Making" by G. E. E. Lindquist, secretary for the Fellowship of Indian Workers in Lawrence, Kansas. Lindquist recommended that Congress review 389 treaties that had created a bureaucratic system characterized by exemptions and restrictions in the form of countless regulations. He also dismissed the popular belief that it was impossible to alter treaties. Lindquist noted that both Congress and the president had constitutional authority to abrogate treaties that had become obsolete through altered conditions.[12]

Lindquist believed the Indian Claims Commission, which allowed tribes to file lawsuits to redress treaty violations and other grievances, provided a unique opportunity to end federal wardship. Common sense called for the commutation of treaties that served no contemporary purpose other than the per capita distribution of small amounts of money or the distribution of calico cloth. He warned that the Seneca and other Indians would cling to the "pretty fiction" they were separate nations until Congress dealt with the anomalous situation of outmoded treaties still in force.[13]

Congress did not revoke treaties. Nonetheless, it applied pressure to make state jurisdiction a desirable alternative to tribal self-determination. The Eightieth Congress forced Indians to pay the salaries of their judges and police or drop these services. Tribes with financial resources assumed this burden. Those less fortunate did not have enough money to hire police, maintain jails, or pay counties for boarding prisoners.[14]

On the Pine Ridge Reservation in South Dakota, the shortage of federal funds led to a breakdown of law and order. Merton Glover, a non-Indian from Porcupine, wrote Senator Karl Mundt that conditions on the reservation had reached a point where people had "no respect for property . . . and very little for life itself." To demonstrate this frightening reality, Glover cited six unsolved murders, recurring episodes of juvenile delinquency, theft of livestock, and vandalism.[15]

Glover blamed New Deal policymakers rather than Congress for the plight of the Oglala Sioux. He was convinced that the socialist tribal government under IRA had canceled a half-century of progress toward the Indians becoming ordinary citizens. He concluded that state jurisdiction over the reservation was urgently needed to correct this deplorable situation and prosecute Indians involved in grand larceny and other crimes.[16]

H. E. Bruce, superintendent of the Winnebago Agency in Nebraska, reported other problems that required immediate attention. In Thurston County, home of the Omaha and Winnebago Indians, the county attorney's office had prosecuted 447 law violations between 1946 and 1948. Sixty-four percent of these cases involved Indians, who made up only 20 percent of the county population.[17]

Superintendent Bruce disliked the New Deal policy of recognizing Indian custom marriage and divorce in the probating of trust estates. This encouraged county officials not to prosecute numerous cases of adultery, fornication, and child desertion. Consequently, Thurston County was burdened with a costly Aid-to-Dependent Children welfare program. For example, in August 1948, 170 Indian children from 72 families received ADC payments, compared to 50 white children from 19 homes. The cost of ADC was three times greater for Indians even though they constituted one-fifth of the county's residents.[18]

Leaders of the Omaha, Santee Sioux, and Winnebago Indians agreed with Superintendent Bruce that Congress should more clearly define state responsibility over Nebraska reservations. Amos Lamson, the chair of the Omaha Tribal Council, told Superintendent Bruce that legislation was required so the state could apply for federal funds to investigate and prosecute recent murders on allotted reservation land. David Frazier, the Santee Sioux chair, also reminded Bruce that Knox County authorities enforced state law on the Santee Sioux and

Ponca Reservations with Indian consent. This valuable service, however, might end if someone raised jurisdictional questions about tribal sovereignty before there was clear authority to enforce state law.[19]

In 1948, Representative Wesley A. D'Ewart of Montana introduced H.R. 4725 to address the question of law and order in Indian country. This bill unilaterally conferred state jurisdiction over criminal offenses committed by or against Indians on reservations. It also permitted state police to enter any reservation to enforce criminal laws but did not deprive any Indian government of jurisdiction over other tribal laws.[20]

D'Ewart's bill encountered opposition at hearings before the House Interior and Insular Affairs Subcommittee, at which Undersecretary of the Interior Oscar Chapman favored alternate legislation. It required Indian consent and allowed state jurisdiction if tribes did not establish proper law enforcement within a specified time. The Pueblo and Mescalero Apache Indians also testified against D'Ewart's bill because it threatened their right to self-determination.[21]

In April 1948, Ruth Muskrat Bronson, the NCAI executive secretary, urged tribes to protect their legal rights. In a memo to NCAI members, she warned that H.R. 4725 did not require Indian consent prior to the imposition of state law. Furthermore, it broke solemn promises made under the Indian Reorganization Act, violated treaties, and ignored executive agreements that recognized the right of tribes to govern themselves.[22]

After listening to this criticism, the House subcommittee reported an amended bill that exempted Arizona and New Mexico Indians from state jurisdiction as long as they were denied their right to vote in local elections. The House passed this legislation and sent it to the Senate, where it was called to the calendar at the end of April but not considered at the request of Senator Joseph O'Mahoney of Wyoming.[23]

Southwestern Indians, who defended their tribal courts and police, had narrowly averted a major defeat. The Iroquois Six Nations were not as fortunate. In March 1945, the New York Senate asked Congress to consider legislation that subjected seven thousand Indians to state civil and criminal jurisdiction. New York senators complained that neither the federal government nor the Iroquois had formulated satisfactory laws to protect reservation residents. They also objected to the *United States v. Forness* federal court decision in 1942, which challenged state authority over Indians.[24]

Senator Hugh Butler of Nebraska responded to these concerns by introducing S.R. 1683, which would give New York jurisdiction over criminal offenses committed by or against Indians on state reservations. LeRoy Snow, a Seneca counselor, opposed this bill because it showed disrespect by a "great sovereign power for the rights of self-determination by one of the small nations of the world that had been permitted for centuries to manage its internal affairs."[25]

Congress paid little attention to Iroquois concerns. Instead, it passed legislation in July 1948 that authorized state jurisdiction without Indian consent. Nonetheless, Congress did continue federal authority over major crimes. It also denied New York the right to tax or alienate restricted Indian land and protected Iroquois hunting and fishing rights.[26]

State power over law and order on New York reservations triggered federal withdrawal. In March 1949, Acting Commissioner William Zimmerman notified Robert T. Landsdale, the state commissioner of social welfare, that the Indian Bureau would not fill a vacant superintendent's position at the Salamanca Indian Agency or continue to provide funds for the clinic at the Thomas Indian School on the Cattaraugus Reservation. A clerk, however, remained on the reservation to distribute lease rentals, annuities, and treaty cloth.[27]

A short time later, Congress considered S.R. 192, which conferred state control over civil law on New York reservations. In July 1949, LeRoy Snow warned Senator O'Mahoney that the Seneca Nation regarded state courts as representing the power of a rival and often antagonistic sovereign power. The Seneca right to self-government included exclusive control over Peacemaker Courts, which dealt with Iroquois internal affairs. New York also had a duty to restore Cayuga payments for land frauds, establish a state claims commission, and respect Seneca laws and treaty rights. After considering Snow's views, O'Mahoney amended S.R. 192 to permit New York Indians to adopt civil codes based on their own traditions within the framework of state law.[28]

Maxwell Garrow, a representative of the Mohawk Nation, wrote the National Congress of American Indians for legal assistance when Congress passed this legislation in 1950. Garrow told James Curry, the NCAI attorney, that the imposition of New York civil and criminal jurisdiction over the Iroquois Six Nations was part of a broader plan to destroy Indian rights. Garrow confided to Curry that the Iroquois would fight until Congress repealed the statutes that permitted state officials to meddle in their domestic affairs.[29]

During the Eighty-first Congress, several bills were introduced to impose state law and order on other tribes. There was support for this legislation in California and Oregon. Purl Willis and Adam Castillo, who represented the Mission Indians of Southern California, and F. G. Collett, a spokesperson for the Indians of California, Inc., favored state jurisdiction because only five thousand out of twenty thousand California Indians lived on reservations or restricted land. For Willis, Castillo, and Collett, the only significant issue was equality under the law guaranteed by the U.S. Constitution.[30]

In May 1951, the Klamath Tribal Council gave its consent for Oregon to assume jurisdiction on the reservation. Boyd J. Jackson and other tribal leaders were convinced that state authorities could help resolve juvenile delinquency problems. They also wanted to stop the expenditure of $34,000 a year from tribal funds to administer law enforcement and use this money for per capita payments to assist needy individuals.[31]

Nevertheless, Indians in Montana and Washington successfully blocked state jurisdiction bills. Rufus Wallowing, chair of the Northern Cheyenne Tribe, traveled to the nation's capital and persuaded Senator James Murray to support the NCAI position that Congress should obtain tribal consent before imposing state law. In March 1951, the fifteen confederated tribes on the Colville Reservation opposed a state jurisdiction bill introduced by Senator Harry P. Cain. They complained that intolerant officials in Snohomish County had illegally forced them to comply with state marriage laws, placed their children in the homes of whites, and arrested Indians for hunting and fishing in areas guaranteed by treaty.[32]

Other tribes that operated Courts of Indian Offenses or IRA tribal courts also fought state jurisdiction. The Red Lake Chippewas of Minnesota, the San Carlos Apaches of Arizona, and the Menominees of Wisconsin either passed resolutions or testified before Congress concerning their satisfaction with tribal law enforcement. For the Crow Tribal Council, continued federal presence on the reservation represented a treaty commitment. It also meant that the tribal court and police, rather than the county attorney in Hardin, Montana, would receive thousands of dollars from local fines.[33]

Secretary of Interior Chapman played an important role in sidetracking legislation in 1951 that conferred state jurisdiction in Indian country. Chapman told members of the House and Senate that tribes should vote to decide if they wanted to come under state supervision or continue to rely on Interior Department law codes and regulations. He also reminded members of Congress that several states would not accept the financial burden for Indian law enforcement.[34]

In February 1952, the Indian Affairs Subcommittee of the House Interior and Insular Affairs Committee held hearings to review the controversy over law and order. The subcommittee spent most of its time discussing a bill introduced by Representative Wesley A. D'Ewart that provided for Indian consent before permitting state jurisdiction on reservations. Members of the subcommittee also examined at length legislation drafted by Commissioner Myer and a controversial proposal to give Indian Bureau police extraordinary power over the lives of tribal people.

At these hearings, D'Ewart testified in favor of H.R. 459, a bill he introduced to confer state authority over criminal offenses committed by or against Indians on reservations. This measure authorized state police to enforce criminal laws without depriving tribal councils of control over civil matters. It also allowed tribes to accept or reject state jurisdiction at referendums and protected Indian hunting and fishing rights.[35]

D'Ewart gave compelling reasons why Congress should extend state jurisdiction. He cited a report from Superintendent E. J. Diehl at the Fort Peck Agency that described how bootlegging and excessive drinking led to the breakdown of law and order. Diehl described parties every night near Poplar, Montana, where Indian men and women fell to the ground drunk. Alcohol abuse also caused abandoned and neglected children, stabbings, and car wrecks.[36]

State authorities found it hard to restore law and order because of a decision by the Montana Supreme Court. In 1951, it released from prison an Indian who was convicted of grand larceny in the Glacier County Court. Because the state had no jurisdiction on the Blackfeet Reservation, the Montana Supreme Court ruled that Peter Tatsey, the defendant, should have been tried in either a federal or tribal court.[37]

When Commissioner Myer appeared before the House subcommittee, he indicated that the Indian Bureau had drafted bills to authorize state jurisdiction in California, Minnesota, Nebraska, Oregon, Washington, and Wisconsin. This did not apply, however, to tribes with a satisfactory record of law enforcement: the Warm Springs Indians in Oregon, the Yakima and Colville Confederated Tribes of Washington, the Red Lake Chippewa of Minnesota, and the Menominee of Wisconsin.[38]

Myer rejected the NCAI contention that Indian consent was necessary before Congress imposed state jurisdiction. He refused to call expensive tribal elections "to get people to vote on an issue that was not tremendously important." The commissioner also feared that outsiders would persuade tribes to oppose state authority even if they had an inadequate law code, court system, and police force.[39]

These legislative proposals repealed the Federal Indian Liquor Law, which prohibited the sale of alcoholic beverages on reservations, but they did not completely eliminate federal wardship. The U.S. government still had jurisdiction over Indians who committed any of ten major crimes or violated other federal laws.[40]

To avoid potential lawsuits, the proposed legislation indicated that states could not interfere with Indian water rights, the tax-free status of restricted property, or hunting and fishing treaty rights. Yet, if Congress decided to terminate the trust on Indian land, the jurisdiction of state courts would apply automatically. In this scenario, federal courts maintained concurrent jurisdiction in case states did not adequately enforce their laws, but tribal authority did not reappear. This outlawed custom marriage, subjected nontrust property to taxation, and disempowered tribal courts and police.[41]

Indians provided conflicting perspectives concerning law and order in their communities. F. G. Collett, a spokesperson for the Indians of California, Inc., disliked concurrent jurisdiction because it remained unclear whether states or the federal government had primary responsibility. He believed that Indians generally should have the right to vote on relinquishing their power but doubted whether this costly procedure was suited to California, where over one hundred bands resided.[42]

John B. Cleveland, the chair of the Colville Business Council, testified that Indians on his reservation paid for their own judges, police, and other law enforcement personnel. He doubted whether Ferris County, one of the poorest in the state, could provide adequate protection for a 1.5-million-acre reservation or effectively remove trespassers from tribal grazing areas. Cleveland endorsed the idea of a referendum because the Colville Indians turned out in large numbers to vote on important issues.[43]

Yakima leaders believed that a separate tribal court was necessary to protect Indians from racial discrimination. Alex Saluskin, chair of the Yakima Tribal Council, emphasized that the state of Washington would not respect hunting, fishing, and other treaty rights. Furthermore, he thought it was inappropriate to tell Indians they must accept state jurisdiction to have the privilege of drinking liquor.[44]

Frank George, the NCAI executive director, recommended two amendments to D'Ewart's bill. The first required at least a 30 percent turnout in tribal elections to clearly determine whether Indians consented to the imposition of state law. The second gave Indians more than one opportunity to vote on this important question. George agreed with Saluskin that the Indian Bureau had made a serious mistake by proposing legislation that gave tribes the right to consume liquor in exchange for not complaining when states took over their powers of self-government.[45]

After George's testimony, the subcommittee considered legislation that Myer had submitted to the House and Senate Judiciary Committees. Both H.R. 6035 and S.R. 2543 permitted federal police officers to search, seize, and arrest Indians for violating federal regulations. These bills were drafted by William B. Benge, a Cherokee attorney and special officer in charge of the Indian Bureau's Division of Community Services.[46]

Benge was concerned about how to address growing law enforcement problems on reservations. Indian Bureau police could only arrest Indians if they violated prohibition and narcotics laws. He tried to remedy this situation by giving police officers the right to carry firearms and authority to deal with a wide variety of criminal activity on reservations.[47]

The subcommittee was aware that Felix Cohen, the AAIA legal counsel, opposed this legislation. In a press release, he had warned that S.R. 2543 gave Indian Bureau law enforcement officers unprecedented power. They could arrest and imprison Indians without a search warrant for violating twenty-two hundred federal regulations beyond the crimes identified in law codes used by Courts of Indian Offenses.[48]

Myer told subcommittee members that he resented Cohen's memorandum because it unnecessarily frightened Indians on several reservations. This defamatory statement also made it extremely difficult for the bureau to work with Indians on the basis of mutual respect and understanding. The commissioner agreed that Indians encountered oversupervision, but he "violently differed" with Cohen about how to change that situation.[49]

Members of the subcommittee sided with Myer on this issue. Norris Poulson of California observed that Cohen's vindictive attitude made him unfit to represent Indians. Toby Morris of Oklahoma thought the commissioner was a person of unimpeachable integrity and one of the ablest administrators in the government. He praised Myer for working closely with the Interior and Insular Affairs Committee to "hammer out a program" that addressed Indian problems.[50]

The last person to appear before the subcommittee was Lewis A. Sigler, the Indian Bureau's chief counsel. He encouraged Congress to broaden Title 18 of the U.S. Code, which authorized federal agents to enforce prohibition on reservations. This would enable tribal police and prohibition officers to arrest Indians who broke criminal laws and regulations that controlled the use of their trust property. These law enforcement officials needed the authority ordinarily conferred on county sheriffs and U.S. marshals to work effectively in large isolated areas where dangerous persons often resided.[51]

After the House hearings ended, Oliver LaFarge asked Chapman to withdraw departmental approval for the commissioner's law and order bills. The AAIA president reminded the secretary of interior that this legislation gave Indian Bureau employees "startling powers of harassment . . . that would be endlessly abused and unquestionably used to enforce subservience." Chapman forwarded this letter to the Indian Bureau.[52]

In early March 1952, the commissioner told LaFarge that the AAIA had acted irresponsibly. Cohen's earlier memo, which falsely claimed that government officials intended to arrest and shoot Indians, had incited tribes into a "frenzy of excitement" and caused them to hate the Indian Bureau. Myer emphasized that tribal leaders had a right to expect sound analysis from the AAIA legal counsel instead of "propaganda diatribes."[53]

This response confirmed LaFarge's belief that Myer had declared a Cold War on Indians. At the annual AAIA meeting in New York, he encouraged members to protect Native American constitutional rights. On 26 March, they passed a resolution that called on President Truman and Congress to repudiate Myer's legislation because it permitted unwarranted intrusions into the lives of tribal people.[54]

Opposition to the commissioner grew when Cohen circulated a letter in April entitled "The Indian Bureau's Drive for Increased Powers." It noted that Undersecretary of the Interior Dale Doty had resigned in protest over Myer's policies. This principled decision did not surprise Cohen because not even the FBI, Secret Service, or federal marshals could arrest people for violating administrative regulations. The commissioner had mistakenly assumed that he could easily frighten Indians even though an increasing number of tribes had employed attorneys, who acted as watchdogs and barked when trespassers threatened Indian rights.[55]

A few days later, Cohen and LaFarge, under the auspices of the AAIA, sent newspapers throughout the United States press releases that were critical of Myer's approach toward law enforcement. This led to a nationwide protest that discredited the commissioner in the eyes of the general public. Feature articles critical of the Indian Bureau appeared in the New York Times, Philadelphia Inquirer, New Orleans Times-Picayune, Houston Post, Gallup Independent, Portland Oregonian, Great Falls Tribune, and Native Voice of British Columbia. Among other things, these editorials chastised Myer for requesting gestapo power to oppress Indian wards.[56]

The commissioner told Secretary Chapman that "the communist-line press" had used news items distributed by the AAIA to discredit the U.S. government. This attempt to smear his opponents did not work. Instead of listening to Myer, Chapman met with Cohen and took the unusual step of asking the Solicitor's Office to recall H.R. 6035 and S.R. 2543. The secretary also made no effort to support the commissioner's six bills that imposed state jurisdiction.[57]

In May 1952, the commissioner wrote Chapman a long letter. In a rare admission of defeat, he agreed not to push for additional authority to enforce federal law on reservations. Nonetheless, Myer saw no future for tribal self-determination. He doubted whether it would be worthwhile "at this late date" to begin the formidable task of codifying departmental law and order regulations for tribal courts and police. Instead, the commissioner preferred to work with

Congress to complete the task of transferring to states the federal responsibility over Indians.[58]

Myer's expectation that all states would eventually control law and order in Indian communities did not become reality. In August 1953, Congress passed Public Law 280, which gave California, Minnesota, Nebraska, Oregon, and Wisconsin civil and criminal jurisdiction in Indian country. This statute pleased those Indians who favored state control to improve police protection and discourage crime on reservations.[59]

Public Law 280 recognized important tribal rights. It exempted the Red Lake Band of Chippewas in Minnesota, Warm Springs Indians in Oregon, the Colville and Yakima tribes in Washington, and the Menominee Indians in Wisconsin from state jurisdiction after they expressed an interest in operating their own judicial systems. Furthermore, Public Law 280 prohibited state jurisdiction over tax-exempt Indian trust property. It acknowledged water and treaty rights, as well as permitting tribal governments to exercise concurrent authority over civil cases if their ordinances were not inconsistent with state law.[60]

The negative aspect of Public Law 280 for many people was that it ended the persistent silence of Congress on law and order in Indian country by upholding state jurisdiction over tribal sovereignty. This statute repudiated Margold's 1934 opinion that the most basic principle of Indian law was that tribes did not have powers delegated by Congress but inherent powers of a limited sovereignty. Section 7 gave the consent of the federal government for all states, at their option, to assume jurisdiction over Indian country through legislation or by amending their statehood acts or constitutions.[61]

Furthermore, Public Law 280 made no provision for tribal consent to recognize the unique status of tribes as sovereignties that existed before the resettlement of America. This pleased Senator Arthur Watkins of Utah, who believed that Public Law 280 ended the New Deal policy of treating tribes as separate nations.[62] The NCAI and those individuals who called for tribal consent before Congress could confer state jurisdiction lost on this issue in the short run. Nevertheless, Congress reversed itself fifteen years later and vindicated their position. It amended Public Law 280 to provide for tribal consent and allowed states to rescind their control over civil and criminal law on reservations.[63]

The foundation for this restoration of tribal authority was laid between 1933 and 1953. During those years, Nathan Margold upheld the inherent sovereign powers of tribes. Felix Cohen codified Indian law, and Indian judges presided over revamped Courts of Indian Offenses and IRA courts. Furthermore, the NCAI and the Iroquois and other tribes defended the right of Indians to separate judicial systems. Later, when federal funds became available and self-determination flourished, Congress recognized this legacy by creating 140 modern tribal courts.[64]

This achievement should not diminish the efforts of those Indians who successfully fought for state jurisdiction in California, Minnesota, Nebraska, Oregon, and Wisconsin. They received assistance from local authorities to address serious law and order problems. Over the years, Alaska, Florida, Idaho, Nevada, and other states used Public Law 280 to provide Indian citizens with police protection.[65] This movement, however, lost momentum when Commissioner Myer refused to allow tribes to vote. From contemporary accounts, it appeared that more tribes would have voluntarily chosen state jurisdiction than mandated under Public Law 280.

The ultimate success of Public Law 280 depended on lifting the restricted status of tribal land. State officials were dissatisfied with this law because it deprived them of an important source of revenue to pay for their newly acquired legal authority over tribal communities. Without special funding from Congress or the right to tax Indian trust property to pay for an expanded criminal justice system, many states would decline the invitation to assume sole financial responsibility for law and order in Indian country.[66]

Commissioner Myer anticipated this dilemma by establishing a Division of Program at the Indian Bureau where government officials began a staged federal withdrawal. They drafted plans that gave individual Indians fee simple ownership of their taxable real estate or placed it under the supervision of state corporations. The first tribal groups targeted for complete independence were California Indians, the Grande Ronde–Siletz and Klamath Indians of Oregon, Paiutes and Utes in Utah, Menominee Indians in Wisconsin, and Missouri River Sioux.

The granting of independence, an important development that included the appointment of Indian consultants to oversee the end of federal wardship, was the climax to a decade of reform to encourage more tribal self-determination. However, the movement for independence floundered because of complex administrative problems associated with Indian claims, trust property, and water rights. There also was continued opposition from the NCAI and other groups that wanted to protect and develop Indian homelands.

10

PROGRAMMING TO END
FEDERAL SUPERVISION

The creation of the bureau's [Division of Program] is the ultimate destruction of Indian community and tribal life . . . and contrary to the best
interests of Indians. RESOLUTION 35, BLACK HILLS SIOUX NATION COUNCIL,
OCTOBER 1951

In January 1952, Commissioner Myer held an interview with radio station WFJL
in Chicago to discuss his plans to give Indians an opportunity to run their
own affairs. He believed there were two general approaches to this problem.
Congress could pass omnibus legislation that abruptly ended Indian Bureau
supervision, or tribal representatives could voluntarily cooperate with officials at
the Interior Department to design withdrawal programs that transferred federal
responsibilities to Indians. The commissioner favored the second option. He
was convinced the Indian Bureau could end the trust with honor by providing
safeguards such as periodic government inspections prior to the formal transfer
of power in three to five years.[1]

Napoleon Bonaparte Johnson endorsed Myer's approach toward self-
determination. In the *Chronicles of Oklahoma*, the NCAI president called for
a staged federal withdrawal from Indian affairs in California, Oklahoma, and
Washington. Johnson observed, however, that many tribes in the Southwest and
elsewhere needed additional economic assistance to run their own affairs. The
only way to solve this problem was for Congress, federal officials, and tribal
representatives to draft long-range rehabilitation plans to hasten the day when
the bureau would no longer exist and all Indian people would be self-supporting
citizens.[2]

Despite support from a prominent Cherokee, Myer found it extremely difficult to diminish the role of the Indian Bureau. His centralization of administrative authority to transfer federal jurisdiction did not make Indians more

self-reliant. By listening to the advice of only a few area office directors, the commissioner isolated himself from the everyday concerns of tribal communities. This made it more difficult to design satisfactory programs for their independence.[3]

In yet another contradiction, Myer increased rather than decreased appropriations for the Indian Bureau to ensure an orderly withdrawal from Indian affairs. Consequently, congressional funding for the bureau rose from $71 million in 1952 to $87 million in 1953. Although most of this money went to human services such as health, education, and welfare, it was impossible to eliminate the influence of a paternalistic federal bureaucracy.[4]

The commissioner's policies were also at odds with the Indian Reorganization Act. Myer was aware that IRA tribes enjoyed rights of self-government that could be diminished or terminated only by specific acts of Congress. He also understood that IRA charters gave tribes the right to prevent the dispossession of their property and that only Congress could revoke this legal empowerment.[5]

Nonetheless, the commissioner appointed a small staff in January 1951 to help area directors formulate plans to end federal jurisdiction over tribal communities. Particular attention was given to California Indians, forty-three Indian bands residing in Western Oregon, and the Ute Indians of Utah. This fit the commissioner's stated objective of encouraging self-determination by progressively curtailing Indian Bureau activities, giving tribes direct control over their trust properties, and asking state and local governments to assume responsibility for Indian health, education, and welfare.[6]

Myer disliked the New Deal policy of reassuming wardship over tribes previously released from federal control by land allotment or executive order. This was especially true in Oregon for over seven hundred members of the Confederated Siletz Tribes, more than five hundred individuals at the Grande Ronde Community, who organized under IRA, and eight hundred descendants of these tribes who left their reservation to settle on eighty-three hundred acres of public domain allotments. Over the years, they had intermarried with non-Indian neighbors, become fluent in English, acquired educational training, and found employment in the private sector of the economy.[7]

The Confederated Siletz Tribes voted against the Indian Reorganization Act. Elwood A. Towner, a Portland attorney and mixed-blood leader of the Tootoo-to-ney Tribe, was an outspoken critic of the Indian New Deal. On speaking engagements with the German-American Bund, he claimed that the IRA was a communist social experiment led by Nathan Margold, Felix Cohen, and other Jewish employees at the Interior Department. Most of the Siletz Indians ignored Towner's inflammatory rhetoric. They welcomed the opportunity to work for the Civilian Conservation Corps and use federal rehabilitation funds to repair roads, build homes, and construct community buildings.[8]

Nevertheless, participation in relief programs did not mean the Siletz Indians favored a tribal alternative to assimilation. In 1945, the Siletz Tribal Council disapproved of a ten-year economic development program proposed by its business committee. The council then asked government officials to distribute all future proceeds from the sale of Siletz timber on a per capita basis. In 1946, Acting Secretary of Interior Oscar Chapman told Senator Wayne Morse that the Indian Bureau would not compel the Siletz Indians to accept federal assistance if they believed that progress came "only through independent individual enterprise."[9]

Two years later, the Interior Department closed the Grande Ronde–Siletz Agency and put the Indians of Western Oregon under the supervision of E. Morgan Pryse. The new director of the Portland Area Office worked closely with Towner to drum up support for federal withdrawal. In April 1951, Towner sent Senators Guy Cordon, Hugh Butler, and George Malone a resolution adopted by Too-too-to-ney Indians that requested a per capita distribution of $58,000 in tribal funds deposited at the U.S. Treasury.[10]

On 12 November 1950, the Siletz General Council met to consider this resolution. Under Towner's influence, the council unanimously asked the federal government to withdraw its supervision while, at the same time, the resolution reaffirmed the Indians' willingness to accept the responsibilities of full American citizenship. For the Siletz this meant freedom from antiquated government regulations as well as the right to spend their own money and sell tribal timberland. One month later Pryse sent Commissioner Myer a report that recommended the termination of federal wardship over Siletz Indians.[11]

The area director then turned his attention to the Grande Ronde Indians. Their 59,759-acre reservation had been established by executive order in 1857. The 546 Indians who resided on this homeland belonged to the Calapooia, Clakamas, Molatta, Nestucca, Rogue River, Santiam Tumwater, Umqua, Wapato, and Yamhill Tribes. After the Civil War, federal officials opened the Grande Ronde Reservation to Euro-American settlers once 269 Indians received land allotments. Before long, all but 830 acres of unproductive and uncleared hillside land passed out of tribal ownership.[12]

The Grande Ronde Confederated Tribes adopted an IRA constitution in 1936 even though only fragments of the reservation remained under their control. They purchased 537 acres of trust land for subsistence gardens and borrowed money to repair homes and operate small fruit canneries. Tribal organization helped these Indians survive the Great Depression, but they did not have enough land or capital for sustained economic development.[13]

Consequently, the Grande Ronde Confederated Tribes decided to terminate federal wardship. In August 1951, Celia Smith, the chair of the four-member Grande Ronde Business Committee, gave her support to a bill written by Pryse. It revoked the Grande Ronde IRA Constitution and By-laws, extended state legal jurisdiction, ended Indian Bureau services, and authorized the secretary of interior to issue fee patents to tribal property. The tribal business committee, however, wanted more time to consider whether to organize a corporation under state law to manage trust land. Furthermore, it asked Congress to recognize Grande Ronde hunting, fishing, and other treaty rights.[14]

Commissioner Myer also believed that historical circumstances made it desirable to withdraw federal services for California Indians. In 1846, at the time of American military occupation of California, more than one hundred thousand Indians from approximately two hundred bands and tribes owned more than 75 million acres of land. In 1852, U.S. commissioners signed eighteen treaties that recognized Indian title to 8.5 million acres of this property, but the Senate, at the request of the state legislature, refused to ratify these treaties.[15]

In subsequent years, 687,000 acres of trust land was set aside by Congress and executive order for eleven thousand Indians who resided on 115 small rancherias, homesteads, and reservations. Most of this real estate consisted of dry grazing land except for the property of twenty-one hundred Indian families with water rights to eight thousand irrigated acres. The Hoopa and Tule River Reservations also had valuable stands of timber appraised in excess of $4.5 million. The remaining thirteen thousand California Indians had migrated to nearby cities to find jobs. This led to racial intermarriage, which dramatically altered the ratio of mixed-bloods and full-bloods. Between 1910 and 1930, full-bloods decreased from 70 to 39 percent of the total Indian population.[16]

Tribal organization under the IRA did not fit the needs of most California Indians who lived on rancherias or small reservations with a population of fewer than two hundred people. Forty-four groups totaling 3,059 individuals voted for IRA, while 43 groups with 5,040 members opposed this legislation. Furthermore, the vast majority of Indians who lived in urban areas remained highly suspicious of the federal government because of a history of broken treaties. They sent F. G. Collett, the executive secretary of the Indians of California, Inc., and Adam Castillo, president of the Mission Indian Federation, to the nation's capital to lobby for termination and a per capita claims settlement.[17]

Officials at the Interior Department listened to these individuals. In 1949, Secretary of Interior Julius Krug asked Walter V. Woehlke, the director of the Sacramento Area Office, to plan for an orderly federal withdrawal from California. Woehlke recommended that Congress help the state provide social services for Indians, issue fee patents on public domain allotments, and transfer within ten years all trust land to individuals or groups organized under state or federal law. He also proposed that Congress authorize per capita payments from a $5 million California claims settlement, except for $1 million to establish a credit fund for impoverished Indians.[18]

After submitting this report, Woehlke accepted a State Department position in Austria. Commissioner Myer then appointed James M. Stewart to direct the Sacramento Area Office. Stewart radically altered Woehlke's proposal by calling for a per capita distribution of the entire $5 million claims settlement and fee patents to unallotted trust land, which could be sold after three years. The only exception was for minors or older people, whose property would remain restricted.[19]

In 1951, Myer sent three agents to California to set the stage for federal withdrawal. Leonard M. Hill and Le Grand B. Ward went to Southern California while G. L. McMillan traveled to Sacramento. While on this tour, they visited with numerous Indian groups and met with state officials to review a resolution passed in May 1951 by the California Senate that encouraged both President Harry Truman and Congress to end restrictions on the freedom of American Indians.[20]

When Hill and Ward returned from California, they informed the commissioner that no consensus existed about how to handle the property and water rights of so many groups. Consequently, Myer decided not to follow the Oregon precedent and ask for Indian consent. Instead, he drafted legislation to give the secretary of interior authority to resolve these complex problems by administrative fiat.[21]

In November 1951, the commissioner established a Division of Program at the Indian Bureau. It was headed by Warren G. Spaulding, the former director of the Aberdeen Area Office. Spaulding hired outside experts in agronomy, economics, forestry, law, and political science to design withdrawal plans not only for California and Oregon Indians but for tribes throughout the United States.[22]

Myer needed additional appropriations from Congress to effectively operate the Division of Program. Congresswoman Reva Beck Bosone helped the commissioner resolve this problem by introducing House Joint Resolution 8 in March 1952. Identical to her earlier resolution, which failed to pass the Senate two years earlier, the 1952 resolution authorized $50,000 for the secretary of interior to study and report to the Eighty-third Congress which tribes were ready to manage their own affairs without federal supervision and which could do so at a later date.[23]

Bosone's second resolution encountered Indian opposition before hearings held by the House Committee on Interior and Insular Affairs. Purl Willis, a spokesperson for the Mission Indians of California, criticized this resolution because it subjected Indians to yet another bureaucratic study. Willis urged committee members to end "the nightmare of perpetual wardship" by passing a resolution that declared all California Indians competent citizens.[24]

The Osage Indians of Oklahoma disliked this resolution for different reasons. They testified in favor of continued federal guardianship to protect oil headrights and tax-free royalties. The Osage feared that if Congress withdrew supervision, state and local officials might try once again to steal their property through dishonesty, fraud, and cheating. They did not want to lose control over oil revenues that represented the source of prosperity for future generations.[25]

Felix Cohen also spoke against the Bosone resolution on behalf of the San Carlos Apaches, Blackfeet, Laguna Pueblo, and All Pueblo Council. The tribal attorney told the committee that the Indians he represented disapproved of Bosone's resolution because it increased rather than diminished Indian Bureau control over their lives. Cohen emphasized that Congress could guarantee self-determination by simply turning over the bureau's vast authority to states, tribal governments, and individual Indians.[26]

Committee members ignored this testimony and reported favorably on H.J.R. 8. In July 1952, Congress passed Bosone's resolution. Myer used the $50,000 authorized by this legislation, plus $150,000 from the bureau's budget, to hire additional staff who devoted their full attention to withdrawal programming.[27]

Employees at the Division of Program soon identified five categories of Indians ready for termination. Group 1 included tribes or bands where a substantial number of Indians had expressed a desire for independence from the federal government. It came as no surprise that California Indians, the Siletz, and Grande Ronde Tribes appeared on this list. More controversial was the inclusion of Indians who resided on the Klamath Reservation in South Central Oregon.[28]

The Klamath first confronted the specter of federal withdrawal in 1947 when Senator Wayne Morse of Oregon introduced S.R. 1222, which lifted restrictions on the sale of tribal timber, grazing land, and pumice deposits valued at $13 million. This bill also gave Indians access to $3 million in tribal funds deposited at the U.S. Treasury. Wade Crawford, a former superintendent and apostle of assimilation, helped draft this legislation. He did not want the Klamath Indians to pay for costly New Deal socialist programs or the administrative expenses associated with federally sponsored tribal self-rule.[29]

There were other reasons why the Klamath Reservation was targeted in 1947 for federal withdrawal. All of the 780 enrolled Klamath, Modoc, and Yahooskin Band of Snake Indians were members of the Klamath General Council. This made it difficult to obtain a quorum to officially conduct tribal affairs. Furthermore, Boyd J. Jackson and Seldon E. Kirk, who led the eight-person business committee, constantly had to deal with problems of mismanagement, political favoritism, and corruption on the Klamath Tribal Loan Board. They discovered that most Indians seemed content to live off unearned income from grazing and timber leases rather than working together to develop tribal resources.[30]

Despite this internal conflict, the business committee met on 5 June and unanimously opposed S.R. 1222. The Klamath General Council met three weeks later and voted 95–4 against federal withdrawal. The council also removed Crawford as one of the Klamath delegates to Congress on grounds of insubordination for proposing legislation to liquidate the reservation.[31]

The Subcommittee on Indian Affairs of the Senate Public Lands Committee held hearings at the Klamath Agency in August 1947. Present were Arthur V. Watkins, chair, Hugh Butler, Ernest MacFarland, and Guy Cordon. Boyd Jackson and other individuals who supported the tribal government testified against S.R. 1222 because it was not sponsored by the general council, dishonored the Klamath Treaty of 1864, ignored boundary claims, threatened tribal control over 860,000 acres of timber, and dispossessed Indians.[32]

Crawford provided a different perspective. He presented a petition signed by 275 people, which recommended ending the federal trust. This document did not persuade the Eightieth Congress to pass S.R. 1222. However, a few years later it attracted the attention of Commissioner Myer and employees at the Division of Program. In this petition, Crawford and his followers argued that five generations were too long for the Klamath Indians to remain under federal wardship. Tribal self-rule made little sense because whites controlled 95 percent of the fee-patented land, only 138,000 out of 1.1 million acres on the reservation remained under Indian ownership, and tribal funds were squandered to subsidize a bankrupt tribal government.[33]

The Division of Program put the Osage Indians of Oklahoma and the Menominees of Wisconsin in group 2, which consisted of tribes with substantial assets. In February 1952, Osage delegates met with Myer to make arrangements to protect the tribe's oil royalties prior to federal withdrawal. At this meeting, the commissioner insisted that the Osages comply with a recent Internal Revenue Service ruling that required Indians to pay taxes on income from restricted property. He also reminded them that "the best country in the world" needed financial support from all citizens to fight communists in North Korea.[34]

A few months later, Myer traveled to Kenosha, Wisconsin, to meet with a skeptical Menominee Advisory Council. He told Gordon Dickie and other tribal leaders to "get down on their knees and thank God" for the large tracts of unallotted timber on the reservation. The commissioner believed that "it would be a sin and a shame" if the Menominees failed to make plans to manage their property without federal oversight. Myer also revealed other deep-seated misgivings when he stated that the bureau and tribe could not afford to make "a major mistake" in planning for the future. Myer tried to hide this sense of uncertainty by announcing that he would not approve per capita payments from the $3 million tribal fund or distribute the $8.5 million Menominee claims award until the council submitted a satisfactory withdrawal plan.[35]

The Missouri River Sioux were in group 3, which consisted of relocated tribes. The Sioux had been uprooted in 1944 when Congress allowed the Army Corps of Engineers to seize large parcels of their land for flood control and reclamation projects. The seven reservations involved in this massive public works project were located in North and South Dakota. Officials at the Division of Program intended to use over $20 million appropriated by Congress to develop rehabilitation programs for these displaced communities.[36]

The Black Hills Sioux Nation Council responded to these developments at a meeting held at Fort Thompson, South Dakota, in October 1951. The council passed a vote of no confidence in Commissioner Myer and Warren Spaulding, the head of Division of Program, for making plans to destroy Indian community and tribal life. David Frazier, the secretary of the council, also indicated that the Sioux had become suspicious, confused, and insecure after learning that the bureau intended to end federal services guaranteed by treaties.[37]

Indians found themselves in group 4 if they received only nominal services and supervision from the Indian Bureau. This included the Sac and Fox of Iowa, several bands in Michigan, and tribes residing in Kansas and Oklahoma. Group 5 targeted an assortment of tribes that were supposedly ready for federal withdrawal: the Ute Indians of Utah, the New Mexico Jicarilla Apaches, the Minnesota Red Lake Band of Chippewas, Indians under the jurisdiction of the Winnebago Agency, and various bands located in western Washington.[38]

The Utes were selected by Commissioner Myer to showcase how tribes could move from the shadow of paternalism to the sunlight of full independence. In November 1950, Myer met with members of the Ute Business Committee at the Phoenix Area Office. They decided to establish a Ute Planning Division and use money from a recent claims settlement to help the tribe manage its own affairs. A few months later, the business committee drafted legislation that Congress approved in August 1951. After President Truman signed this bill, he congratulated the Utes for developing "an eminently sound" program to prepare for full participation in the affairs of the nation.[39]

Public Law 120 authorized the Utes to rehabilitate the Uintah and Ouray Reservation prior to ending the federal trust. The Ute Business Committee used the tribe's claims award to make per capita payments to alleviate poverty, establish a $1.25 million loan fund, and set aside over $1 million for educational services and wildlife management. It also purchased fifty-five hundred acres of land, remodeled and constructed new homes, and upgraded the quality of grazing lands. Mixed-bloods led by Reginald O. Curry received a disproportionate share of these benefits.[40]

Myer's five categories of tribes ready to end federal wardship differed in important ways from the lists prepared by Commissioner John Collier and Acting Commissioner William Zimmerman. They did not mention important criteria for withdrawal programming, such as the degree of acculturation, the requirement of tribal consent, or the ability of tribes to make a decent standard of living. Instead, claims awards and tribal assets played a more important role in calculations made by the Division of Program.

In May 1952, the Association on American Indian Affairs sponsored an Institute on American Indian Assimilation in Washington DC. At this conference, Oliver LaFarge, the AAIA president, discussed the ramifications of Myer's policies that were designed to remake Indians in the image of Euro-Americans. He emphasized that partial or complete assimilation should be a voluntary Indian decision. In reference to Myer's withdrawal programming, LaFarge observed that a clear line should be drawn between persuasion and guidance that resulted in coercion. He warned that if Indians and non-Indians did not make a better effort to understand each other, assimilation would turn into "the negative of destruction."[41]

The firestorm that LaFarge predicted began in April 1952 when Commissioner Myer drafted a withdrawal bill for California Indians that received bipartisan support. This legislation, S.R. 3005, declared it the policy of Congress to terminate, as quickly as possible, federal services and supervision of Indians in the state of California. All Indians, except for the Agua Caliente Band, were required to apply for fee patents to their restricted allotments and trust land. This real estate, which included the corporate property of IRA tribes, was tax-exempt for only five years.[42]

Furthermore, the secretary of interior was authorized to issue fee patents "without application or consent" and distribute per capita the cash proceeds from the sale of this property. Water rights to irrigated land could be transferred to Indian owners or held in trust by "some other person or agency." Once wardship ended, Secretary Chapman was required to issue a proclamation that gave Indians the same rights and responsibilities as other California citizens.[43]

A clear majority of the seven thousand Indians who resided on 115 rancherias, public domain allotments, and reservations did not consent to Myer's bill to end federal supervision. At a California Conference of Indians and other meetings, they recommended amendments to protect their hunting and fishing rights. According to the commissioner, 2,106 individuals representing six groups favored this legislation while 111 people from five bands clearly voiced their opposition. He did not mention that thousands of Indians expressed disinterest or disapproval by refusing to vote.[44]

In June 1952, the Senate Subcommittee on Interior and Insular Affairs held hearings on Myer's termination bill. Ellen Norris, Robert Cromwell, and Linwood Ward, who represented the Indians of California, Inc., spoke out against S.R. 3005. They doubted whether Myer intended to promptly end federal supervision because he had requested over $3 million to administer their affairs. These Indian leaders were especially upset by the commissioner's unilateral decision in February 1951 to set aside $1 million of their $5 million claims settlement to pay for withdrawal programming.[45]

Frank George, the NCAI executive director, was the next person to testify. He condemned Myer for drafting termination legislation without meaningful input or consent from California Indians. George noted that tax-exempt land was a valuable property right guaranteed by treaties and other agreements. He emphasized that the successful transition from federal wardship to self-determination depended on whether officials at the Indian Bureau listened to tribal people and whether Congress upheld its constitutional and moral responsibility to promote the well-being of Indian communities (pl. 24).[46]

After the hearings ended, Senator Clinton P. Anderson of New Mexico asked Myer to respond to this adverse testimony. On 20 June, the commissioner told Anderson that federal supervision over Indians would never end if the government first had to resolve all problems. Myer reminded Anderson that tribal governments did not exist beyond congressional control. Congress should give the Indian Bureau authority to circumvent obsolete and unworkable IRA charters so it could implement withdrawal programming. These arguments did not convince Anderson to report favorably on S.R. 3005. The senator wanted more time to consider the views of different Indian groups.[47]

Objections raised by Senator Guy Cordon of Oregon also forced the Senate subcommittee to defer action on H.R. 7489. This termination bill would end federal supervision over the Confederated Siletz and Grande Ronde Tribes. It would give the secretary of interior authority to issue fee patents, incorporate trust property under state law, or distribute per capita the proceeds from the sale of this land without tribal consent.[48]

The commissioner ignored this criticism of his all-or-nothing approach toward Indian self-determination. Instead, he ordered the Division of Program to proceed with federal withdrawal. By the summer of 1952, officials at the Indian

Bureau had drafted termination bills for the following tribal groups in sixteen states besides California and Oregon:

Western Washington	32 tribes
Michigan	L'Anse, Bay Mills, Hannahville, and Isabella Indians
Wisconsin	Menominee Indians
Minnesota	Red Lake Chippewa Indians
New York	Six Iroquois Nations
Iowa	Sac and Fox Indians
Idaho	Nez Percé and Coeur d'Alene Indians
Kansas	Iowa, Kickapoo, Potawatomie, and Sac and Fox Indians
Oklahoma	Osage and Quapaw Indians
Utah	Uintah and Ouray Indians
Colorado	Consolidated Ute Indians
New Mexico	Jicarilla Apaches
North Dakota	Fort Berthold Indians
Montana	Flathead Indians
Texas	Alabama and Coushatta Indians
Louisiana	Chitimacha Indians[49]

Most of these groups were part of a semi-acculturated or predominately acculturated Indian population previously identified at congressional hearings by Commissioner Collier and Assistant Commissioner Zimmerman. Important exceptions were the Colorado Utes, Fort Berthold Indians, Utes on the Uintah and Ouray Reservation, and Red Lake Chippewas. Zimmerman had thought these Indians should remain under guardianship for an indefinite period of time.[50]

Furthermore, Myer refused to meet with the National Advisory Committee on Indian Affairs to discuss withdrawal programming. This isolated him from Ruth Muskrat Bronson, Louis Bruce, and other people who were interested in Indian self-determination. By May 1951, nine of the eleven persons on the committee had resigned because Congress prohibited the Interior Department from paying their travel expenses or in protest over the commissioner's policies.[51]

Secretary Chapman viewed the committee's demise as an opportunity to meet directly with Indian consultants because the government could reimburse their travel expenses. In April 1952, he reviewed a staff recommendation to create an Indian Advisory Board composed of leaders from tribal groups with the largest population. This board would confer with the secretary of interior on proposed legislation, administrative orders, and regulations concerning Indian affairs.[52]

Chapman rejected this idea and accepted a proposal written by Newton Edwards, a community specialist at the Division of Land Utilization. Edwards suggested that the secretary appoint Indian consultants based on merit to avoid problems concerning representation. They also would have no authority to speak on behalf of tribal governments or give embarrassing information to the press.[53]

Another feature of Edwards's plan was that different Indian groups could discuss topics such as federal withdrawal, and there was no obligation to invite them back for a second meeting. Edwards told Chapman that, as a general rule, government officials should formulate policies prior to meeting with consultants and not permit votes. To avoid negative publicity, the Interior Department would release only brief summaries of these meetings to newspapers. This would prevent unexpected reactions to new policies while allowing Indians "with no axe to grind" to participate in decisions that affected their lives.[54]

On 26 June 1952, Secretary Chapman and Commissioner Myer met with ten Indian consultants at the Interior Department. The agenda of this two-day conference concerned withdrawal programming, the transfer of Indian education to public schools, law and order, and relocation. The Indians who attended were Sam Ahkeah, Navajo; Henry Cottier, Oglala Sioux; Reginald Curry, Uintah–Ouray Ute; Popovi Da, San Ildefonso Pueblo; James Frechette, Menominee; Frank George, Nez Percé; Abel Paisano, Laguna Pueblo; Herman St. Clair, Shoshone; Davis Tyner, Shawnee; and Carl Whiteman Jr., Fort Berthold.[55]

They spent most of their time sharing information about how to independently manage tribal affairs. Frechette discussed Menominee plans to determine the exact cost of administrative services and decide whether to turn expensive tribal programs over to state and local governments. Whiteman noted that Fort Berthold leaders wanted to spend $2.5 million of their claims award for reservation economic development. Nonetheless, tribal members voted in favor of per capita payments. Da and Paisano reported that Pueblo Indians refused to draft long-range termination plans unless Congress appropriated more money for this purpose.[56]

Curry reviewed the Ute withdrawal program. His tribe had voted to use claims money to establish a planning board that coordinated efforts to end federal supervision. Furthermore, the Utes had taken responsibility for twenty Indian Bureau services, started a housing project for sixty families, consolidated small parcels of land into economic units, and distributed per capita payments. Less successful was a tribal revolving credit fund because many Utes saw no reason to repay loans made with their own money.[57]

Sam Ahkeah, chair of the Navajo Tribal Council, also reported significant progress. He discussed a program to restore the range, manage livestock, operate a sawmill, and purchase trading posts. Ahkeah indicated that the Navajos had bought trucks to haul ore and wanted to develop other enterprises such as wool preparation, weaving, pottery, and silver work. In another positive development, the FBI provided special training for twenty-six Navajo police officers while the tribe paid New Mexico to deputize six officers to protect Navajos living off the reservation. Ahkeah believed that the tribe's most serious challenge was to locate classrooms for fifteen thousand children.[58]

On the last day of the conference, the consultants recommended that the federal government, whenever possible, sell fee-patent land to tribal governments to protect reservation resources. They also asked Myer if his controversial California and Oregon termination bills established a precedent. The commissioner replied that Indians in both states had requested federal withdrawal. When he promised to meet with tribes before drafting additional legislation, skeptical consultants insisted that the federal government not remove the trust from Indian land.[59]

Three days after these tribal leaders went home, the House passed H.R. 698, which authorized the Committee on Interior and Insular Affairs to investigate the Indian Bureau. A short time later, Representative Toby Morris from Oklahoma asked Commissioner Myer to prepare a detailed report on how the bureau had fulfilled its trust obligation. The commissioner was instructed to provide a list of Indian groups qualified to manage their own affairs and identify Indian Bureau services that Congress should discontinue or transfer to other government agencies.[60]

Myer was eager to comply with H.R. 698. His decision to move ahead with federal withdrawal did not have tribal approval. Many Indians believed that it was desirable to transfer health and education programs to states because they hoped to secure better services. Thousands of people also wanted to manage their own funds and sell, lease, and mortgage real estate. But it was a much more serious matter to implement a sweeping policy that abolished the trust status of most Indian property in the United States. Self-determination, in this instance, would end the advantages of tax-exempt property, threaten tribal security, violate treaties, and destroy the concept of self-rule under IRA.[61]

Believing that he knew what was best for Indians, Myer ignored this problem and stood by his conviction that the federal trust had retarded the Indians' political, social, and economic development. In early August 1952, the commissioner sent a memo to all Indian Bureau officials that discussed his decision to push ahead, unilaterally, with programming to dismantle the reservation system. Myer made it clear that if Indians refused to cooperate with him, the Division of Program would draft withdrawal bills without their approval.[62]

Thoroughly alarmed tribal leaders expressed their concern about this approach to self-determination at a second conference with Secretary Chapman and Commissioner Myer in mid-September 1952. The twelve Indian consultants who attended this meeting were George Adams, Skokomish; Alfred Chalepah, Kiowa-Apache; Frank George, Nez Percé; Jasper Long, Crow; Floyd Maytubby, Chickasaw; Charles Reevis, Blackfeet; Richard LaRoche, Lower Brule Sioux; Thomas Segundo, Papago; Henry L. Vicente, Jicarilla Apache; Ed Wilson, Chippewa; Albert Yava, Hopi; and Maxwell Yazzi, Navajo. Despite the effort by Newton Edwards and other government officials to minimize their influence, these individuals strongly disagreed that it was time to end federal guardianship (pl. 25).[63]

The consultants recommended that the Indian Bureau not abruptly abandon its trust over tribal property. Otherwise, a large amount of unrestricted land would be lost by tax default. Before the bureau transferred its services, they wanted the Interior Department to guarantee that other governmental agencies and states would honor treaty commitments to protect elderly and other at-risk people from undue hardship. Furthermore, these tribal leaders rejected Myer's recommendation to sell and divide the proceeds of their heirship land. Instead, they wanted to purchase this property for tribal use and revoke the congressional policy that prohibited tribes in certain western states from purchasing real estate for landless Indians.[64]

The NCAI, which favored certain aspects of federal withdrawal, also opposed this attempt to abruptly end federal supervision. On 26 September, Frank George, the NCAI executive director, sent an open letter to all tribal chairs warning that a radical change had occurred in Indian affairs because the commissioner had ignored treaty rights and had threatened to draft withdrawal bills without Indian consent. George urged tribal officials to immediately inform members of Congress whether they wanted to end the federal trust and to suggest that if these politicians refused to follow their advice, it would be appropriate to vote for other candidates in the November election.[65]

In October 1952, Myer replied to George in an open letter sent to all tribal councils. The commissioner stated that he would recommend immediate termination for tribes that believed the bureau had handicapped their advancement, modify existing trust relations with tribes that favored this approach, and work with tribes that wanted to assume some bureau responsibilities without ending the trust relationship. He concluded with a threat to unilaterally forward Division of Program recommendations to Congress if tribes rejected this compromise. Indians, of course, were free to make their own legislative recommendations.[66]

Two months later, Myer submitted a sixteen-hundred-page document to the Indian Affairs Subcommittee containing statistical data on tribes as well as voluminous material on legislation, statutes, and treaties affecting Indians. This report gave the false impression that most tribes were ready to independently manage their own affairs, and it hid complex problems associated with ending the federal trust. The commissioner called for an inventory of Indian property modeled after William the Conqueror's Domesday Survey of England in 1086 to enable Congress to complete land allotment and abolish tribal governments.[67]

Myer addressed with considerable candor the many issues that Congress would have to confront prior to complete federal withdrawal. He indicated that the concept of guardianship had evolved from colonial laws, royal proclamations, the Northwest Ordinance, and treaties. Over the years, Congress had broadened the trust from the protection of Indian property to a complex pattern of responsibilities.[68]

The commissioner told Congress that the Indian Bureau faced a dilemma in carrying out its trust obligations. The rights of allotted Indians often conflicted with tribal interests. The trust also represented a legal disability for competent Indians and involved high administrative costs. On the other hand, as long as Indian land remained restricted, it was desirable to encourage tribal economic development by authorizing long-term leases, to transfer submarginal, ceded, and public domain land to certain reservations, and to stop the loss of subsurface rights through mineral entry under public land laws.[69]

The commissioner found it difficult to provide a definitive statement about which tribes were ready for complete independence. The bureau had begun intensive withdrawal programming and submitted termination bills at the request of California and Oregon Indians. Little more could be accomplished under present law until Congress passed legislation to address the diverse needs of each tribal group. Furthermore, many tribes were unprepared to manage their own affairs. Others, such as the New York Iroquois, argued that services and protection they enjoyed under the federal trust represented permanent vested legal rights. They insisted that Congress recognize their sovereignty by continuing to distribute treaty cloth.[70]

Myer made several other important observations. Congress would have to examine treaty rights, settle Indian possessory claims in southeastern Alaska, and resolve the problem of heirship land. It also had to decide how to fund Indian health, education, and welfare. This was an especially troublesome issue because many states refused to provide social services due to the low assessed value of Indian real estate. Finally, Congress would have to establish modern tribal business corporations and authorize appropriations for the gigantic task of relocating up to 50 percent of the Indian population.[71]

Frustrated by the commissioner's refusal to consult with them, Indians voted in large numbers for President Dwight D. Eisenhower. Myer submitted his resignation in January 1953 with the expectation of keeping his job because of bipartisan congressional support. Two months later, Republican officials at the Interior Department refused to reappoint the commissioner after concluding that he had "outlived his usefulness."[72]

Myer was unable to successfully bring far-reaching changes to Indian affairs because, like President Truman, he tried to resolve deep-seated problems and issues of substance through bureaucratic reorganization and coercion. Impatient with the Indians' slow progress toward assimilation, Myer used the Division of Program as a panacea to impose his personal definition of freedom and emancipation on a diverse tribal population. The commissioner gave lip service to the principle of self-determination but did not understand that Indians had the right to disapprove of his policies.[73]

Myer's assimilationist program was based on the ethnocentric assumption that all Americans should be alike. He was evasive about the right of Indians to retain the values of their choice because he believed that Indian cultures were static and unsuited to the modern world. The commissioner looked forward to the elimination of Indianness through population dispersal and the triumph of homogenous middle-class urban industrial civilization. In effect, he offered white civilization for land, but he never explained how the government could bring the Indians equality by dissolving their tribal communities, depriving them of their property, and threatening their cultural heritages.[74]

Myer also took a hard-headed approach to the issue of whether to continue the federal trust. Essential to his position was the idea that it was impossible to have guardianship without federal paternalism. The commissioner concluded that it would be unrealistic to ask states to assume Indian Bureau services and still keep restricted tribal property. Myer believed that treaties, which were designed to protect Indians, also perpetuated conditions of dependency and poverty. He feared that Indians would never voluntarily relinquish the trust relationship because it provided special social services and protected their tax-exempt land.[75]

It was the commissioner's judgment that Congress, which granted the trust, must determine how long it would continue. His withdrawal programs paved the way in 1953 for House Concurrent Resolution 108, which expressed the desire of Congress to end federal wardship, close the Indian Bureau in several states, target certain tribes for federal withdrawal, and grant them all the rights and responsibilities of other citizens.[76]

Myer's departure was a victory for American Indian political activists who since the 1940s had demanded the right of self-determination. They would continue to insist that the voice of Indian people should be final in changes of federal jurisdiction, treaty relations, control over natural resources, and the prerogative of tax-exempt property. Consequently, only twelve tribal groups representing 13,263 individuals agreed to sever their trust relationship with the U.S. government.[77]

EPILOGUE

In January 1953, a few months prior to his premature death, Felix Cohen wrote an article for *Yale Law Journal* that detailed the erosion of Indian rights during the last three years of the Truman administration. In this provocative essay, Cohen cited numerous examples of how Dillon S. Myer had expanded federal control over every aspect of Indian life accompanied "by the soft music" of liquidating the Indian Bureau. He also noted that the commissioner's deceptive administrative approach toward self-determination was also used in the Soviet Union, where officials assumed vastly enlarged powers to justify "the withering of the state."[1]

Cohen regretted that so many people viewed Indians as either romantic or comic figures without contemporary significance. He pointed out that Indians in American society and Jews in Germany played similar roles. Like the miner's canary, the Indians marked "shifts from fresh air to poison gas" in the political atmosphere and the rise and fall of the democratic faith in the United States. Cohen was convinced that this trend toward autocratic rule, which Myer epitomized, would continue until a new generation of Americans showed "a higher respect for inexpert humans or lower respect for expert administrators."[2]

Commissioner Myer was convinced that Cohen had written an unbalanced, inaccurate, and misleading account of his record at the Indian Bureau. He tried to set the record straight by writing lengthy point-by-point rebuttals to many of Cohen's statements in his private papers. For instance, Myer claimed that Cohen had falsely charged him with a stealthy attempt to enlarge Indian Bureau powers under the cloak of withdrawal programming. To dispel this idea, the commissioner cited his earlier public offer to advance Indian self-determination by helping tribes develop long-range plans to terminate federal control over Indian affairs.[3]

In his defense, Myer failed to mention important issues concerning the erosion of Indian rights that were missing from Cohen's article. For example, there was no reference to Solicitor Nathan Margold's opinions circumventing the intent of Congress when it passed the IRA, Justice Department opposition to Cohen's *Handbook of Federal Indian Law*, the adverse impact of stock reduction and New Deal educational policies on the Navajos, the vote by native groups not to extend the reservation system to Alaska, the Hoover Commission report, or the breakdown of law and order in Indian country. Cohen also overlooked the negative consequences of his feud with James Curry, problems associated with the NCAI's solicitation of claims contracts, and the financial and other problems of IRA governments.

The conflict between Cohen and Myer reflected the different perspectives of termination held by Indian leaders. For Ruth Muskrat Bronson, George Pambrun, Rufus Sago, Avery Winnemucca, and other Indians, federal withdrawal offered hope that the government would honor its promise of self-rule under IRA. This meant that consultation by superintendents with tribal councils would be more than a mere formality. Furthermore, federal officials would have to delete restrictions written into IRA constitutions and charters that gave the secretary of interior greater, not less, control over Indian affairs.[4]

Self-determination in the form of termination also appealed to Native Americans who wanted to manage their own affairs as citizens of states. Joseph Bruner, Adam Castillo, Reginald O. Curry, Napoleon Bonaparte Johnson, Elwood A. Towner, and Wade Crawford were not interested in the IRA tribal alternative to assimilation. For them, termination of the trust offered a unique opportunity for a claims settlement and a per capita distribution of tribal assets not under the control of patronizing federal bureaucrats.

By 1953, termination was no longer an attractive policy because federal policymakers continued to ignore the richness and variety of human life and to stereotype Indians. Victorious and self-confident after World War II, the American people believed that their superior civilization was destined to triumph over the world.[5] Consequently, the concept of tribal self-rule was redefined to discourage socialism and the legal separateness of quasi-sovereign Indian nations. Native Americans, as well as other conquered people, would be required to accept the political ideology of the U.S. Constitution. In addition, they would be asked to adopt middle-class values associated with the liberal tradition and to achieve social mobility in a capitalist economic system.[6]

After 1945, most Americans did not think of Indian reservations as permanent homelands with their own dynamic histories and cultures. Instead, they stereotyped reservations as outmoded concentration camps for captive people, rural slums, or backwaters where conquered tribes required outside assistance to obtain their freedom from an antiquated form of colonial rule. Reservations, with their communal land tenure, also were obstacles to building military installations, dams, lumber mills, and the allocation of fisheries and other resources that symbolized the march of progress in the American West and Alaska Territory.[7]

Commissioner Myer agreed with those people who saw Indians only in terms of their deficiencies when compared to the civilization of European settlers. In his autobiography, the commissioner stereotyped Indians as a primitive people. Furthermore, he characterized their homelands as overpopulated poorhouses where corrupt Indian politicos exploited hapless neighbors who were dependent on the largess of a federal welfare state.[8] These ethnocentric beliefs, and his experience as director of the War Relocation Authority, explain why Myer encouraged Indians in California, Oregon, Utah, Wisconsin, and elsewhere to terminate their status as wards, relocate to more prosperous cities, and develop long-range plans to secure a greater measure of self-determination as citizens of states.

Many members of Congress joined with Myer to stereotype Native Americans. For instance, Senator Hugh Butler of Nebraska asked what would happen if European immigrants in the United States were treated like Indians. Butler emphasized that no other American minority would tolerate being wards of a special federal agency, restrictions on their property, the impoundment of trust funds in the U.S. Treasury, or separate credit facilities, police, and courts to ensure compliance with bureaucratic orders. For Butler, and many other Americans, the only solution to ending the artificial segregation of Indians was to dismantle the Indian Bureau and repeal the IRA.[9]

Charles Russell, the director of the American Museum of Natural History, also used a settler's analogy to turn tribal people into a white man's Indian. In January 1953, at the seventieth annual meeting of the Indian Rights Association, he indicated that all Americans, including Indians, traced their ancestry to immigrants. Because the cultural integration of the United States had reached a higher stage than in any other country, Russell concluded it was a mistake for tribal people to dream of returning to a romanticized past. Instead, their future was extricably woven into the life of tomorrow's America.[10]

This definition of self-determination, which stressed conformity with mainstream society, appeared in August 1953 when the Eighty-third Congress by unanimous consent adopted House Concurrent Resolution 108. As one scholar has observed, this resolution did not even mention the word "termination."

Instead, it was the culmination of a decade of inconclusive reform to restructure Indian affairs. H.R. 108 resembled a Fourth of July address: it proclaimed the confidence of Congress in republican virtue by reaffirming a longstanding commitment to end the Indians' status as wards and to grant them full American citizenship.[11]

In addition, H.R. 108 called for the abolition of the Indian Bureau in California, Florida, New York, and Texas. It was the intent of Congress to free the Indians in these four states as well as the Montana Flatheads, Klamath Indians of Oregon, Wisconsin Menominees, Kansas and Nebraska Potawatomis, and North Dakota Turtle Mountain Chippewas from all the limitations associated with federal control. By targeting so few groups, Congress showed considerable restraint and some uncertainty. For instance, when H.R. 108 reached the floor of the House, the Osage and Iowa Indians were removed from the list of emancipated tribes. In response to queries about the meaning of this resolution, Congressman Wesley D'Ewart, the chair of the Subcommittee on Indian Affairs, also promised to hold hearings to listen to tribes that wanted to maintain their trust relationship with the United States.[12]

For the National Congress of American Indians, H.R. 108 was extremely disappointing. The NCAI definition of self-determination differed in important respects from the use of that term by Commissioner Myer or Congress. By linking tribal governments to a pan-Indian political structure, the NCAI had reaffirmed the permanence of Indian communities. It also asked all Americans to respect Indian cultural values and treaty rights, support reservation economic development, and put an end to stereotyping Indian people.[13]

Ruth Muskrat Bronson, Frank George, Napoleon Bonaparte Johnson, John Rainer, and Avery Winnemucca played an important role in the early years of the NCAI. They emphasized that the federal trust, tax-exempt land, and tribal courts were vested legal rights. These individuals also insisted that Congress obtain Indian consent before it passed legislation that threatened tribal property rights, permitted state jurisdiction in Indian country, or authorized federal withdrawal.

James Curry, the Irish-American socialist attorney from Chicago, was a driving force behind NCAI political activism. He upheld the right of Indians to exist as nations within a nation. Curry defended the possessory claims of Indians in southeastern Alaska, helped Avery Winnemucca evict settlers from Pyramid Lake Paiute land, and worked behind the scenes with Rufus Sago to empower the IRA tribal government on the Mescalero Apache Reservation. Furthermore, Curry took the lead in asserting the constitutional right of tribes to hire independent legal counsel, not only to prepare claims litigation but to represent other concerns of independent Indian communities.

Sam Ahkeah, the chair of the Navajo Tribal Council, was part of the movement to help Indians regain control over their own destiny. With the assistance of the NCAI and the Navajo Coordinating Committee, Ahkeah forced Congress to confront the issue of universal education for Indian children and approve a long-range plan to rehabilitate the Navajo Reservation. The political and economic progress of the Navajos after World War II demonstrated that tribal communities, if given a chance and adequate support, could successfully manage their affairs and contribute to modern American society.

Felix Cohen played a key role in the postwar drive to encourage Native American self-determination. He believed that the most important task of his generation was to find patterns by which people of different racial, religious, and economic backgrounds could live in harmony and contribute to each other's prosperity. For Cohen, the U.S. Constitution was an instrument of intercultural integration that expanded freedom and democracy for all citizens except for occasional setbacks during periods of national hysteria.[14]

Through experience, Cohen discovered that terminating the colonial status of American Indians was an extremely complicated political assignment. During the New Deal, he took several important initiatives to advance Indian self-rule. Cohen drafted solicitor's opinions on the inherent powers of tribes, organized Indian communities under IRA constitutions and charters, and issued a law code for autonomous tribal courts. Nonetheless, he soon became disillusioned because administrators at the Indian Bureau refused to relinquish their authority to tribal councils. Instead, they followed the quaint idea that indirect colonial rule was equivalent to democratic self-government.

Cohen tried to rectify this deplorable situation. He published the *Handbook of Federal Indian Law* to better identify tribal legal rights and helped establish the Indian Claims Commission, which led to the growth of the NCAI and a new assertiveness in Indian politics. Unfortunately, these efforts did not prevent officials in the Truman administration from running roughshod over the possessory claims of Haida and Tlingit Indians. Before Cohen resigned from the Interior Department in protest, he encouraged the inhabitants of Kake to resist this form of American imperialism. Led by Frank Johnson, they defended their right under the Alaska Reorganization Act to cut and market timber in the Tongass National Forest.

Overdependence on the wisdom of colonial administrators and neglect of Indian perspectives became an acute problem after 1950, when President Truman appointed Dillon S. Myer instead of an Indian as commissioner. Myer took an all-or-nothing approach to self-determination that gave tribes little choice but to end the federal trust. Furthermore, he regulated attorney contracts to silence Cohen and Curry, who favored tribal self-rule under federal protection. Myer cooperated with western members of Congress who wanted to promote economic development at the expense of Indian rights, and he openly interfered with the operation of IRA tribal councils that were obstacles to termination.

Products of their time, President Truman, Secretary Chapman, and Commissioner Myer took bold steps to end colonial rule throughout Indian America. They launched an aggressive campaign to assimilate Indians, which included relocation to cities and the promise of equality as citizens of states. These efforts, which culminated in H.R. 108 and Public Law 280, ultimately made little headway because Native American leaders increasingly demanded a voice in decisions that impacted on the lives of their followers.

The Indian political resurgence that began during the New Deal and accelerated after 1945 had dramatic consequences. It made termination an obsolete national policy and set the stage for the drive toward more self-determination during the 1960s and 1970s. More importantly, the cultural persistence of Indian communities was assured in the United States during the second half of the twentieth century, based on a separate political sovereignty and control over tribal resources.[15]

NOTES

1. ON A NEW TRAIL

1. Diary, Reel 5, 15 February 1942, 6345–46, Harold L. Ickes Papers.

2. Alison R. Bernstein, *American Indians and World War II*, 89; Kenneth Philp, *John Collier's Crusade for Indian Reform*, 205; John Collier to William Zimmerman, 25 May 1944, Box 14, Secretary of the Interior Oscar L. Chapman Office Records; and "Statement on Proposed Decentralization of Bureau of Indian Affairs," 1950, Box 155, Dillon S. Myer Desk Files.

3. Senate, *Analysis of Statement of Commissioner of Indian Affairs in Justification for Appropriations for 1944 and Liquidation of Indian Bureau*, 78th Cong., 1st sess., 11 June 1943, S. Rept. 310, 1–22; and House Committee on Indian Affairs, *Hearings on H.R. 166: Bill to Authorize Investigation*, pt. 1, 1–5.

4. Bernstein, *American Indians and World War II*, 112; Stephen Cornell, *Return of the Native*, 115–20; and Dorothy Parker, *Singing an Indian Song*.

5. Bernstein, *American Indians and World War II*, 122; and Diary, Ickes Papers, Reel 6, 6 January 1945, 9455, and 21 January 1945, 9499–9500.

6. Senate Committee on Indian Affairs, *Hearings on Nomination of William A. Brophy*, 20, 27, and 28 February and 1 March 1945, 8–11, 25, 73, 78–79.

7. Senate Committee on Indian Affairs, *Hearings on Nomination of William A. Brophy*, 34–35, 37, 47, 49, 57, 136–42.

8. Senate Committee on Indian Affairs, *Hearings on Nomination of William A. Brophy*, 141–42, 149; and Library of Congress, *Aspects of Indian Policy*, 1–29.

9. Kenneth Philp, ed., *Indian Self-Rule*, 17.

10. "Judge Nathan Margold Dies Unexpectedly," *Washington Star*, 16 December 1947, Box 93, Felix S. Cohen Papers; and Mortimer Riemer to James E. Curry, 7 May 1938, Box 105, James E. Curry Papers; Lucy Krammer Cohen, "Biography of Felix S. Cohen," 345–50; and "Felix Cohen Dead; Aided U.S. Indians," *New York Times*, 20 October 1953, Box 96, Cohen Papers.

11. Felix S. Cohen to Nathan R. Margold, 7 May 1947, Box 88, Cohen Papers; Jim Cork,

"Obituary of Morris Raphael Cohen," *Socialist Call*, 10 February 1947, Box 87, Cohen Papers; Newspaper Clipping, "Morris Cohen Is Dead in Capital," 30 January 1947, Box 96, Cohen Papers; Lewis S. Feurer, "Morris Cohen's Last Book," Box 96, Cohen Papers.

12. Theodore H. Haas, "Felix Cohen — Fighter for Indian Rights," Box 91, Cohen Papers; and Ken Meiklejohn to Felix S. Cohen, 28 October 1948, Box 88, Cohen Papers. In 1940, Cohen resigned from the National Executive Board of the National Lawyers Guild. He was convinced that communism and fascism both accepted the doctrine that the end justifies the means, which included lying and assassination. Felix S. Cohen to Lester P. Schoene, Box 77, Cohen Papers.

13. Felix S. Cohen, "Socialism and Myth of Legality," 3, 11–12, 18, 22–23.

14. Cohen, "Socialism and Myth of Legality," 27–28, 31–32.

15. Commissioner John Collier to Superintendents, Tribal Councils, and Individual Indians, Memorandum on Indian Self-Government, 20 January 1934, Box 13, Cohen Papers; and Laurence M. Hauptman, "Africa View," 359–74.

16. Hauptman, "Africa View."

17. For an extended analysis of the Wheeler-Howard Bill, consult Vine Deloria Jr. and Clifford Lytle, *Nations Within*, 66–79, 266–70; and Philp, *John Collier's Crusade for Indian Reform*, 141–43.

18. For a full account of the Indian congresses, see Deloria and Lytle, *Nations Within*, 101–21; and Philp, *John Collier's Crusade for Indian Reform*, 145–54.

19. House, *Report with Respect to House Resolution Authorizing Investigation*, 1035–39.

20. Nathan R. Margold, "The Powers of an Indian Tribe," 25 October 1934, Box 8, Cohen Papers.

21. Margold, "Powers of an Indian Tribe," Cohen Papers.

22. Margold, "Powers of an Indian Tribe," Cohen Papers.

23. Margold, "Powers of an Indian Tribe," Cohen Papers. Consult Deloria and Lytle, *Nations Within*, 154–70, for a discussion of how Nathan R. Margold's rulings gave life to the IRA.

24. Margold, "Powers of an Indian Tribe," Cohen Papers; Felix S. Cohen to William L. Paul Jr., Box 90, Cohen Papers; and "Legal Doctrine," Box 1, Cohen Papers.

25. Solicitor Nathan R. Margold, Memorandum for the Secretary, undated, Box 7, Cohen Papers.

26. Charlotte T. Westwood to Commissioner of Indian Affairs, 11 July 1936, Box 43, Cohen Papers; John Collier, Circular 3123, Membership in Indian Tribes, 18 November 1935, Box 90, Cohen Papers. For a case study of the Sioux under IRA, see Thomas Biolsi, *Organizing the Lakota*.

27. Attorney [name unknown], Memo on Indian Organization for Fowler Harper, 15 January 1937, Box 3, Cohen Papers; Outline of Tribal Constitutions and Bylaws, undated,

Box 8, Cohen Papers; and A Form of Corporate Charter, 25 September 1935, Box 104, Cohen Papers.

28. Nathan R. Margold, Memorandum on the Power of the Secretary to Make Regulations Concerning the Conduct of Indians, 1935, Box 1, Cohen Papers.

29. Margold, Memorandum on Power of Secretary, Cohen Papers.

30. Department of Interior Press Release, 8 January 1935, Box 3, Cohen Papers.

31. Comments upon the Original Draft of the Law and Order Regulations, Cohen Papers.

32. Comments upon Original Draft, Cohen Papers; and Courts of Indian Offenses, Law and Order Regulations, 1935, Code of Tribal Offenses, Sections 1–38, Box 1, Boyd J. Jackson Papers.

33. John Collier to the Tribal Councils of Organized Tribes through the Superintendent, Law and Order Codes for Organized Tribes, undated circular, Box 107, Curry Papers.

34. Form of Approval of Constitution and Bylaws, November 1934, Box 7, Cohen Papers.

35. James E. Curry to Felix S. Cohen, 9 October 1935, Box 104, Curry Papers. Curry resigned from the National Lawyers Guild because this organization refused to state that it was not dominated or sponsored by communists. James E. Curry to Hugh Butler, 1 September 1951, Box 210, Hugh Butler Papers.

36. James E. Curry to John Collier, 26 April 1936, Box 104, Curry Papers.

37. James E. Curry to Felix S. Cohen, 27 June 1936, Box 43, Cohen Papers.

38. James E. Curry, Principles of Cooperation, Indian Service Credit Section, undated, Box 107, Curry Papers.

39. James E. Curry to Felix S. Cohen, 27 January 1937, Box 43, Cohen Papers; and James E. Curry, Memorandum for the Acting Solicitor, 1 March 1938, Box 108, Curry Papers.

40. Laurence M. Hauptman, *Iroquois and the New Deal*, 47, 97.

41. Report to the Commissioner of Indian Affairs on the Work of Assistant Solicitor Cohen in Oklahoma, 8–24 March 1937, Box 8, Cohen Papers.

42. Felix S. Cohen, Memorandum for the Acting Assistant Attorney General, 13 May 1939, Box 11, Cohen Papers.

43. Felix S. Cohen, Memorandum for Norman Littell, Assistant Attorney General, 1 November 1939, Box 14, Cohen Papers; and Peter Iverson, *Navajo Nation*, 53–54.

44. Felix S. Cohen, Memorandum for Solicitor, 10 February 1940, Box 14, Cohen Papers.

45. Cohen, Memorandum for Solicitor, 10 February 1940, Cohen Papers; and Cohen, Memorandum for Littell, 1 November 1939, Cohen Papers.

46. Cohen, Memorandum for Solicitor, 10 February 1940, Cohen Papers.

47. Cohen, Memorandum for Solicitor, 10 February 1940, Cohen Papers; and Felix S. Cohen, *Handbook of Federal Indian Law*, xxi–xxix.

48. House Committee on Indian Affairs, *Hearings on H.R. 166: Bill to Authorize Investigation,* pt. 1:24; and Deloria and Lytle, *Nations Within,* 145.

49. House Committee on Indian Affairs, *Hearings on H.R. 166: Bill to Authorize Investigation,* pt. 1:24–25.

50. For discussion of the shortcomings of the IRA, consult Lawrence C. Kelly, "Indian Reorganization Act," 291–312; Kenneth R. Philp, "Termination," 165–80; Graham D. Taylor, *New Deal and American Indian Tribalism*; and William Zimmerman Jr., "Economic Status of Indians in United States," 108–20.

51. House Committee on Indian Affairs, *Hearings on H.R. 166: Bill to Authorize Investigation,* pt. 1:59–60.

52. Bernstein, *American Indians and World War II,* 22, 59, 64, 86. This topic is also discussed in Jere Franco, "Native Americans in World War II" (Ph.D. diss.).

53. Bernstein, *American Indians and World War II,* 88–89, 110.

54. Mary L. Rogers, Report to the Board of Directors from the Administrative Committee, 1 November 1942, 11–12, Association on American Indian Affairs (AAIA) Papers.

55. Oliver LaFarge, ed. *Changing Indian,* 166–74.

56. Royal B. Hassrick, "American Indian in Tomorrow's America," 3–4.

57. Hassrick, "American Indian in Tomorrow's America," 8–9.

58. Hassrick, "American Indian in Tomorrow's America," 7, 10, 12.

59. G. E. E. Lindquist, *Indian Wardship,* 16, 27–28, copy in Box 2, Cohen Papers; and J. C. McCaskill to Mrs. Fred Bennett, 8 April 1943, Cohen Papers.

60. Lindquist, *Indian Wardship,* 13, 29, 32, 37–38.

61. House Committee on Indian Affairs, *Hearings on H.R. 166: Bill to Authorize Investigation,* pt. 1:2, 16–21.

62. House Committee on Indian Affairs, *Hearings on H.R. 166: Bill to Authorize Investigation,* pt. 1:61–63.

63. Bernstein, *American Indians and World War II,* 113; and Parker, *Singing an Indian Song,* 106.

64. Ruth Muskrat Bronson, *Indians Are People Too,* 5, 23–27, 123. For a full discussion of Bronson's interest in both tribal heritage and American citizenship, consult Gretchen Grace Harvey, "Cherokee and American" (Ph.D. diss.), 1–244.

65. Bronson, *Indians Are People Too,* 28–30, 80–81, 120–21. For additional contemporary views on Indian wardship, consult O. G. Villard, "Wardship and the Indian," 397–98; and O. K. Armstrong, "Set American Indians Free," 47–52.

66. Mark L. Burns to Tribal Leaders, 16 October 1944, Box 1, National Congress of American Indians (NCAI) Papers; and Bernstein, *American Indians and World War II,* 113–14.

67. Bernstein, *American Indians and World War II,* 116–17. For a discussion of elite theory, consult Nicholas C. Peroff, *Menominee Drums,* 28–46.

68. "Little Sketches of Convention Folks," 1944, Box 1, NCAI Papers; and "Minutes of the National Congress of American Indians Convention," Denver, 15–18 November, 1944, NCAI Papers.

69. NCAI *Newsletter* 2 (July 1945): 2, Box 1, Jackson Papers; and NCAI, 6–9 November 1946, 1–5, Department of Interior Central Files.

70. "Indians of Today: Napoleon B. Johnson," Box 10, NCAI Papers; "Common Sense Solution of Indian Problem," *Oklahoma City Times*, 16 December 1948, and Newspaper Clipping, "Sooner Indian Views Change," Box 2, NCAI Papers.

71. "Mrs. Bronson Speaking," *Our Times and National Missions*, April 1944, 4, Box 2, NCAI Papers; and Bernstein, *American Indians and World War II*, 121.

72. Albert L. Hurtado and Peter Iverson, eds., *Major Problems in American Indian History*, 480–81; and Charles F. Wilkinson, *American Indians, Time, and the Law*, 4, 57–59.

2. SETTLING TRIBAL CLAIMS

1. Bernstein, *American Indians and World War II*, 162–63.

2. *New York Times*, "President Truman Signs Claims Bill," 14 August 1946, 27; and Parker, *Singing an Indian Song*, 108.

3. Napoleon Bonaparte Johnson to All Indian Tribes, 13 August 1948, Box 1, NCAI Papers.

4. NCAI, Convention Call, 6–9 November 1945, Box 104, Joseph C. O'Mahoney Papers.

5. James E. Curry to the NCAI, 17 October 1951, Box 12, NCAI Papers.

6. John T. Vance, "Congressional Mandate and Indian Claims Commission," 327; and Harvey Daniel Rosenthal, "Their Day in Court" (Ph.D. diss.), 26.

7. House Committee on Indian Affairs, *Hearings on H.R. 1198 to Create Indian Claims Commission*, 81, 107–9.

8. Rosenthal, "Their Day in Court" (Ph.D. diss.), 30–31.

9. Lewis Meriam, *Problem of Indian Administration*, 468, 807–11.

10. Purl Willis, "California Indians Win Partial Victory in Court of Claims," 4–6; and House Committee on Indian Affairs, *Hearings on H.R. 1198 to Create Indian Claims Commission*, 177.

11. Rosenthal, "Their Day in Court" (Ph.D. diss.), 50, 88. For an analysis of Ernest Wilkinson's role as Ute attorney, consult Warren R. Metcalf, "Arthur V. Watkins and Indians of Utah" (Ph.D. diss.), 61–94.

12. Rosenthal, "Their Day in Court" (Ph.D. diss.), 101; and Philp, *John Collier's Crusade for Indian Reform*, 171–72.

13. "Indian Ferment," *Newsweek* 14 (11 September 1939), 27; and Joseph Bruner to John Collier, 23 November 1939, Box 2, Office Files of John Collier.

14. John Collier, Memorandum on H.R. 5921, 76th Cong., 1st Sess., 20 April 1939, and S.R. 2206, 21 April 1939, Box 2, Collier Office Files.

15. Division of Information Press Release, 7 September 1939, Box 2, Collier Office Files.

16. Harold L. Ickes to Usher L. Burdick, 28 April 1939, Box 2, Collier Office Files.

17. House Committee on Indian Affairs, *Hearings on H.R. 1198 to Create Indian Claims Commission*, 105; and Resolution, Joseph Bruner, American Indian Federation, 14 January 1945, Box 110, O'Mahoney Papers.

18. Rosenthal, "Their Day in Court" (Ph.D. diss.), 102–6.

19. House Committee on Indian Affairs, *Hearings on H.R. 166: Bill to Authorize Investigation*, pt. 1:48.

20. House Committee on Indian Affairs, *Hearings on H.R. 1198 to Create Indian Claims Commission*, 164–66.

21. House Select Committee, *Report of Select Committee to Investigate Indian Affairs*, 1–7.

22. House Select Committee, *Report of Select Committee to Investigate Indian Affairs*, 6–7; and Answer to Questions Asked by the Committee on Indian Affairs, House of Representatives, 10 June 1944, RG 3, Karl E. Mundt Papers.

23. House Select Committee, *Report of Select Committee to Investigate Indian Affairs*, 6–7; and Answer to Questions Asked by Committee on Indian Affairs, Mundt Papers.

24. Napoleon Bonaparte Johnson, "National Congress of American Indians," 3.

25. House Committee on Indian Affairs, *Hearings on H.R. 1198 to Create Indian Claims Commission*, 1–2.

26. House Committee on Indian Affairs, *Hearings on H.R. 1198 to Create Indian Claims Commission*.

27. The editors of *Reader's Digest* to Mrs. Ed MacLean, 7 September 1945, Box 118, Ickes Papers.

28. Armstrong, "Set American Indians Free," 47–49.

29. Armstrong, "Set American Indians Free," 56.

30. Armstrong, "Set American Indians Free," 15–17.

31. House Committee on Indian Affairs, *Hearings on H.R. 1198 to Create Indian Claims Commission*, 55–56.

32. House Committee on Indian Affairs, *Hearings on H.R. 1198 to Create Indian Claims Commission*, 15–17.

33. House Committee on Indian Affairs, *Hearings on H.R. 1198 to Create Indian Claims Commission*, 25–28.

34. House Committee on Indian Affairs, *Hearings on H.R. 1198 to Create Indian Claims Commission*, 29–34.

35. House Committee on Indian Affairs, *Hearings on H.R. 1198 to Create Indian Claims Commission*, 69–70.

36. House Committee on Indian Affairs, *Hearings on H.R. 1198 to Create Indian Claims Commission*, 69–70.

37. House Committee on Indian Affairs, *Hearings on H.R. 1198 to Create Indian Claims Commission*, 79–83.

38. House Committee on Indian Affairs, *Hearings on H.R. 1198 to Create Indian Claims Commission*, 113–15.

39. House Committee on Indian Affairs, *Hearings on H.R. 1198 to Create Indian Claims Commission*, 121–25.

40. House Committee on Indian Affairs, *Hearings on H.R. 1198 to Create Indian Claims Commission*, 121–25.

41. House Committee on Indian Affairs, *Hearings on H.R. 1198 to Create Indian Claims Commission*, 149.

42. House Committee on Indian Affairs, *Hearings on H.R. 1198 to Create Indian Claims Commission*, 152–55.

43. House Committee on Indian Affairs, *Hearings on H.R. 1198 to Create Indian Claims Commission*, 157–58.

44. House Committee on Indian Affairs, *Hearings on H.R. 1198 to Create Indian Claims Commission*, 160.

45. Oscar L. Chapman to Louis O'Marr, 7 April 1952, Box 3520, Indian Claims, General, Department of Interior Central Files.

46. Robert J. Donovan, *Conflict and Crisis*, 181–82.

47. Harold L. Ickes to Harold D. Smith, 20 November 1945, Box 3520, Department of Interior Central Files.

48. Harold D. Smith, Memorandum for the President, 21 February 1946, Box 64, Indian Claims Commission Papers.

49. Harry S. Truman, Memorandum for the Director of the Budget, 25 February 1946, Harry S. Truman Official Files.

50. Bernstein, *American Indians and World War II*, 161.

51. *Congressional Record*, 79th Cong., 2d sess., 20 May 1946, 92, pt. 4:5311–16.

52. *Congressional Record* 92, pt. 4:5311–16.

53. *Congressional Record* 92, pt. 4:5318–19, 10403.

54. Senate Committee on Indian Affairs, *Hearings on H.R. 4497 to Create Indian Claims Commission*, 15.

55. Senate Committee on Indian Affairs, *Hearings on H.R. 4497 to Create Indian Claims Commission*, 24–26.

56. Senate Committee on Indian Affairs, *Hearings on H.R. 4497 to Create Indian Claims Commission*, 23.

57. Senate Committee on Indian Affairs, *Hearings on H.R. 4497 to Create Indian Claims Commission*, 18, 36, 77.

58. Willis, "California Indians Win Partial Victory," 4.

59. Senate Committee on Indian Affairs, *Hearings on H.R. 4497 to Create Indian Claims Commission*, 23, 83.

60. Senate Committee on Indian Affairs, *Hearings on H.R. 4497 to Create Indian Claims Commission*, 53–73; and House Conference Report 2693, *Creating Indian Claims Commission*, 79th Cong., 2d sess., 27 July 1946, Box 154, RG 75, William A. Brophy Desk Files.

61. House Conference Report 2693, *Creating Indian Claims Commission*, Brophy Desk Files.

62. House Conference Report 2693, *Creating Indian Claims Commission*, Brophy Desk Files.

63. House Conference Report 2693, *Creating Indian Claims Commission*, Brophy Desk Files.

64. Ernest L. Wilkinson to Joseph C. O'Mahoney, 1 August 1946, Box 104, O'Mahoney Papers.

65. Wilkinson to O'Mahoney, O'Mahoney Papers.

66. "Julius A. Krug," in *Current Biography: Who's News and Why, 1943*, ed. Judith Graham (New York: W. W. Wilson, 1944), 362–66.

67. NCAI, Convention Call, 6–9 November 1946, Oklahoma City, Box 104, O'Mahoney Papers.

68. Rosenthal, "Their Day in Court" (Ph.D. diss.), 135.

69. Julius A. Krug to President Truman, 1 August 1946, Box 64, Indian Claims Commission Papers.

70. Krug to Truman, 1 August 1946, Truman Official Files.

71. White House Press Release, Statement by the President, 13 August 1946, Truman Official Files.

72. White House Press Release, 13 August 1946, Truman Official Files; and Clayton R. Koppes, "From New Deal to Termination," 544.

73. Napoleon Bonaparte Johnson to All Indian Tribes, 1 November 1946, Box 107, Curry Papers.

74. Ruth M. Bronson, Urgent Message, 17 January 1947, Curry Papers.

75. Summary of Recommendations Made to the President for Appointments to the Indian Claims Commission, 1947, Box 65, File: Endorsements, Truman Official Files; Julius A. Krug to William A. Brophy, 5 August 1946, Box 7, Correspondence File, 1946–49, Julius A. Krug Papers; Oscar L. Chapman to President Truman, 22 August 1946, Box 58, Administrative Correspondence Files, 1939–58, Office of the Solicitor, Records; and William A. Brophy to Julius A. Krug, 14 August 1946, General Office Files of Assistant Secretary G. G. Davidson, 1946–50, Box 8, General Office File, RG 48, Washington National Records Center (WNRC).

76. Summary of Recommendations Made to the President, File: Endorsements, Truman Official Files; Editorial Notes, "Section 2 of the Indian Claims Commission Act," 389; and Rosenthal, "Their Day in Court" (Ph.D. diss.), 68, 124.

77. Rosenthal, "Their Day in Court" (Ph.D. diss.), 145.

78. Vance, "Congressional Mandate and Indian Claims Commission," 333–35.

79. Rosenthal, "Their Day in Court" (Ph.D. diss.), 180–81.

80. Mastin G. White to William A. Brophy, 24 May 1948, Box 58, Administrative Correspondence Files, 1939–58, Indian Claims Commission Act, 1946–48, Office of the Solicitor, Records.

81. Synoptic Survey of the Data on the Survival of Indian and Part-Indian Blood in the Eastern Part of the United States, Legislative Reference Department, 1945, 1–41, Box 101, O'Mahoney Papers.

82. Nancy O. Lurie, "Indian Claims Commission," 107.

83. Rosenthal, "Their Day in Court" (Ph.D. diss.), 186–87.

84. Rosenthal, "Their Day in Court" (Ph.D. diss.), 101, 147–48, 170–72; and Indian Claims Commission, Annual Report, 1972, Box 3, Edward A. Milligan Papers.

85. Rosenthal, "Their Day in Court" (Ph.D. diss.), 154.

86. Metcalf, "Arthur V. Watkins and Indians of Utah" (Ph.D. diss.), 14–21, 54, 292–97.

87. Rosenthal, "Their Day in Court" (Ph.D. diss.), 186–87.

3. ALASKA

1. William A. Brophy to Don C. Foster, 5 July 1946, Box 2, William A. Brophy Papers; and Department of Interior Press Release, 15 August 1946, Box 23, Cohen Papers.

2. Senate Committee on Interior and Insular Affairs, Hearings on S.R. 2037 and S.J.R. 162: Repeal Act, 415–16.

3. Senate Committee on Interior and Insular Affairs, Hearings on S.R. 2037 and S.J.R. 162: Repeal Act, 13.

4. Fowler Harper, Memorandum for Oscar L. Chapman, 27 April 1944, Box 13, Indians: Alaska, Chapman Office Records.

5. K. Crichton, "Storm over Alaska," 20; and Senate Committee on Interstate and Foreign Commerce, Hearings on S.R. 1446: Salmon Trap Sites, 11–12.

6. Warner W. Gardner to Julius A. Krug, 30 January 1947, Box 1, Indians: Alaska, Chapman Office Records; and Warner W. Gardner to Julius A. Krug, 12 March 1947, Chapman Office Records.

7. Warner W. Gardner to Alfred E. Widmark, 10 June 1946, Box 21, Cohen Papers.

8. Felix S. Cohen to Henry Cohen, 17 September 1947, Box 63, Curry Papers.

9. Warner W. Gardner to Julius A. Krug, 10 January 1947, Box 1, Indians: Alaska, Chapman Office Records.

10. Warner W. Gardner to Julius A. Krug, 12 March 1947, Indians: Alaska, Chapman Office Records.

11. Walter R. Goldschmidt and Theodore H. Haas, *Report to Commissioner of Indian Affairs*, 1–173, copy in Box 22, Cohen Papers; and Stephen W. Haycox, "Economic Development and Indian Land Rights in Modern Alaska," in *Alaska Anthology*, ed. Stephen W. Haycox and Mary Childers Mangusso, 343–44.

12. Goldschmidt and Haas, *Report to Commissioner of Indian Affairs*, iv, 1–5.

13. Goldschmidt and Haas, *Report to Commissioner of Indian Affairs*, iv, 1–5.

14. Charles M. Wright to Senator Julius A. Krug, 5 February 1947, Box 129, Indians: Alaska, Chapman Office Records.

15. Julius A. Krug to Senator Arthur H. Vandenberg, 11 June 1947, Box 129, Indians: Alaska, Chapman Office Records.

16. Senate Committee on Interstate and Foreign Commerce, *Hearings on S.R. 1446: Salmon Trap Sites*, 1–5, 12.

17. Senate Committee on Interstate and Foreign Commerce, *Hearings on S.R. 1446: Salmon Trap Sites*, 4, 18–19.

18. Senate Committee on Interstate and Foreign Commerce, *Hearings on S.R. 1446: Salmon Trap Sites*, 3–4.

19. Senate Committee on Interstate and Foreign Commerce, *Hearings on S.R. 1446: Salmon Trap Sites*, 14, 15, 22, 26. Ninety percent of the voters favored the abolition of fish traps in this 1948 referendum. Harold L. Ickes, "On Frisking the Alaska Indians," 19.

20. Senate Committee on Interstate and Foreign Commerce and House Committee on Merchant Marine and Fisheries, *Hearings on S.R. 1446 and H.R. 3859: Salmon Trap Sites*, 96, 111, 133, 153, 183, 191, 213, 243.

21. Senate Committee on Interstate and Foreign Commerce and House Committee on Merchant Marine and Fisheries, *Hearings on S.R. 1446 and H.R. 3859: Salmon Trap Sites*, 189–91.

22. Senate Committee on Interstate and Foreign Commerce and House Committee on Merchant Marine and Fisheries, *Hearings on S.R. 1446 and H.R. 3859: Salmon Trap Sites*, 191–96.

23. Senate Committee on Interstate and Foreign Commerce and House Committee on Merchant Marine and Fisheries, *Hearings on S.R. 1446 and H.R. 3859: Salmon Trap Sites*, 195–97.

24. Senate Committee on Interstate and Foreign Commerce and House Committee on Merchant Marine and Fisheries, *Hearings on S.R. 1446 and H.R. 3859: Salmon Trap Sites*, 195–97.

25. Ruth Muskrat Bronson, "Shall We Repeat Indian History in Alaska?" 1–11.

26. Haycox, "Economic Development and Indian Land Rights in Modern Alaska," in

Haycox and Mangusso, eds., *Alaska Anthology*, 344; E. L. Bartlett to James E. Curry, 29 May 1947, Box 26, Cohen Papers; and House Committee on Agriculture, *Hearings on H.J.R. 205 to Authorize Secretary to Sell Timber*, 16, 189.

27. James E. Curry to Ruth M. Bronson, 30 April 1947, Box 13, NCAI Papers.

28. Charles M. Wright to Judge Napoleon Bonaparte Johnson, 1 May 1947, Box 10, NCAI Papers; and James E. Curry and Charles M. Wright to the Tlingit and Haida Indians of Southeastern Alaska, 15 April 1947, Box 26, Cohen Papers.

29. Curry and Wright to Tlingit and Haida Indians, Cohen Papers; and Haycox, "Economic Development and Indian Land Rights in Modern Alaska," in Haycox and Mangusso, eds., *Alaska Anthology*, 346–47.

30. Ruth Bronson to James E. Curry, 15 May 1947, Box 138, Curry Papers; and Wright to Johnson, 1 May 1947, NCAI Papers.

31. For a full discussion of this and other events leading to the passage of the Tongass Timber Act, consult Haycox, "Economic Development and Indian Land Rights in Modern Alaska," in Haycox and Mangusso, eds., *Alaska Anthology*, 336–63 (reprinted from *Western Historical Quarterly*).

32. Haycox, "Economic Development and Indian Land Rights," in Haycox and Mangusso, eds., *Alaska Anthology*, 350.

33. House Committee on Agriculture, *Hearing on H.J.R. 205 to Authorize Secretary to Sell Timber*, 1–2.

34. House Committee on Agriculture, *Hearing on H.J.R. 205 to Authorize Secretary to Sell Timber*, 2–3.

35. House Committee on Agriculture, *Hearing on H.J.R. 205 to Authorize Secretary to Sell Timber*, 13.

36. House Committee on Agriculture, *Hearing on H.J.R. 205 to Authorize Secretary to Sell Timber*, 5–6, 8.

37. House Committee on Agriculture, *Hearing on H.J.R. 205 to Authorize Secretary to Sell Timber*, 13.

38. House Committee on Agriculture, *Hearing on H.J.R. 205 to Authorize Secretary to Sell Timber*, 54.

39. House Committee on Agriculture, *Hearing on H.J.R. 205 to Authorize Secretary to Sell Timber*, 77–82.

40. Alaska Pulp Timber Bill, Report of Alaskan Native Witnesses on Their Visit to Washington during June and July 1947, Box 61, Curry Papers; and William Paul Sr. to Don Foster, 24 June 1947, Box 63, Curry Papers.

41. House Committee on Agriculture, *Hearings on H.J.R. 205 to Authorize Secretary to Sell Timber*, 150–61.

42. Alaska Pulp Timber Bill, Report of Alaskan Native Witnesses, Curry Papers.

43. Ernest Gruening to Julius A. Krug, 18 September 1947, Box 1, Interdepartmental Committee on Alaska, Chapman Office Records; and reprint, Ruth M. Bronson, "Drama in Alaska," *New York Herald Tribune*, 8 August 1947, Box 8, James E. Murray Papers.

44. Felix S. Cohen, "Open Season on Alaskan Natives," 4–8; and James E. Curry to Felix S. Cohen, 11 August 1947, Box 63, Curry Papers.

45. Henry Cohen to James E. Curry, 16 September 1947, Box 62, Curry Papers; and James E. Curry to Henry Cohen, 13 December 1947, Curry Papers.

46. James E. Curry to the Puget Sound Pulp and Timber Company, 9 September 1947, Box 62, Curry Papers. In 1955, in *Tee-Hit-Ton Indians v. the United States*, the Court of Claims rejected the possessory claims of Tlingit Indians and James Curry's argument that the Fifth Amendment of the U.S. Constitution applied to the taking of Indian property. Congress later addressed this problem in the Alaska Native Claims Settlement Act of 1971. John R. Wunder, "*Retained by the People*," 115–18.

47. Felix S. Cohen to Secretary Julius A. Krug, 2 October 1947, Box 27, Cohen Papers.

48. Cohen to Krug, 2 October 1947, Cohen Papers.

49. Mastin G. White to Secretary Julius A. Krug, 15 October 1947, Box 27, Cohen Papers; and Department of Interior Press Release, 16 October 1947, Box 46, Cohen Papers.

50. Senate Committee on Interior and Insular Affairs, *Hearings on S.R. 2037 and S.J.R. 162: Repeal Act*, 74–79; NCAI Press Release, "Indians Take Over Alaskan Timber Sales," 12 November 1947, Box 63, Curry Papers; and James E. Curry to Harold L. Ickes, 25 October 1947, Box 62, Curry Papers.

51. Felix S. Cohen, Memorandum for the Files, 10 December 1947, Box 42, Cohen Papers; and "Copy of Felix S. Cohen's Resignation and Acceptance by Secretary Julius Krug," *Ketchikan (Alaska) Daily News*, 30 December 1947, Box 90, Cohen Papers.

52. Felix S. Cohen, "Breaking Faith with Our First Americans," 1–7.

53. "Sawmill at Kake Expected to Prove Test Case for Taking of Timber in Alaska," *Ketchikan Daily News*, 23 January 1948, Box 27, Cohen Papers; and Felix S. Cohen, Memorandum for the File, 19 May 1948, Cohen Papers.

54. Press Release, Kake, Alaska, 5 April 1948, Cohen Papers; and Cohen, "Breaking Faith with Our First Americans," 1–7.

55. Senate Committee on Interior and Insular Affairs, *Hearings on S.R. 2037 and S.J.R. 162: Repeal Act*, 1–2. Senator Hugh Butler's parochial settler views, anti–New Deal conservatism, and anti-communist perspectives are discussed in Justus F. Paul, *Senator Hugh Butler and Nebraska Republicanism*.

56. Senate Committee on Interior and Insular Affairs, *Hearings on S.R. 2037 and S.J.R. 162: Repeal Act*, 542, 547.

57. Senate Committee on Interior and Insular Affairs, *Hearings on S.R. 2037 and S.J.R. 162: Repeal Act*, 313.

58. Hugh Butler to Julius A. Krug, 3 March 1948, Box 24, Cohen Papers.

59. Senate Committee on Interior and Insular Affairs, *Hearings on S.R. 2037 and S.J.R. 162: Repeal Act*, 572, 575.

60. Senate Committee on Interior and Insular Affairs, *Hearings on S.R. 2037 and S.J.R. 162: Repeal Act*, 569–70, 590.

61. Senate, *Rescinding Certain Orders of Secretary of Interior Establishing Indian Reservations in Alaska*, copy in Box 24, Cohen Papers; and Report of James E. Curry, General Counsel to the NCAI Denver Convention, 12 December 1948, Box 12, NCAI Papers.

62. Message from the President of the United States, Statehood for Alaska, 80th Cong., 2d sess., 21 May 1948, Box 40, Stephen Springharn Papers.

63. House Committee on Public Lands, *H.R. 7002: Bill to Settle Land Claims in Alaska*, copy in Box 61, Curry Papers.

64. House Committee on Public Lands, *H.R. 7002: Bill to Settle Land Claims in Alaska*, Curry Papers; and Frances Lopinsky to Ruth M. Bronson, 29 January 1949, Box 61, Curry Papers.

65. James E. Curry to Secretary of State George C. Marshall, 22 September 1948, Box 27, Curry Papers; and Charter of the United Nations (San Francisco, 1946), 23–24.

66. Conference no. 2, Native Claims Bill, 10 December 1948, Alaska Development Program, Box 73, Krug Papers; and Felix S. Cohen to Oliver LaFarge, 28 April 1949, Box 154, RG 75, Brophy Desk Files.

67. Memorandum from the National Advisory Committee on Indian Affairs to Julius A. Krug, 4 March 1949, Box 68, Krug Papers. Advisory committee members besides LaFarge and Bronson were Mark Dawber, executive secretary, Home Missions Council; E. P. Carville, former Nevada governor and senator; W. Carson Ryan, professor of education, University of North Carolina; Clyde Kluckhohn, professor of anthropology, Harvard; Roland Renne, president, Montana State College; Ruth Kirk, General Federation of Women's Clubs; Barry Goldwater, Goldwater Department Store; and Louis R. Bruce, Mohawk dairy farmer and executive secretary of the NCAI. Department of Interior, *Annual Report of the Commissioner*, 1949, 363–64.

68. Memorandum from the National Advisory Committee on Indian Affairs to Krug, 4 March 1949, Krug Papers.

69. James E. Curry to Cyrus Peck, 20 May 1949, Box 61, Curry Papers; and Stephen Springharn to Clark M. Clifford, 28 April 1949, Box 1, Clark M. Clifford Files.

70. Springharn to Clifford, 28 April 1949, Clifford Files.

71. David K. Niles, Memorandum for President Truman, 2 May 1949, Box 1, Alaska Indian Claims, Philleo Nash Files; and Harry S. Truman to Julius A. Krug, 4 May 1949, Box 40, Springharn Papers.

72. Clayton Koppes, "Oscar L. Chapman" (Ph.D. diss.), 169–70.

73. Koppes, "Oscar L. Chapman" (Ph.D. diss.); and William E. Warne to Harold L. Ickes, 30 January 1950, Box 28, Cohen Papers.

74. William E. Warne to Harold L. Ickes, 6 December 1949, Box 64, Alaska Native Rights, Department of Interior Central Files; Ernest Gruening to Oscar L. Chapman, 12 January 1950, Box 211, Butler Papers; and Department of Interior Press Release, "Krug Reserves Barrow Area," 30 November 1949, Box 46, Cohen Papers.

75. Report of James E. Curry, NCAI Papers.

4. FAIR DEAL FOR NAVAJOS

1. Newspaper Clipping, "Navajo Delegates Leave for Washington to Air Reservation Problems," 11 May 1946, Box 101, O'Mahoney Papers.

2. Notes on the meeting of the Navajo Tribal Delegation, Proceedings of the Delegation of the Navajo Tribal Council, 13–25 May 1946, 2–4, Box 22, RG 75, WNRC.

3. Notes on Navajo Tribal Delegation, 6–10, WNRC.

4. Notes on Navajo Tribal Delegation, 8–9, WNRC.

5. Notes on Navajo Tribal Delegation, 9–10, WNRC.

6. Notes on Navajo Tribal Delegation, 11–13, WNRC.

7. Notes on Navajo Tribal Delegation, 11–13, WNRC.

8. Notes on Navajo Tribal Delegation, 11–13, WNRC.

9. Notes of Navajo Tribal Delegation, 18–21, WNRC; and George Boyce, *When Navajos Had Too Many Sheep*, 193.

10. Members of the Native American Church to President Harry S. Truman, 15 July 1946, Box 19, RG 75, WNRC.

11. For a discussion of how stock reduction made the Navajos a dependent people, consult Richard White, *Roots of Dependency*, 250–314.

12. Bernstein, *American Indians and World War II*, 49, 67–68, 133–37.

13. Will Rogers Jr., "Starvation without Representation," 36; and Ruth F. Kirk, "Navajo's Tragedy," 176–81.

14. Pamphlet, *More about Navajo Education*, New Mexico Association on Indian Affairs, November 1946, Box 191, RG 75, WNRC.

15. Boyce, *When Navajos Had Too Many Sheep*, 178–79; and Kirk, "Navajo's Tragedy," 176–81.

16. Department of Interior, Post-War Resources Institute, Washington DC, 5–9 November 1945, Box 14, Chapman Office Records.

17. Department of Interior, Post-War Resources Institute, Chapman Office Records.

18. William A. Brophy to Ward Shepard, 15 May 1945, Chapman Office Records; and Ward Shepard, "Reorienting Indian Education and Extension in the Wake of the Wheeler-Howard Act," 15 August 1934, Box 40, Cohen Papers.

19. Ward Shepard, "New Grotons on the Old Navajo Desert: A Critical Analysis of Fiscal Sky-Writing," 8 November 1946, Box 8, Brophy Papers.

20. William A. Brophy to Mrs. Stanley Manlove, 19 June 1946, Box 2, Brophy Papers.

21. William A. Brophy to Julius A. Krug, Report on Southwestern Trip, 18 September 1946, Box 191, RG 75, WNRC; Willard W. Beatty to Washington Office, 26 September 1946, Box 191, Navajo, RG 75, WNRC. For a firsthand account of the Special Navajo Education Program, consult Hildegard Thompson, *Navajos Long Walk for Education*, 88–117.

22. Brophy to Krug, Report on Southwestern Trip, WNRC; Margaret Szasz, *Education and the American Indian*, 116–17; Boyce, *When Navajos Had Too Many Sheep*, 197–200; and "Report on the Navajo Experiment at Sherman Institute, 1946–1947," Box 191, Navajo, RG 75, WNRC.

23. Boyce, *When Navajos Had Too Many Sheep*, 175–76.

24. Secretary Krug's Talk to the Navajo Council, 16 September 1946, Box 3452, Department of Interior Central Files.

25. George I. Sanchez, *People*, 25–28, 33–38.

26. Sanchez, *People*, 37–38, 45.

27. Szasz, *Education and the American Indian*, 117; and Department of Interior Press Release, "A School for 2,000 Navajos," 27 May 1949, Box 174, Navajo, RG 75, WNRC.

28. Carl Carmer, ed., Editorial, "Navajo Institute Report," 1–3; and Boyce, *When Navajos Had Too Many Sheep*, 178–80.

29. Boyce, *When Navajos Had Too Many Sheep*, 210–13.

30. Congressional Hearing, 21 October 1947, Navajo Agency, Window Rock, Arizona, 5–6, Box 170, RG 75, WNRC; and William E. Warne, The Navajo: Problem and Plan, 21 October 1947, Box 154, Brophy Desk Files.

31. Warne, Navajo, Brophy Desk Files; and William E. Warne to Secretary Julius A. Krug, 17 December 1947, Box 3452, Department of Interior Central Files.

32. Warne to Krug, 17 December 1947, Department of Interior Central Files; and Harry S. Truman to Secretary Julius A. Krug, 10 November 1947, Box 937, Truman Official Files.

33. Press Release, Statement by the President, 2 December 1947, Box 937, Truman Official Files; and Secretary Julius A. Krug, Report to the President on the Conditions of the Navajo Indians, 2 December 1947, Truman Official Files.

34. Summary of Navajo Developments, 8 April 1949, Box 174, Navajo, RG 75, WNRC; and Lucy W. Adams to All Navajo Traders, the Navajo Employment Service, 26 March 1948, Box 3453, Navajo Administrative, Department of Interior Central Files.

35. Krug, Report to the President, Truman Official Files; and Jonathan M. Steere, "Navajo Rehabilitation," 1–7.

36. "NCAI Considers Indian Office Change: Ahkeah Blames U.S. for Plight," *Gallup Independent*, 6 December 1947, Box 2, NCAI Papers.

37. Napoleon Bonaparte Johnson to Sam Ahkeah, 1 January 1948, NCAI Papers.

38. Lucy W. Adams to Elizabeth Chief, 19 August 1949, Box 50, Cohen Papers; Sam

Ahkeah, Exhibit H on Elizabeth Chief, 19 October 1949, Cohen Papers; and Felix S. Cohen to Elizabeth Chief, 10 March 1950, Cohen Papers.

39. "Indian Council Attorney Tells Navajo to Defy Grazing Rules," *Arizona Daily Star*, 25 February 1948, Box 121, Curry Papers; and Donald L. Parman, *Navajos and the New Deal*, 289.

40. Minutes of the Proceedings of the Fifth NCAI Annual Convention, 13–16 December 1948, Denver, Box 2, NCAI Papers.

41. Rogers, "Starvation without Representation," 38–40.

42. Rogers, "Starvation without Representation," 38–40.

43. Robert K. Carr to Members of the President's Committee on Civil Rights, Civil Rights of American Indians, 6 June 1947, Box 15, President's Committee on Civil Rights, Truman Official Files; and Testimony by D'Arcy McNickle before the President's Committee on Civil Rights, 15 May 1947, Box 138, Curry Papers.

44. Felix S. Cohen, "Indian Wardship," 9.

45. NCAI Press Release, Indian Vote Means Social Security, 6 August 1948, Box 152, Curry Papers; Felix S. Cohen to Philleo Nash, 5 October 1950, Box 23, Nash Files; and Department of Interior, *Annual Report of the Commissioner*, 1949, 361.

46. Nathan R. Margold, The Applicability of the Social Security Act to Indians, 22 April 1936, Box 13, Indians: Social Security, Chapman Office Records.

47. R. M. Tisinger to William Zimmerman, 10 September 1941, Chapman Office Records; and William Zimmerman to Julius A. Krug, Box 3528, Indian Office, Department of Interior Central Files.

48. All Pueblo Council Press Release, Indians Win Social Security, 17 June 1947, Box 30, Nash Files; Felix S. Cohen to the Officers of the All Pueblo Council, 19 October 1950, Box 23, Nash Files.

49. Felix S. Cohen, "Our Country's Shame," copy in J. Howard McCrath Papers; and William Zimmerman to Secretary Julius A. Krug, 22 July 1948, Box 3528, Department of Interior Central Files.

50. NCAI Press Release, 21 September 1948, NCAI Papers; *Frank Mapatis vs. Oscar R. Ewing*, U.S. District Court for the District of Columbia, NCAI Papers.

51. Secretary Julius A. Krug, Report on the Long-Range Program of Navajo Rehabilitation, March 1948, Box 3451, Department of Interior Central Files.

52. Krug, Report on the Long-Range Program, Department of Interior Central Files; and Secretary Julius A. Krug to Richard F. Harless, 19 May 1948, Box 3453, Department of Interior Central Files.

53. Sam Ahkeah to John Tabor, 19 March 1948, Box 30, Nash Files.

54. Ahkeah to Tabor, 19 March 1948, Nash Files.

55. Ahkeah to Tabor, 19 March 1948, Nash Files; Richard Drinnon, *Keeper of Concentration Camps*, 40; and Donald Parman, *Navajos and the New Deal*, 283.

56. Boyce, *When Navajos Had Too Many Sheep*, 231; and Robert A. Hecht, *Oliver LaFarge and the American Indian*, 183–84.

57. Proceedings of the Navajo Advisory Committee, 16 October 1948, 64, 67, RG 75, WNRC.

58. Proceedings of the Navajo Advisory Committee, 16 October 1948, 62, 66–69, WNRC.

59. William Zimmerman to Sam Ahkeah, 24 November 1948, Box 3453, Department of Interior Central Files.

60. "Aerial Shuttle Relieves Snow-Marooned Indians," *Arizona Daily Star*, February 1949, Box 121, Curry Papers; "Snow Stricken Navajo Tribe Facing Disease, Hunger, Cold," 2 February 1949, Curry Papers; "State Haylift Hits Peak Day," 7 February 1949, Curry Papers.

61. Report of Relief Activities of the American National Red Cross on the Navajo-Hopi Reservations, Spring 1949, Box 211, Butler Papers.

62. Hecht, *Oliver LaFarge and the American Indian*, 185; Rehabilitation of the Navajo and Hopi Tribes, Veto Message from the President of the United States, Returning S.R. 1407, 81st Cong., 1st sess., 17 October 1949, Box 938, Truman Official Files.

63. Hopi Chieftains to President Harry S. Truman, 28 March 1949, Box 99, Hopi, RG 75, WNRC.

64. John H. Province to Oscar L. Chapman, Analysis of Section 9 of the Navajo–Hopi Rehabilitation Bill, S.R. 1407, 3 October 1949, Box 14, Indian Affairs, Chapman Office Records; and Rehabilitation of the Navajo and Hopi Tribes, Truman Official Files.

65. Clinton P. Anderson to Harold L. Ickes, 25 July 1949, Box 62, Ickes Papers.

66. Minutes of the Navajo Tribal Council Meeting, 11–14 October 1949, Box 172, Navajo, RG 75, WNRC.

67. Minutes of the Navajo Tribal Council Meeting, 11–14 October 1949, 5, 11, 17, WNRC.

68. Minutes of the Navajo Tribal Council Meeting, 10 June 1949, 45–46, WNRC.

69. Minutes of the Navajo Tribal Council Meeting, 10 June 1949, 38, WNRC.

70. Minutes of the Navajo Tribal Council Meeting, 10 June 1949, 47–49, 65, WNRC.

71. Sam Ahkeah to Reva Beck Bosone, 16 September 1949, Box 17, Reva Beck Bosone Papers.

72. Sam Ahkeah to Members of the Joint Conference Committee, 16 September 1949, Bosone Papers; Ernest W. McFarland and Toby Morris to Julius A. Krug, 13 October 1949, Box 41, Springharn Papers; and Eleanor Roosevelt, "To Arms, Indians: The Congressmen Are Coming," *Washington Daily News*, 5 October 1949.

73. John Collier to Clark M. Clifford, 12 October 1949, Box 7, Clifford Files; Eleanor Roosevelt to Harry S. Truman, 16 October 1949, Box 937, Truman Official Files; and Harold L. Ickes to President Harry S. Truman, 10 October 1949, Box 938, Truman Official Files.

74. Oliver LaFarge to Harry S. Truman, 8 October 1949, Box 938, Truman Official Files; and Hecht, *Oliver LaFarge and the American Indian*, 187–88.

75. Minutes of the Navajo Tribal Council Meeting, 11–14 October 1949, WNRC.

76. Minutes of the Navajo Tribal Council Meeting, 11–14 October 1949, 23, WNRC.

77. Minutes of the Navajo Tribal Council Meeting, 11–14 October 1949, 27, 36–37, WNRC.

78. Minutes of the Navajo Tribal Council Meeting, 11–14 October 1949, 46–53, WNRC.

79. Minutes of the Navajo Tribal Council Meeting, 11–14 October 1949, 57–59, 62, WNRC.

80. Julius A. Krug to Frank Pace, 15 October 1949, Box 31, Nash Files; Charles S. Murphy to President Harry S. Truman, 17 October 1949, Box 41, Springharn Papers; and Harold L. Ickes to John Collier, 15 October 1949, Box 62, Ickes Papers.

81. Harry S. Truman to Harold L. Ickes, 25 October 1949, Box 90, Ickes Papers; and Harry S. Truman, Veto Message to the Senate, 17 October 1949, Box 938, Truman Official Files.

82. Truman, Veto Message, Truman Official Files; and Statement by President Harry S. Truman, 19 April 1950, Box 41, Springharn Papers.

83. Remarks of the President to a Group from the Navajo Tribal Council in the Rose Garden, 21 February 1952, Box 23, Nash Files.

84. Jonathan M. Steere, "Crucial Needs of Navajo Indians Presented by Superintendent Allan Harper," 2; and Kenneth R. Philp, ed., *Indian Self-Rule*, 89.

85. Jonathan M. Steere, "Appropriations–1953," 5.

5. EMANCIPATION

1. Consult Frederick E. Hoxie, *Final Promise*, for an analysis of how this assimilation movement was altered after 1900 to make Indians a peripheral people.

2. For a discussion of how American political ideology was linked to the Cold War, see Thomas G. Paterson, *On Every Front*, 69–83.

3. Vernon D. Northrop to William A. Brophy, 27 April 1945, Box 14, Indian Office, Chapman Office Records.

4. Memorandum from Fred H. Daiker, 1 April 1946, Box 7, S. Lyman Tyler Papers.

5. Minutes of the Meeting of the Tribal Council of the Confederated Salish and Kootenai Tribes of the Flathead Reservation, 16 September 1946, Box 8, Indian Affairs, Davidson General Office Files.

6. Minutes of the Meeting of the Tribal Council, 16 September 1946, Davidson General Office Files; and Dorothy R. Parker, "D'Arcy McNickle," 4.

7. Minutes of the Meeting of the Tribal Council, 16 September 1946, Davidson General Office Files.

8. Charles M. Wright to William A. Brophy, 18 June 1947, Box 8, Indian Affairs, Davidson General Office Files.

9. Paul L. Fickinger to William Zimmerman, 2 January 1948, Box 3531, Administrative Reorganization, Department of Interior Central Files.

10. Senate Committee on Civil Service, *Hearings on S.R. 41: Officers and Employees*, 79–80, 96, 245, 249, 251, 255, 257.

11. House Committee on Indian Affairs, *Hearings on H.R. 166: Bill to Authorize Investigation*, pt. 2:61–63.

12. Senate Committee on Civil Service, *Hearings on S.R. 41: Officers and Employees*, 544–45.

13. Senate Committee on Civil Service, *Hearings on S.R. 41: Officers and Employees*, 547, 569. For an estimate of the number of people included in Zimmerman's three groups, see John H. Province, The Withdrawal of Federal Supervision over the American Indian, February 1949, Box 4, J. W. Wellington Papers.

14. Senate Committee on Civil Service, *Hearings on S.R. 41: Officers and Employees*, 585–91.

15. Department of Interior, *Annual Report of the Commissioner*, 1947, 351–52.

16. House Committee on Public Lands, *Hearings on H.R. 2958, H.R. 2165, and H.R. 1113: Emancipation of Indians*, 1–7, 33, 52.

17. Haven Emerson, Statement on H.R. 1113 to Emancipate United States Indians in Certain Cases, 1948, Box 8, Murray Papers.

18. Haven Emerson to Helen Gahagen Douglas, 25 February 1948, Box 512, AAIA Papers; and Haven Emerson to Arthur V. Watkins, 14 January 1948, Box 51, AAIA Papers.

19. Oscar L. Chapman to Senator Hugh Butler, 13 January 1948, Box 130, AAIA Papers; and Julius A. Krug to Senator Hugh Butler, 4 May 1948, Box 71, Curry Papers.

20. Chapman to Butler, 13 January 1948, Curry Papers; and Emerson to Watkins, 14 January 1948, AAIA Papers.

21. Department of Interior Press Release, "California Chosen for Test of Indian Policy," 11 February 1948, Box 71, Curry Papers.

22. William E. Pemberton, *Bureaucratic Politics*, 79–89.

23. Bureau of Indian Affairs, Information Circular, June 1948, Box 3, Wellington Papers.

24. Commission on Organization of Executive Branch of Government, *Report on Social Security, Education, and Indian Affairs*, 1–2, 54–55, 62–69, 156; and Commission on Organization of the Executive Branch of Government, *Final Commission Report on Indian Affairs*, 17 December 1948, 1–160, Box 22, Indian Affairs, Dean Acheson Papers.

25. Commission on Organization, *Final Commission Report on Indian Affairs*, 2, 57, 61, 68, 72, 103–7, Acheson Papers.

26. Commission on Organization, *Final Commission Report on Indian Affairs*, 7, 69, Acheson Papers.

27. Commission on Organization, *Final Commission Report on Indian Affairs*, 5–7, Acheson Papers.

28. Commission on Organization, *Final Commission Report on Indian Affairs*, 6–7, 87, 91, 97–99, Acheson Papers.

29. Commission on Organization, *Final Commission Report on Indian Affairs*, 6, 72, 82–86, Acheson Papers.

30. Commission on Organization, *Final Commission Report on Indian Affairs*, 5, 121–28, Acheson Papers.

31. Commission on Organization, *Final Commission Report on Indian Affairs*, 139, Acheson Papers.

32. Commission on Organization, *Final Commission Report on Indian Affairs*, 63–67, 154–59, Acheson Papers.

33. Commission on Organization, *Final Commission Report on Indian Affairs*, 9, 164–69, Acheson Papers.

34. Commission on Organization, *Final Commission Report on Indian Affairs*, 14–15, Acheson Papers; and Commission on Organization, *Report on Social Security, Education, and Indian Affairs*, 77, 79, 80.

35. Commission on Organization, *Report on Social Security, Education, and Indian Affairs*.

36. Address by William Zimmerman Jr. before the Annual Meeting of the Home Missions Council, Buck Hill Falls, Pennsylvania, 12 January 1949, Box 4, Wellington Papers.

37. Address by Zimmerman, Wellington Papers.

38. William Warne to Julius A. Krug, 9 February 1949, Box 68, Krug Papers; and Julius A. Krug to William Warne, 20 December 1949, Box 32, Krug Papers.

39. Dillon S. Myer, *Autobiography of Dillon S. Myer*, University of California, Regional Oral History Office, 1970, 244–45; and E. Raymond Ormsby to Harry Truman, 6 April 1949, Box 58, Truman Official Files.

40. Qualifications of John Ralph Nichols as Commissioner of Indian Affairs, 24 February 1949, Box 58, Truman Official Files; Newspaper Clipping, "Educator Is Named Indian Affairs Chief," 16 March 1949, Truman Official Files; and Harold L. Ickes to Clinton P. Anderson, 2 August 1949, Box 62, Ickes Papers.

41. Ruth M. Bronson to Julius A. Krug, 10 June 1949, Advisory Committee, Indian Affairs, Department of Interior Central Files.

42. William Langer, "Notes on Confirmation," 1949, Box 216, William Langer Papers; and Hugh Butler to John R. Nichols, 22 March 1949, Box 211, Butler Papers.

43. Department of Interior, *Annual Report of the Commissioner*, 1949, 338–39.

44. Department of Interior, *Annual Report of the Commissioner*, 1949, 341–42, 345, 348, 351, 353, 355; and Statement of Commissioner John R. Nichols, Bureau of Indian Affairs, 1949, Box 154, Desk Files of John R. Nichols.

45. Statement of Nichols, 1949, Nichols Desk Files.

46. Statement of Nichols, 1949, Nichols Desk Files.

47. Digest of Statement of John R. Nichols, Commissioner of Indian Affairs, 1949, Box 102, AAIA Papers; and Memorandum on Appropriation Bills for 1949–50, Box 102, AAIA Papers.

48. John R. Nichols to Central Office Staff, 15 August 1949, Box 154, Nichols Desk Files.

49. John Collier to Superintendents, Tribal Councils, All Indian Service Personnel, Circular 3537, Planning, RG 3, Mundt Papers.

50. John R. Nichols to Central Office Staff, 15 August 1949, Box 154, Nichols Desk Files.

51. Nichols to Central Office Staff, 15 August 1949, Nichols Desk Files; and Department of Interior, *Annual Report of the Commissioner*, 1949, 337.

52. AAIA Press Release, Current Issues in Indian Affairs, June 1949, Box 22, Nash Files.

53. Felix S. Cohen, Memorandum on Recent Legislative Developments in Indian Affairs, 21 June 1950, Box 23, Nash Files.

54. Elmer B. Staats to Senator Joseph C. O'Mahoney, 15 May 1950, Box 2, Murray Papers; and F. J. Lawton to Joseph C. O'Mahoney, 21 December 1950, RG 3, Mundt Papers.

55. Hugh Butler to Mrs. Charles H. Dietrich, 28 September 1949, Box 211, Butler Papers; and George W. Malone, "Tear Up the Indian Bureau by the Roots," Reprint, *Congressional Record*, 81st Cong., 2d sess., 17 October 1949, Box 17, Bosone Papers.

56. Forrest E. Cooper to William Langer, 31 January 1947, Box 179, Langer Papers.

57. Address by Theodore H. Haas, Sixth Convention of the NCAI, Rapid City, South Dakota, 22 September 1949, Box 9, Tyler Papers.

58. AAIA Press Release, "Why an Institute on American Indian Self-Government," 8 April 1949, Box 66, Cohen Papers; and Guest List Dais, Cohen Papers.

59. Speech by John Collier, 8 April 1949, Institute on American Indian Self-Government, Box 4, Wellington Papers.

60. Felix S. Cohen, "Indian Self-Government," 3–12.

61. Cohen, "Indian Self-Government."

62. Cohen, "Indian Self-Government."

63. Allan G. Harper, "Economic Factors in Self-Government," 18–21.

64. Theodore H. Haas, "Administration and Self-Government," 40–43.

65. Haas, "Administration and Self-Government," 40–43.

66. John F. Embree, "Indian Bureau and Self-Government," 11–14; and Philp, *John Collier's Crusade for Indian Reform*, 207.

67. Embree, "Indian Bureau and Self-Government," 11–14.

68. Embree, "Indian Bureau and Self-Government," 11–14.

69. Oliver LaFarge, Restatement of Program Policy in Indian Affairs, 8 February 1950, Box 77, Nash Files.

70. Alexander Lesser, Comment on LaFarge Statement, 8 February 1950, Nash Files.

71. Lesser, Comment on LaFarge Statement, Nash Files.

72. Certificate of Incorporation of ARROW, 1 July 1949, Box 107, Curry Papers; Maurice Rosenblatt, Introduction: A Summary Discussion to Organize ARROW, 23 November 1949, Curry Papers.

73. Will Rogers Jr., "Launching of ARROW: National Organization to Rehabilitate Indians," 10 October 1949, Box 22, Nash Files.

74. Jonathan M. Steere, "Governors' Conference on Indian Affairs," 5; and *New York Times*, 15 March 1950, 35; 13 May 1950, 17; 21 May 1950, 67.

75. Steere, "Governors' Conference on Indian Affairs," 3.

76. *Washington Star*, March 1950, 23; and Jonathan M. Steere, "New Commissioner of Indian Affairs," 2–3.

6. PATERNALISM TO INDEPENDENCE

1. "Dillon S. Myer," in *Current Biography: Who's News and Why, 1947*, ed. Anna Roethe (New York: W. W. Wilson, 1948), 462–63. For a critical assessment of Myer's formative years, consult Richard Drinnon, *Keeper of Concentration Camps*, 11–25.

2. Drinnon, *Keeper of Concentration Camps*, 80–116; and Edward Spicer, Asael T. Hansen, Katherine Luomara, and Marvin Opler, *Impounded People*, 17–21.

3. Myer, *Autobiography*, 252–54; and William E. Warne, "Plight of the American Indian," 45.

4. Address by Commissioner Dillon S. Myer before the Western Governors Conference, Phoenix, 9 December 1952, Box 155, Myer Desk Files; Dillon S. Myer, *Program of Bureau of Indian Affairs*, 12; and Dillon S. Myer to the Secretary of Interior, 20 March 1953, Box 2, Government Agencies File, Dillon S. Myer Papers.

5. Myer, *Program of Bureau of Indian Affairs*, 1–3.

6. Myer, *Program of Bureau of Indian Affairs*, 13.

7. Myer, *Program of Bureau of Indian Affairs*, 13–15.

8. Theodore H. Haas to Oscar L. Chapman, 5 June 1950, Box 136, AAIA Papers; General Washington Situation, 16 February 1952, AAIA Papers; Dillon S. Myer, "Cohen Statement," undated, Box 2, Myer Papers; Jonathan M. Steere, "Zimmerman Transferred from Indian Service," 5–6; Harold L. Ickes to William Denman, 4 September 1951, Box 62, Ickes Papers; and Clayton R. Koppes, "Oscar L. Chapman" (Ph.D. diss.), 174.

9. Steere, "Zimmerman Transferred from Indian Service," 5–6.

10. Reva Beck Bosone, "Ladies and Gentlemen of the Radio Audience" (undated), Box 10, Bosone Papers; Statement of Reva Beck Bosone, Answering Criticism of H.R. 490, 26 September 1950, Box 17, Bosone Papers; and House Committee on Public Lands, *Authorizing Study with Regard to Qualifications of Indian Tribes*, copy in Box 17, Bosone Papers.

11. Remarks by Dillon S. Myer, Billings Area Conference, 22 August 1950, Box 4,

Wellington Papers; and Dillon S. Myer to Charles de Y. Elkus, 4 August 1950, Box 155, Myer Desk Files.

12. Oscar L. Chapman to J. Hardin Peterson, 25 July 1950, Box 62, Ickes Papers.

13. Editorial, "Indians Might Do Better with Less Protection," *Saturday Evening Post* 223 (23 July 1950): 10, Box 17, Bosone Papers.

14. Frank Tom-Pee-Saw to Reva Bosone, 12 August 1950, Box 17, Bosone Papers; F. G. Collett to Joseph C. O'Mahoney, 15 August 1950, Bosone Papers; and James E. Curry to Frank McCulloch, 19 September 1950, Box 62, Ickes Papers.

15. Ruth Bronson to Harold L. Ickes, 16 September 1950, Ickes Papers.

16. William Fire Thunder, Press Release, 5 October 1950, Box 17, Bosone Papers.

17. Harold L. Ickes to John Collier, 22 July 1950, Box 62, Ickes Papers; Harold L. Ickes to President Harry S. Truman, 1 September 1950, Ickes Papers; and Harry S. Truman to Harold L. Ickes, 8 September 1950, Box 90, Ickes Papers.

18. Senate, *Congressional Record*, 15 December 1950, 16769, Box 17, Bosone Papers.

19. Remarks by Commissioner Myer, 22 August 1950, Box 4, Wellington Papers; and Address of Commissioner Dillon S. Myer to the Navajo Tribal Council, 13 September 1950, Myer Desk Files.

20. Statement of Commissioner Dillon S. Myer before the NCAI, Bellingham, Washington, 29 August 1950, Box 155, Myer Desk Files.

21. Discussion Period with Commissioner Dillon S. Myer, 29 August 1950, Box 2, NCAI Papers.

22. Cohen, "Our Country's Shame"; Department of Interior, Annual Report of the Commissioner, 1948, 391, and 1950, 364; House Committee on Interior and Insular Affairs, *Hearings on State Legal Jurisdiction in Indian Country*, 45–48; and Senate Committee on Indian Affairs, *Hearings on Nomination of William A. Brophy*, 133–45. Also consult Peter Iverson, "Building toward Self-Determination," 162–73.

23. Newspaper Clipping, "Rogers for Myer for Indian Post," 5 January 1949, Box 121, Curry Papers; and Avery Winnemucca to James E. Curry, 13 October 1950, Box 144, Curry Papers.

24. House Committee on Public Lands, *Emancipation of Indians*, 4–5, 12–32, 62–63, 77, 93, 103–4, 121–22, 157, 163–64.

25. Felix S. Cohen to Louis R. Bruce Jr., 21 April 1950, Box 64, Office of the Solicitor, Records; Laurence Hauptman, *Iroquois and the New Deal*, 177–83; and Louis R. Bruce Jr., "Indian Trail to Success," 77–80, copy in Box 10, NCAI Papers.

26. "A Condensed History of the Governors' Interstate Indian Council," Menominee Study Committee, Box 4, Wisconsin State Historical Society, Madison; and Editorial, "New Trails for Indians?" 507–8.

27. "Condensed History of the Governors' Interstate Indian Council," Wisconsin State Historical Society.

28. "Condensed History of the Governors' Interstate Indian Council," Wisconsin State Historical Society; Newspaper Clipping, *Santa Fe New Mexican*, 15 August 1952; and "Liquidation of Indian Service Is Requested," *Miles City (Montana) Star*, 11 December 1951, Box 55, AAIA Papers; and Proceedings of Fourth National Meeting, Governors' Interstate Indian Council, Helena, Montana, 10–11 December 1951, Box 18, Wayne Morse Papers.

29. Department of Interior, *Annual Report of the Commissioner*, 1952, 392; and Newspaper Clipping, "Ruling from Indians to Spend Own Money," 27 June 1951, Box 62, Ickes Papers.

30. Department of Interior, *Annual Report of the Commissioner*, 1952.

31. Department of Interior, *Annual Report of the Commissioner*, 1951, 368–69, and 1952, 405. For a discussion of Indian migration during the early years of the twentieth century, consult Lewis Meriam, *Problem of Indian Administration*, 667–742.

32. Myer, "Cohen Statement," undated, 30, Myer Papers.

33. Newspaper Clipping, "Indian Bureau Moves to Transfer Functions," February 1953, Box 3, Wellington Papers; and Dillon S. Myer to All Area Directors, 21 March 1952, Box 2, Myer Papers.

34. Myer to All Area Directors, 21 March 1952, Myer Papers.

35. Robert M. Kvasnicka and Herman J. Viola, eds., *Commissioners of Indian Affairs*, 193–202; and Hoxie, *Final Promise*, 189–90.

36. Department of Interior, *Annual Report of the Commissioner*, 1951, 360–61; Newspaper Clipping, "Chapman Appoints Woman to Head Indian Education," 25 January 1952, Box 5, Richard Searles Desk Files.

37. Francis Paul Prucha, *Great Father*, 704; and "Oscar L. Chapman," *Current Biography, 1949*, ed. Anna Roethe (New York: W. W. Wilson, 1950), 102.

38. Oscar L. Chapman to President Harry S. Truman, 9 November 1951, Box 58, Truman Official Files; Department of Interior, *Annual Report of the Commissioner*, 1951, 377, and 1952, 399; and Prucha, *Great Father*, 2:1153.

39. Dillon S. Myer, "Identical Letters Sent to All Area Directors," 18 February 1953, Box 2, Myer Papers.

40. Dillon S. Myer to Secretary of the Interior, 20 March 1953, Myer Papers; Haven Emerson to Senator Joseph C. O'Mahoney, 27 May 1952, Box 210, Butler Papers; Oscar L. Chapman to A. E. Miller, January 1953, Box 2, Myer Papers; and Prucha, *Great Father*, 2:1073.

41. Address by Commissioner Dillon S. Myer before the Combined Assemblies of the Division of Christian Life and Work of the National Council of Churches of Christ, Buck Hill Falls, Pennsylvania, 12 December 1951, Box 155, Myer Desk Files.

42. D'Arcy McNickle, "Its Almost Never Too Late," *Christian Century*, 20 February

1957, 1–7, Box 4, Murray Papers; and Oliver LaFarge to President Harry S. Truman, 27 August 1951, Box 938, Truman Official Files.

43. Napoleon Bonaparte Johnson to President Harry S. Truman, 27 August 1951, Truman Official Files; and William D. Hassett to Napoleon Bonaparte Johnson, 20 September 1951, Truman Official Files.

44. Address by Dillon S. Myer before the Combined Assemblies, 12 December 1951, Myer Papers. Other disadvantaged groups besides Indians that migrated from rural areas to cities between 1940 and 1960 were southern African Americans, Spanish Americans, and whites from Appalachia. For an introduction to the literature on this subject, consult Daniel O. Price and Melanie Sikes, *Rural-Urban Migration Research in the United States*, 1–250.

45. Address by Dillon S. Myer before the Combined Assemblies, 12 December 1951, Myer Papers; and Dillon S. Myer, "The Federal Government and the States in Indian Administration," Phoenix, 9 December 1952, Box 2, Myer Papers.

46. Newspaper Clipping, *New Town News*, 10 September 1953, Box 506, Langer Papers; Address by Dillon S. Myer before the Western Governors Conference, Phoenix, 9 December 1952, Box 155, Myer Desk Files; and "The Voluntary Relocation Program of the Bureau of Indian Affairs," 1955, Box 86, AAIA Papers.

47. Ruth M. Bronson to James E. Curry, 3 September 1948, Box 117, Curry Papers; James E. Curry, Draft of Letter to Roy Mobley, 25 September 1948, Curry Papers; Roy Mobley to Curry, Cohen, and Bingham, 3 April 1948, Curry Papers.

48. Regular Meeting of the Business Committee, 16 September 1949, Box 118, Curry Papers.

49. Regular Meeting of the Business Committee, 16 September 1949, Curry Papers; and Constitution and Bylaws of the Apache Indians of the Mescalero Reservation, 1936, Box 97, Cohen Papers.

50. James E. Curry to Rufus Sago, 3 January 1950, Box 118, Curry Papers.

51. Curry to Sago, 3 January 1950, Curry Papers; and Regular Meeting of the Business Committee, 16 September 1949, Curry Papers.

52. James E. Curry to Rufus Sago, 27 September 1949, Box 117, Curry Papers; Newspaper Clipping, "Mescalero Agent Voted Support," 4 October 1949, Curry Papers; Henry Weihofen to James E. Curry, 28 August 1950, Box 118, Curry Papers; and James E. Curry to Wheeler Tissnolthtos, 9 January 1950, Curry Papers.

53. Rufus Sago to Senator George D. Aiken, Box 117, 17 October 1949, Curry Papers; James E. Curry to John H. Provinse, 4 October 1949, Curry Papers; and James E. Curry to William J. McFarland, 25 October 1949, Curry Papers.

54. Henry Weihofen to James E. Curry, 28 August 1950, Box 118, Curry Papers; and Ruth Bronson, *Report on the Findings of a Special Subcommittee to Investigate the Status*

of Tribal Self-Government at the Mescalero Apache Reservation, November 1950, Curry Papers.

55. Weihofen to Curry, 28 August 1950, Curry Papers; and Bronson, *Report on Findings of Special Subcommittee*, Curry Papers.

56. Myer, *Autobiography*, 265, 267, 286–87, 291.

57. Myer, *Autobiography*, 265, 278; and Dillon S. Myer to Eric Hagberg, 19 September 1950, Box 119, Curry Papers.

58. Myer to Hagberg, 19 September 1950, Curry Papers.

59. Myer to Hagberg, 19 September 1950, Curry Papers.

60. Report on Conference of Mescaleros with Commissioner Myer, 4 October 1950, Box 118, Curry Papers.

61. John C. Rainer to Dear Friends, 20 November 1950, Curry Papers; and Bronson, *Report on Findings of Special Subcommittee*, Curry Papers.

62. Bronson, *Report on Findings of Special Subcommittee*, Curry Papers.

63. Abel Paisano to Napoleon Bonaparte Johnson, 18 December 1950, Curry Papers.

64. Department of Interior Press Release, 2 February 1951, Box 119, Curry Papers; Wheeler Tissnolthtos, Mescalero Council Adopts Resolutions Concerning John Crow, Other Matters, Resolution 365, 10 February 1951, Curry Papers; and Dillon S. Myer to James E. Curry, undated, Box 68, Curry Papers.

65. Stanley J. Underdal, "On the Road to Termination" (Ph.D. diss.), 164–65.

66. E. Reesman Fryer to Dillon S. Myer, 23 June 1950, Box 144, Curry Papers.

67. Oliver LaFarge to the AAIA Board of Directors, November 1950, Box 3, AAIA Papers; and Ruth Bronson to Oliver LaFarge, 30 September 1950, AAIA Papers.

68. Dillon S. Myer to E. Raymond Armsby, 24 November 1950, AAIA Papers.

69. Oliver LaFarge to AAIA Board of Directors, November 1950, Box 3, AAIA Papers.

70. "President Truman Acts to Protect Paiute Indians," NCAI *Washington Bulletin*, October-November 1950, Box 3, Murray Papers.

71. Patrick McCarran to Ruth M. Bronson, 1949, Box 210, Butler Papers.

72. McCarran to Bronson, 1949, Butler Papers.

73. "The National Congress of American Indians: An Indian Bureau Organization and How It Was Formed," by Individuals Opposed to the Exploitation of Indians, 1 June 1947, Box 10, Usher L. Burdick Papers.

74. Leta Smart, Registration Pursuant to Los Angeles County Ordinance 5578, 1950, Box 210, Butler Papers; and Thomas Largo to Napoleon Bonaparte Johnson, 27 October 1951, Butler Papers.

75. LaFarge to AAIA Board of Directors, November 1950, AAIA Papers.

76. "President Truman Acts to Protect Paiute Indians," Murray Papers; Harold L. Ickes to Glen Coy Kendall, 8 October 1950, Box 62, Ickes Papers; and "McCarran and the Paiute Indians," 13 October 1950, Box 155, Myer Desk Files.

77. NCAI Press Release, 15 October 1950, Box 155, Myer Desk Files; Underdal, "On the Road to Termination" (Ph.D. diss.), 170; Alexander Lesser, Memorandum for the Record, 9 November 1950, Box 47, AAIA Papers; and E. Reesman Fryer to John C. Rainer, 7 November 1950, Box 62, Ickes Papers.

78. Jonathan M. Steere, "Indians' Free Choice of Attorneys Threatened," 4–5.

7. RIGHT TO EMPLOY COUNSEL

1. Statement by Commissioner Dillon S. Myer, before a Subcommittee of the Senate Committee on Interior and Insular Affairs, 21 January 1952, Box 2, Myer Papers.

2. Vern Haugland, Press Release, 24 October 1950, Box 67, Curry Papers; and James E. Curry to Napoleon Bonaparte Johnson, 9 April 1947, Box 12, NCAI Papers.

3. James E. Curry to Oscar L. Chapman, 26 March 1950, Box 3518, Department of Interior Central Files.

4. James E. Curry to Felix S. Cohen, 21 January 1948, Box 122, Curry Papers; and James E. Curry, Confidential Memorandum for the File, 3 February 1949, Box 107, Curry Papers.

5. Curry to Cohen, 21 January 1948, Curry Papers; and Curry, Confidential Memorandum for File, 3 February 1949, Curry Papers.

6. James E. Curry to Oscar L. Chapman, 18 April 1950, Box 3518, Department of Interior Central Files.

7. James E. Curry to Alexander Lesser, 19 April 1949, Box 153, Curry Papers; and James E. Curry, Memorandum for File, 6 January 1948, Box 108, Curry Papers.

8. Curry, Confidential Memorandum for File, 3 February 1949, Curry Papers.

9. Walter J. Fried to James E. Curry, 10 February 1949, Curry Papers; and Curry, Confidential Memorandum for File, 3 February 1949, Curry Papers.

10. James E. Curry to Frances Lopinsky, 20 June 1949, Curry Papers; and James E. Curry, Memorandum for Federal Bureau of Investigation, 15 November 1949, Curry Papers.

11. James E. Curry, Memorandum for File, 1 August 1949, Curry Papers; James E. Curry, Telephone Conversation, 25 August 1949, Curry Papers.

12. NCAI Resolution, 3 September 1949, Curry Papers.

13. James E. Curry, Memorandum for Charles M. Wright, 13 October 1949, Curry Papers; and James E. Curry, Memorandum for File, 31 July 1949, Curry Papers.

14. James E. Curry to Oscar L. Chapman, 26 March 1950, Box 3518, Attorneys and Agents, Department of Interior Central Files.

15. Statement by Myer, before a Subcommittee, 21 January 1952, Myer Papers.

16. Statement by Myer, before a Subcommittee, 21 January 1952, Myer Papers.

17. Department of Interior, Regulations Governing Negotiation and Execution of Attorney Contracts with Indian Tribes, 2 May 1938, Box 3517, Attorneys and Agents, Department of Interior Central Files.

18. Statement by Myer, before a Subcommittee, 21 January 1952, Myer Papers; and James E. Curry to Oscar L. Chapman, 28 September 1950, Box 3518, Attorneys and Agents, Department of Interior Central Files.

19. Newspaper Clipping, "Attorney Answers Attack Levelled by Indian Bureau," 25 October 1950, *Reno Evening Gazette*, Box 22, Nash Files.

20. NCAI Press Release, 24 October 1950, Dale Doty Papers; and John C. Rainer, Memorandum concerning Employment of Tribal Attorneys, 1 November 1950, Box 8, Doty Papers.

21. Dillon S. Myer to Bureau Officials and Tribal Officials, 9 November 1950, Contracts between Attorneys and Indian Tribes, Box 2, Myer Papers; and Statement by Myer, before a Subcommittee, 21 January 1952, Myer Papers.

22. Myer to Bureau Officials and Tribal Officials, 9 November 1950, Myer Papers.

23. Myer to Bureau Officials and Tribal Officials, 9 November 1950, Myer Papers.

24. Martha L. Jay to Senator James E. Murray, 4 December 1950, Box 1, Murray Papers.

25. Statement by Commissioner Dillon S. Myer on Proposed Attorney Contract Regulations, December 1952, Box 2, Myer Papers; and "Memorandum on the Right of Indian Tribes to Counsel," 14 December 1950, Myer Papers.

26. "Memorandum on Right of Indian Tribes," 14 December 1950, Myer Papers.

27. "Memorandum on Right of Indian Tribes," 14 December 1950, Myer Papers.

28. "Memorandum on Right of Indian Tribes," 14 December 1950, Myer Papers.

29. Isaac C. Sutton to Oscar L. Chapman, 5 January 1951, Box 67, Curry Papers; Dillon S. Myer to Roswell P. Barnes, 16 January 1951, Box 155, Myer Desk Files; Edith B. Ricketson to Oscar L. Chapman, 29 January 1951, Box 3518, Attorneys and Agents, Department of Interior Central Files; Elizabeth Roe-Cloud to Oscar L. Chapman, 31 January 1951, Box 17, Bosone Papers; and Clarence Wesley, "San Carlos Apache Tribe Seeks Equal Rights," 1.

30. Oliver LaFarge to President Harry S. Truman, 20 February 1951, Box 22, Nash Files; John Rainer to President Harry S. Truman, 20 February 1951, Box 938, Truman Official Files.

31. Memorandum, Pyramid Lake Attorney Contract Situation, 2 March 1951, Box 22, Nash Files; and David K. Niles to John Rainer, 9 April 1951, Box 938, Truman Official Files.

32. Harold L. Ickes to John Collier, 21 March 1951, Box 62, Ickes Papers; and Bureau of Indian Affairs Press Release, 20 March 1951, Box 8, Doty Papers.

33. Dillon S. Myer, Memorandum on the Right of Indian Tribes to Counsel—An Answer to the Memorandum of 14 December 1950, Issued by the Joint Efforts Law Firms and Others, 16 March 1951, Box 2, Myer papers.

34. Myer, Memorandum on the Right of Indian Tribes to Counsel, 16 March 1951, Myer Papers.

35. Myer, Memorandum on the Right of Indian Tribes to Counsel, 16 March 1951,

Myer Papers; and Patrick McCarran to Oscar L. Chapman, 23 February 1951, Box 3519, Attorneys and Agents, Department of Interior Central Files.

36. Ruth M. Bronson, Memorandum for Mr. Ickes on Dillon Myer's Administration of Indian Affairs, April 1951, Box 62, Ickes Papers; and Harold L. Ickes, "Justice in a Deep Freeze," copy in Doty Papers.

37. Mastin G. White to Oscar L. Chapman, Authority of the Secretary Respecting the Approval of Contracts between Indian Tribes and Attorneys, 22 June 1951, Box 8, Doty Papers.

38. White to Chapman, 22 June 1951, Doty Papers.

39. Oscar L. Chapman, "Notice of Proposed Rule-Making: Code of Federal Regulations," 1 August 1951, Box 3517, Attorneys and Agents, Department of Interior Central Files.

40. Charles L. Black Jr. to Oscar L. Chapman, 7 August 1951, Box 3519, Attorneys and Agents, Department of Interior Central Files; and Alexander Lesser to Oscar L. Chapman, 7 September 1951, Box 5, Richard Searles, Department of Interior Central Files.

41. Elizabeth B. Roe Cloud to Oscar L. Chapman, 24 October 1951, Box 10, NCAI Papers; and Napoleon Bonaparte Johnson to Oscar L. Chapman, undated, NCAI Papers.

42. Mastin G. White to Oscar L. Chapman, 12 July 1951, Box 3519, Attorneys and Agents, Department of Interior Central Files.

43. Avery Winnemucca to Oscar L. Chapman, 20 September 1951, Box 12, NCAI Papers.

44. Avery Winnemucca to the Pyramid Lake Tribal Council, Report of Delegation to Washington to Obtain Approval of Attorney Contract and Restoration of Land Rights, October 1951, Box 63, Ickes Papers; and Dillon S. Myer, Executive Order 556, The Conduct of Tribal Government, 7 March 1951, Box 62, Ickes Papers.

45. Dillon S. Myer to Burton Ladd, 26 September 1951, Box 145, Curry Papers; and Avery Winnemucca to Alma Mayer, 18 October 1951, Curry Papers.

46. Avery Winnemucca to the Pyramid Lake Tribal Council, Report of Delegation to Washington, October 1951, Box 63, Ickes Papers; Avery Winnemucca to John Collier, 1 November 1951, Ickes Papers; and Winnemucca's Report on New York Trip, 19 December 1951, Box 146, Curry Papers.

47. Winnemucca's Report on New York Trip, 19 December 1951, Curry Papers.

48. Winnemucca's Report on New York Trip, 19 December 1951, Curry Papers.

49. Harry S. Truman to Governor John Bonner, 4 December 1951, Box 938, Truman Official Files.

50. American Bar Association, Report of Special Committee on Contracts of Lawyers with Indian Tribes, Hearing on Proposed Regulations to Govern Indian Tribal Contracts, 3–4 January 1951, 197–202, Department of Interior Central Files.

51. American Bar Association, Report of Special Committee, Department of Interior

Central Files; and Felix S. Cohen, Memorandum on American Bar Association Report on Commissioner Myer's Proposed Attorney Regulations, Box 10, NCAI Papers.

52. Myer, *Autobiography*, 303; Underdal, "On the Road to Termination" (Ph.D. diss.), 211; and Koppes, "Oscar L. Chapman" (Ph.D. diss.), 248.

53. "Two Capital Hearings Set to Air Rules for U.S. Indian Lawyers," *New York Times*, 9 November 1951, 1; and Myer, *Autobiography*, 303.

54. Newspaper Clipping, "In War We Were Men; Now They Think We Are Savages," *Washington Daily News*, 3 January 1952, Box 8, Doty Papers; and Newspaper Clipping, "Navajo Describes Indian Service as a Liability," *Albuquerque Journal*, 4 January 1952, Box 27, Papers of Joel D. Wolfsohn.

55. Martha Jay, "Witnesses Unanimous in Opposition," 1; and Statement of Harold L. Ickes, Hearing on Proposed Regulations to Govern Indian Tribal Attorney Contracts, 3–4 January 1952, Box 3517, 276–77, Department of Interior Central Files.

56. Hearing on Proposed Regulations, 3–4 January 1952, 16–25, Department of Interior Central Files.

57. Hearing on Proposed Regulations, 3–4 January 1952, 26–42, Department of Interior Central Files.

58. Hearing on Proposed Regulations, 3–4 January 1952, 81–86, Department of Interior Central Files.

59. Hearing on Proposed Regulations, 3–4 January 1952, 117–20, Department of Interior Central Files.

60. Hearing on Proposed Regulations, 3–4 January 1952, 174–76, Department of Interior Central Files.

61. Hearing on Proposed Regulations, 3–4 January 1952, 184, Department of Interior Central Files.

62. Hearing on Proposed Regulations, 3–4 January 1952, 192–94, Department of Interior Central Files.

63. Hearing on Proposed Regulations, 3–4 January 1952, 242–48, Department of Interior Central Files.

64. Hearing on Proposed Regulations, 3–4 January 1952, 242–48, Department of Interior Central Files.

65. Hearing on Proposed Regulations, 3–4 January 1952, 283, Department of Interior Central Files.

66. Hearing on Proposed Regulations, 3–4 January 1952, 66–70, Department of Interior Central Files.

67. Hearing on Proposed Regulations, 3–4 January 1952, 50–55, Department of Interior Central Files.

68. Hearing on Proposed Regulations, 3–4 January 1952, 294–325, Department of Interior Central Files.

69. Hearing on Proposed Regulations, 3–4 January 1952, 294–325, Department of Interior Central Files.

70. Hearing on Proposed Regulations, 3–4 January 1952, 294–325, Department of Interior Central Files.

71. Dillon S. Myer to Dale Doty, 16 January 1952, Box 155, Myer Desk Files.

72. Statement by Myer, before a Subcommittee, 21 January 1952, Myer Papers.

73. Statement by Myer, before a Subcommittee, 21 January 1952, Myer Papers.

74. Oscar L. Chapman to Dillon S. Myer, 24 January 1952, Box 155, Myer Desk Files.

75. Dillon S. Myer to Oscar L. Chapman, 28 January 1952, Box 3519, Department of Interior Central Files; Alden Stevens to Oscar L. Chapman, 18 February 1952, Department of Interior Central Files; and Myer, "Cohen Statement," undated, Myer Papers.

76. Koppes, "Oscar L. Chapman" (Ph.D. diss.), 249; James E. Curry to Lorena Burgess, 29 June 1952, Box 60, Curry Papers; and Napoleon Bonaparte Johnson to James E. Curry, 21 July 1952, Box 12, NCAI Papers.

77. Senate, *Attorney Contracts with Indian Tribes*, 24–25, copy in Box 3519, Attorneys and Agents, General, Department of Interior Central Files. For additional information on the Anderson subcommittee and James Curry, consult Koppes, "Oscar L. Chapman" (Ph.D. diss.), 247–55; and Underdal, "On the Road to Termination" (Ph.D. diss.), 204–18.

78. Senate, *Attorney Contracts with Indian Tribes*, 6–7, 9, 10, 12, 13, Department of Interior Central Files.

79. Senate, *Attorney Contracts with Indian Tribes*, 4, 6–7, Department of Interior Central Files.

80. Wilkinson, *American Indians, Time, and the Law*, 1–6, 59.

81. Underdal, "On the Road to Termination" (Ph.D. diss.), 220–21; and Sidney W. Robinson to Burton Ladd, 31 March 1952, Box 146, Curry Papers. For a discussion of how the Paiutes and other contemporary Indians have shaped their own destiny and upheld the principle of tribal sovereignty, see Fergus M. Bordewich, *Killing the White Man's Indian*.

8. BLACKFEET DECLARE INDEPENDENCE

1. George Pambrun, Press Release, 14 April 1951, Box 22, Nash Files; and Drinnon, *Keeper of Concentration Camps*, 218–19. In 1945, Adam Castillo, president of the California Mission Indian Federation, took a similar position. He criticized the Indian Bureau for not giving California Indians immediate control over their money and property after they won a claims judgment against the U.S. government. Willis, "California Indians Win Partial Victory in Court of Claims," 4–5.

2. Statement of George Pambrun, Senate Interior and Insular Affairs Committee, 15 April 1952, Box 82, AAIA Papers.

3. Cohen also represented the Omahas, Oglala Sioux, Hualapais, San Carlos Apaches, and All Pueblo Council. Statement of Pambrun, Senate Interior and Insular Affairs Committee, 15 April 1951, AAIA Papers; and Sister Providencia to Felix S. Cohen, 6 June 1950, Box 88, Cohen Papers.

4. Oscar L. Chapman to Henry Magee, 28 February 1950, Box 3380, Blackfeet Administration, Department of Interior Central Files.

5. Chapman to Magee, 28 February 1950, Department of Interior Central Files.

6. Oscar L. Chapman to Henry Magee, 7 April 1950, Box 3380, Blackfeet Administration, Department of Interior Central Files.

7. Paul L. Fickinger to Dillon S. Myer, 9 June 1950, Department of Interior Central Files.

8. Oscar L. Chapman to Oliver LaFarge, 11 July 1950, Box 3380, Blackfeet Administration, Department of Interior Central Files; and Paul L. Fickinger to Blackfeet Tribal Business Council, 6 June 1950, Department of Interior Central Files.

9. Fickinger to Blackfeet Tribal Business Council, 6 June 1950, Department of Interior Central Files.

10. Paul L. Fickinger to Blackfeet Tribal Business Council, 9 June 1950, Box 87, AAIA Papers.

11. Dale E. Doty to Joseph C. O'Mahoney, 25 August 1950, Box 2, Murray Papers.

12. J. L. Sherburne to Oliver LaFarge, 16 June 1950, Box 85, AAIA Papers.

13. Sherburne to La Farge, 16 June 1950, AAIA Papers.

14. George Pambrun, Memorandum for Senator James E. Murray, 4 December 1950, Box 8, Murray Papers.

15. Felix S. Cohen to Dillon S. Myer, 13 September 1950, Box 85, AAIA Papers.

16. Pambrun, Memorandum for Murray, 4 December 1950, Murray Papers; Drinnon, *Keeper of Concentration Camps*, 217; and Department of Interior Press Release, Superintendent Appointed at Blackfeet Agency, 22 November 1950, Box 46, Cohen Papers.

17. Pambrun, Memorandum for Murray, 4 December 1950, Murray Papers.

18. Statement of Pambrun, Senate Interior and Insular Affairs Committee, 15 April 1952, Box 82, AAIA Papers; and Circular, "Attention, Blackfeet Members," 6 September 1950, Box 88, Cohen Papers.

19. Statement of Pambrun, Senate Interior and Insular Affairs Committee, 15 April 1952 AAIA Papers.

20. Statement of Pambrun, Senate Interior and Insular Affairs Committee, 15 April 1952, AAIA Papers.

21. Testimony of Joseph Brown, Member of the Blackfeet Business Council, before the House Subcommittee of the Committee on Appropriations, 28 February 1951, Box 3, Wellington Papers.

22. Testimony of Brown, 28 February 1951, Wellington Papers.

23. Press Release, "Indian Bureau Inciting Montana Range War," 5 February 1951, Box

23, Nash Files; and Newspaper Clipping, "Topics of the Times: Blackfeet on Warpath," 21 February 1951, Box 88, AAIA Papers.

24. Press Release, "Indian Bureau Inciting Montana Range War," 5 February 1951, Nash Files.

25. Testimony of Myer, House Subcommittee on Appropriations, 9 March 1951, Wellington Papers.

26. Press Release, 14 April 1951, Box 22, Nash Files; and Dillon S. Myer to George Pambrun, 19 April 1951, Box 2, Myer Papers.

27. Drinnon, *Keeper of Concentration Camps*, 218; and Press Release, 14 April 1951, Nash Files.

28. Drinnon, *Keeper of Concentration Camps*, 21.

29. Myer to Pambrun, 19 April 1951, Myer Papers.

30. Myer to Pambrun, 19 April 1951, Myer Papers.

31. Myer to Pambrun, 19 April 1951, Myer Papers.

32. Felix S. Cohen, "The Democratic Faith in 1951: Address before the Yale Philosophy Club," January 1951, Box 69, Cohen Papers.

33. Extension of Remarks by Senator James E. Murray, Appendix to the *Congressional Record*, 82d Cong., 1st sess., A5424–32.

34. Remarks by Murray, *Congressional Record*; and Bernstein, *American Indians and World War II*, 124.

35. *Congressional Record*, 82d Cong., 1st sess., A5424–32.

36. *Congressional Record*, 82d Cong., 1st sess., A5424–32.

37. *Congressional Record*, 82d Cong., 1st sess., A5424–32.

38. "An Indian Declaration of Independence," November 1951, Box 155, Myer Desk Files.

39. Statement of Pambrun, Senate Interior and Insular Affairs Committee, 15 April 1952, AAIA Papers.

40. Statement of Pambrun, Senate Interior and Insular Affairs Committee, 15 April 1952, AAIA Papers.

41. Statement of Pambrun, Senate Interior and Insular Affairs Committee, 15 April 1952, AAIA Papers.

42. Statement of Pambrun, Senate Interior and Insular Affairs Committee, 15 April 1952, AAIA Papers; and Graham D. Taylor, *New Deal and American Indian Tribalism*, 55–57.

43. Taylor, *New Deal and American Indian Tribalism*, 55–57, and Philp, *John Collier's Crusade for Indian Reform*, 165–66.

44. James E. Murray to Louis Plenty Treaty, 16 May 1951, Box 3, Murray Papers.

45. Statement of Pambrun, Senate Interior and Insular Affairs Committee, 15 April 1952, AAIA Papers.

46. Murray to Plenty Treaty, 16 May 1951, Murray Papers.

47. Dillon S. Myer to Oscar L. Chapman, 28 May 1952, Box 3380, Blackfeet Administration, Department of Interior Central Files.

48. Amendment 3, Constitution and Bylaws, Blackfeet Tribe, Box 22, Nash Files.

49. Myer to Chapman, 28 May 1952, Blackfeet Administration, Department of Interior Central Files; and Mastin G. White to Oscar L. Chapman, Vote on Proposed Amendment 3 to the Blackfeet Constitution, 18 July 1952, Blackfeet Administration, Department of Interior Central Files.

50. Guy Robertson to Walter Wetzel, 30 April 1952, Box 22, Nash Files; and Newspaper Clipping, "Blackfeet Tribe Asks Governor Bonner for State Protection against Indian Bureau Interference in Local Elections," 1 May 1952, Nash Files.

51. Robertson to Wetzel, 30 April 1952, Nash Files; and Myer to Chapman, 28 May 1952, Department of Interior Central Files.

52. Guy Robertson, "To the Members of the Blackfeet Tribe," 30 April 1952, Box 22, Nash Files.

53. Walter S. Wetzel to Oscar L. Chapman, 1 May 1952, Box 22, Nash Files.

54. Wetzel to Chapman, 1 May 1952, Nash Files.

55. Wetzel to Chapman, 1 May 1952, Nash Files.

56. Philleo Nash, Memorandum for Files, 9 May 1952, Box 2, Nash Files; and Oscar L. Chapman to Mike Mansfield, 26 June 1952, Nash Files.

57. Nash, Memorandum for Files, 9 May 1952, Nash Files.

58. Myer to Chapman, 28 May 1952, Department of Interior Central Files.

59. Louis Plenty Treaty to Harry S. Truman, 9 May 1952, Box 22, Nash Files.

60. Felix S. Cohen to Oscar L. Chapman, 26 May 1952, Box 3380, Blackfeet Administration, Department of Interior Central Files.

61. James E. Murray to Oscar L. Chapman, 28 May 1952, Blackfeet Administration, Department of Interior Central Files.

62. Dillon S. Myer to Oscar L. Chapman, 27 May 1952, Blackfeet Administration, Department of Interior Central Files.

63. White to Chapman, 18 July 1952, Department of Interior Central Files.

64. White to Chapman, 18 July 1952, Department of Interior Central Files.

65. White to Chapman, 18 July 1952, Department of Interior Central Files.

66. Dillon S. Myer to Oscar L. Chapman, 7 August 1952, Blackfeet Administration, Department of Interior Central Files.

9. STATE JURISDICTION

1. House Committee on Interior and Insular Affairs, *Hearings on H.R. 459, H.R. 3235, and H.R. 3624: State Legal Jurisdiction*, 1–5.

2. Lewis Meriam, *Problem of Indian Administration*, 748–49, 757.

3. Lawrence F. Schmeckebier, *Office of Indian Affairs*, 259–60; Meriam, *Problem of*

Indian Administration, 769–70; and Cohen, ed., *Handbook of Federal Indian Law*, 359–60.

4. Schmeckebier, *Office of Indian Affairs*, 262–64. Consult William T. Hagan, *Indian Police and Judges*, for a comprehensive analysis of early efforts to provide law enforcement on reservations.

5. Deloria and Lytle, *Nations Within*, 158–60.

6. Commission on Organization, *Final Commission Report on Indian Affairs*, 51–53, Acheson Papers.

7. Louis Mueller, Summary: Present Police Organization, 1935, Box 2, Cohen Papers; Lem Towers to Louis Mueller, 1 May 1935, Cohen Papers; and Reuben Neill, Walter Lewis, and M. K. Clark to Commissioner of Indian Affairs, 13 June 1935, Cohen Papers.

8. E. Adamson Hoebel, "Problem of Iroquois Law and Order," 12–13.

9. Hoebel, "Problem of Iroquois Law and Order," 14–16.

10. Hoebel, "Problem of Iroquois Law and Order," 18–20.

11. Commission on Organization, *Final Commission Report on Indian Affairs*, 141–44, Acheson Papers.

12. G. E. E. Lindquist, "Indian Treaty Making," 417, 423. For a scholarly and more comprehensive analysis of the significance of treaties, consult Francis Paul Prucha, *American Indian Treaties*.

13. Lindquist, "Indian Treaty Making," 437–39.

14. Commission on Organization, *Final Commission Report on Indian Affairs*, 143, Acheson Papers.

15. Merton Glover to Karl E. Mundt, 12 July 1950, RG 1, Mundt Papers.

16. Glover to Mundt, 12 July 1950, Mundt Papers.

17. H. E. Bruce to Commissioner of Indian Affairs, 7 March 1949, Box 211, Butler Papers.

18. Bruce to Commissioner, 7 March 1949, Butler Papers.

19. Bruce to Commissioner, 7 March 1949, Butler Papers.

20. House Committee on Interior and Insular Affairs, *Hearings on H.R. 459, H.R. 3235, and H.R. 3624: State Legal Jurisdiction*, 9–10.

21. Haven Emerson to Hugh Butler, 26 April 1948, Box 8, Murray Papers.

22. Ruth M. Bronson to Members of the NCAI, 3 April 1948, Box 103, AAIA Papers; and James E. Curry to NCAI, 23 July 1948, Box 125, O'Mahoney Papers. Indian tribes consented to giving up jurisdiction over criminal offenses in Kansas (1940), on the Devils Lake Reservation, North Dakota (1946), and on the Sac and Fox Reservation, Iowa (1948); and House Committee on Interior and Insular Affairs, *Hearings on H.R. 459, H.R. 3235, and H.R. 3624: State Legal Jurisdiction*, 9.

23. James E. Curry to NCAI, 23 July 1948, Box 125, O'Mahoney Papers.

24. House Committee on Public Lands, *Conferring Jurisdiction on State of New York*,

copy in Box 21, Morse Papers; and Laurence M. Hauptman, *Formulating American Indian Policy in New York State,* 14–16.

25. LeRoy Snow and Glenn B. Coykendall to Senator Joseph C. O'Mahoney, 29 July 1949, Box 39, AAIA Papers.

26. House Committee on Public Lands, *Conferring Jurisdiction on State of New York,* 3–4, Morse Papers.

27. William Zimmerman Jr. to Robert T. Lansdale, 28 March 1949, Box 211, Butler Papers.

28. Snow and Coykendall to O'Mahoney, 29 July 1949, AAIA Papers.

29. James E. Curry to Xavier Bullhead, 14 July 1951, Box 1, Murray Papers.

30. House Committee on Interior and Insular Affairs, *Hearings on H. R. 459, H.R. 3235, and H.R. 3624: State Legal Jurisdiction,* 61–79, 98–99, 101–6.

31. Forrest E. Cooper to Wayne Morse, 31 July 1951, Box 21, Morse Papers.

32. Curry to Bullhead, 14 July 1951, Murray Papers; and Giles C. Evans to Senator Harry Cain, 9 August 1951, Box 938, Truman Official Files.

33. Curry to Bullhead, 14 July 1951, Murray Papers.

34. Oscar L. Chapman to Senator Joseph C. O'Mahoney, 30 March 1950, Box 211, Butler Papers.

35. House Committee on Interior and Insular Affairs, *Hearings on H.R. 459, H.R. 3235, and H.R. 3624: State Legal Jurisdiction,* 1, 5.

36. House Committee on Interior and Insular Affairs, *Hearings on H.R. 459, H.R. 3235, and H.R. 3624: State Legal Jurisdiction,* 7–8.

37. House Committee on Interior and Insular Affairs, *Hearings on H.R. 459, H.R. 3235, and H.R. 3624: State Legal Jurisdiction,* 7–9, 14–15, 40–41.

38. House Committee on Interior and Insular Affairs, *Hearings on H.R. 459, H.R. 3235, and H.R. 3624: State Legal Jurisdiction,* 25–26.

39. House Committee on Interior and Insular Affairs, *Hearings on H.R. 459, H.R. 3235, and H.R. 3624: State Legal Jurisdiction,* 26–27.

40. House Committee on Interior and Insular Affairs, *Hearings on H.R. 459, H.R. 3235, and H.R. 3624: State Legal Jurisdiction,* 28–33.

41. House Committee on Interior and Insular Affairs, *Hearings on H.R. 459, H.R. 3235, and H.R. 3624: State Legal Jurisdiction,* 29; and Felix S. Cohen, Supplementary Memorandum on Bills to Subject Indians to State Jurisdiction, 4 March 1952, Box 103, AAIA Papers.

42. House Committee on Interior and Insular Affairs, *Hearings on H.R. 459, H.R. 3235, and H.R. 3624: State Legal Jurisdiction,* 101–5.

43. House Committee on Interior and Insular Affairs, *Hearings on H.R. 459, H.R. 3235, and H.R. 3624: State Legal Jurisdiction,* 83–85.

44. House Committee on Interior and Insular Affairs, *Hearings on H.R. 459, H.R. 3235, and H.R. 3624: State Legal Jurisdiction*, 83–85.

45. House Committee on Interior and Insular Affairs, *Hearings on H.R. 459, H.R. 3235, and H.R. 3624: State Legal Jurisdiction*, 87–88.

46. House Committee on Interior and Insular Affairs, *Hearings on H.R. 459, H.R. 3235, and H.R. 3624: State Legal Jurisdiction*, 43.

47. Bureau of Indian Affairs Press Release, 26 August 1950, Box 46, Cohen Papers.

48. Felix S. Cohen, "Memorandum on Bill Authorizing the Indian Bureau to Seize, Search, Arrest and Shoot Indians," 1 February 1952, Box 2, Myer Papers.

49. House Committee on Interior and Insular Affairs, *Hearings on H.R. 459, H.R. 3235, and H.R. 3624: State Legal Jurisdiction*, 51–52, 56–57.

50. House Committee on Interior and Insular Affairs, *Hearings on H.R. 459, H.R. 3235, and H.R. 3624: State Legal Jurisdiction*, 52, 54.

51. House Committee on Interior and Insular Affairs, *Hearings on H.R. 459, H.R. 3235, and H.R. 3624: State Legal Jurisdiction*, 57–60.

52. Oliver LaFarge to Oscar L. Chapman, 26 February 1952, Box 155, Myer Desk Files.

53. Dillon S. Myer to Oliver LaFarge, 11 March 1952, Myer Desk Files; and Statement by Commissioner of Indian Affairs Dillon S. Myer, Concerning Felix S. Cohen's Memorandum on S.R. 2543, undated, Box 2, Myer Papers.

54. Resolution on Pending Law Enforcement Bills S.R. 2543 and H.R. 6035, AAIA Annual Meeting, 26 March 1952, Box 1, Murray Papers.

55. Felix S. Cohen, "The Indian Bureau's Drive for Increased Police Powers," 3 April 1952, Box 27, Wolfsohn Papers.

56. Press Comment on Indian Bureau Police Bill, undated, Box 22, Nash Files; and Newspaper Clipping, "Bill on American Indians Decried as Threatening Unfair Arrests," 14 April 1952, Box 27, AAIA Papers.

57. Dillon S. Myer to Secretary Oscar L. Chapman, 5 August 1952, Box 155, Myer Desk Files; Dillon S. Myer to Secretary Oscar L. Chapman, 26 May 1952, Box 155, Myer Desk Files; and Felix S. Cohen, Report on Indian Legislation in the Second Session of the 82d Congress, 7 July 1952, Box 102, AAIA Papers.

58. Myer to Chapman, 26 May 1952, Myer Desk Files.

59. *Federal Indian Legislation and Policies: Workshop on American Indian Affairs* (University of Chicago, Department of Anthropology, 1956), 78–81.

60. *Federal Indian Legislation and Policies*, 78–81.

61. *Federal Indian Legislation and Policies*, 78–81.

62. Prucha, *Great Father*, 2:1046.

63. Prucha, *Great Father*, 2:1108. For an analysis of the impact of Public Law 280 on tribes after 1953, consult Carole E. Goldberg, "Public Law 280," 535–94.

64. Sharon O'Brien, *American Indian Tribal Governments*, 203–4.

65. For a discussion of this topic, consult Theodore W. Taylor, *States and Their Indian Citizens*, 36–37.

66. O'Brien, *American Indian Tribal Governments*, 277; and Goldberg, "Public Law 280," 538.

10. TO END FEDERAL SUPERVISION

1. "Answers to Three Questions Posed by Charles Sebastian," Station WFJL, Chicago, 10 January 1952, Box 2, Myer Papers.

2. Napoleon Bonaparte Johnson, "National Congress of American Indians," 140–48.

3. Larry J. Hasse, "Termination and Assimilation" (Ph.D. diss), 127.

4. Jonathan M. Steere, "Indian Bureau Policy Jeopardizes Indian Rights and Welfare," 5; and Oscar L. Chapman to President Harry S. Truman, 9 November 1951, Box 58, Truman Official Files.

5. Dillon S. Myer to Secretary Oscar L. Chapman, 3 January 1952, Box 155, Myer Desk Files.

6. House, *Report with Respect to House Resolution Authorizing Investigation*, 16–17.

7. *Congressional Record*, 82d Cong., 2d sess., 10 April 1952, 98, 3919–20; and E. Morgan Pryse, "Withdrawal of Federal Supervision: Grande Ronde and Siletz Jurisdiction — State of Oregon," December 1950, Portland Area Office, Box 8, Robert K. McCormick Papers.

8. Pryse, "Withdrawal of Federal Supervision, McCormick Papers; and Philp, *John Collier's Crusade for Indian Reform*, 201–2.

9. Oscar L. Chapman to Senator Wayne Morse, 7 May 1946, Box 19, Morse Papers.

10. E. Morgan Pryse to Elwood A. Towner, 24 May 1951, Box 210, Butler Papers; and *Congressional Record*, 82d Cong., 2d sess., 10 April 1952, 98, 3920.

11. *Congressional Record*, 82d Cong., 2d sess., 10 April 1952, 98, 3920; and Resolution of the Confederated Tribes of the Siletz Indians, 12 November 1950, Box 8, McCormick Papers.

12. Pryse, "Withdrawal of Federal Supervision," McCormick Papers.

13. Pryse, "Withdrawal of Federal Supervision," McCormick Papers.

14. Resolution of the Confederated Grande Ronde Tribes Business Committee, 21 August 1951, Box 8, McCormick Papers.

15. *Congressional Record*, 82d Cong., 2d sess., 10 April 1952, 98, 3920–22.

16. *Congressional Record*, 82d Cong., 2d sess., 10 April 1952, 98, 3920–22.

17. G. E. E. Lindquist, *Indian Wardship*, 49–54, Box 2, Cohen Papers.

18. Walter V. Woehlke, Report on a Program for the Termination of Indian Bureau Activities in the State of California, June 1949, Box 1, Sacramento California Agency: 10 Year Plan, RG 75, WNRC.

19. Dillon S. Myer to Walter V. Woehlke, 6 May 1952, Box 155, Myer Desk Files; and House, *Report with Respect to House Resolution Authorizing Investigation*, 200–202.

20. House, *Report with Respect to House Resolution Authorizing Investigation*, 200–202.

21. House, *Report with Respect to House Resolution Authorizing Investigation*, 200–202.

22. Haase, "Termination and Assimilation," 144–45; and Department of Interior, *Annual Report of the Commissioner*, 1952, 393.

23. *Congressional Record*, 82d Cong., 2d sess., 18 March 1952, 98, Appendix A, 2945–46, Box 8, copy in Bosone Papers.

24. Purl Willis to John R. Murdock, 10 March 1952, Box 17, Bosone Papers.

25. *Congressional Record*, 82d Cong., 2d sess., 1 July 1952, 98, 8826–27, Bosone Papers.

26. Statement by Felix S. Cohen on H.J.R. 8 before the House Committee on Interior and Insular Affairs, 14 March 1952, Bosone Papers.

27. House, *Authorizing and Directing the Secretary of Interior to Study the Respective Tribes*, copy in Box 155, Myer Desk Files.

28. Department of Interior, *Annual Report of the Commissioner*, 1952, 394–95.

29. Donald L. Fixico, *Termination and Relocation*, 34; and Verne F. Ray, "Klamath Oppose Liquidation," 15–22.

30. Proceedings of Official General Council Meeting, 31 July 1947, Box 158, Klamath, RG 75, WNRC; Oscar L. Chapman to Senator Joseph C. O'Mahoney, 15 March 1946, Box 102, WNRC; William Zimmerman to Boyd J. Jackson, 14 November 1949, Box 2, Jackson Papers; and Raymond H. Bitmey, Memorandum for Klamath Tribal Loan Board, 15 September 1949, Jackson Papers.

31. Ray, "Klamath Oppose Liquidation," 16–17.

32. Ray, "Klamath Oppose Liquidation," 21–22.

33. Ray, "Klamath Oppose Liquidation"; and Hearing at Klamath Falls, Oregon, 18 August 1947, on S.R. 1222 for the Purpose of Liquidating the Klamath, Box 158, Klamath, RG 75, WNRC.

34. Dillon S. Myer to Ruth M. Bronson, 12 March 1952, Box 155, Myer Desk Files.

35. Minutes of an Open Meeting of the Menominee Advisory Council, 2 July 1952, Box 162, Myer Desk Files.

36. Department of Interior, *Annual Report of the Commissioner*, 1952, 394. For a critical analysis of this reclamation effort, consult Michael L. Lawson, *Damned Indians*.

37. Resolution 35, Black Hills Sioux Nation Council, Box 210, Butler Papers.

38. Department of Interior, *Annual Report of the Commissioner*, 1952, 395.

39. "Varied Plans Seek Indians' Welfare," *New York Times*, 3 November 1951, section C, 7; Metcalf, "Arthur V. Watkins and Indians of Utah" (Ph.D. diss.), 111–24; and Press Release, Statement by President, 21 August 1951, Box 46, Cohen Papers.

40. Metcalf, "Arthur V. Watkins and Indians of Utah" (Ph.D. diss.), 111–24.

41. Edward Lindeman to Dillon S. Myer, 6 March 1952, Box 155, Myer Desk Files; and AAIA, Institute on American Indian Assimilation, Washington DC, 8–10 May 1952, 20 April 1952, Box 22, AAIA Papers.

42. *Congressional Record*, 82d Cong., 2d sess., 10 April 1952, 98, 3919–22.

43. *Congressional Record*, 82d Cong., 2d sess., 10 April 1952, 98, 3919–22.

44. *Congressional Record*, 82d Cong., 2d sess., 10 April 1952, 98, 3919–22.

45. Ellen Norris, Robert Cromwell, Linwood Ward, to Hugh Butler, 11 June 1952, Box 210, Butler Papers; "Indians of California and Taxpayers Should Be Freed from Indian Bureau," 4 July 1952, Box 10, Burdick Papers; "California Indians Demand Immediate Cutting of Wardship Chains," 12 March 1952, Burdick Papers; and Dillon S. Myer to Eleanor Roosevelt, 6 February 1951, Box 155, Myer Desk Files.

46. Statement of Frank George, before House Interior and Insular Affairs Committee, 11 June 1952, Box 12, NCAI Papers.

47. Dillon S. Myer to Senator Clinton P. Anderson, 20 June 1952, Box 2, Myer Papers.

48. Joseph C. O'Mahoney to William K. Coblentz, 16 July 1952, Box 130, AAIA Papers; Oliver LaFarge to Alexander Lesser, 24 June 1952, AAIA Papers; and James E. Curry to Frank George, 29 May 1952, Box 123, NCAI Papers.

49. House, *Report with Respect to House Resolution Authorizing Investigation*, 16–17; and Hasse, "Termination and Assimilation" (Ph.D. diss.), 144–46.

50. House, *Report with Respect to House Resolution Authorizing Investigation*, 16–17.

51. Ruth Kirk to Mark Dawber, 14 November 1949, Box 3527, Department of Interior Central Files; William Warne to Oscar L. Chapman, 6 December 1949, Department of Interior Central Files; Minutes of Fourth Meeting of National Advisory Committee on Indian Affairs, 8–9 December 1949, Department of Interior Central Files; Myer, "Cohen Statement," 38, Myer Papers; Dillon S. Myer to Ruth Kirk, 5 July 1950, Box 3527, Department of Interior Central Files; and Oliver LaFarge to Secretary Oscar L. Chapman, 8 May 1951, Box 2, Myer Papers.

52. Executive Order, Establishment of Indian Advisory Board on Indian Affairs, 13 May 1952, Box 3527, Department of Interior Central Files.

53. Newton W. Edwards to Dale Doty, 18 April 1952, Department of Interior Central Files; and "Tentative Agenda for Meeting with Indian Consultants," Box 3577, 1951–52, Searles Desk Files.

54. Edwards to Doty, 18 April 1952, Department of Interior Central Files.

55. "Notes on Discussions with Indian Consultants," 26–27 June 1952, Box 29, Wolfsohn Papers.

56. "Notes on Discussions with Indian Consultants," 26–27 June 1952, Wolfsohn Papers.

57. "Notes on Discussions with Indian Consultants," 26–27 June 1952, Wolfsohn Papers.

58. "Notes on Discussions with Indian Consultants," 26–27 June 1952, Wolfsohn Papers.

59. "Notes on Discussions with Indian Consultants," 26–27 June 1952, Wolfsohn Papers.

60. House, *Report with Respect to House Resolution Authorizing Investigation*, 1–2, 14; and John Murdock to Toby Morris, 7 July 1952, Box 17, Bosone Papers.

61. Oliver LaFarge to AAIA Board of Directors, 30 September 1952, Box 32, AAIA Papers;

and Proceedings, Governors' Interstate Indian Council, 10–11 December 1951, Morse Papers.

62. Commissioner Dillon S. Myer to All Bureau Officials, 5 August 1952, Box 2, Myer Papers.

63. Notes on Discussions with Indian Consultants to the Secretary of Interior, 15–16 September 1952, Box 3527, Department of Interior Central Files.

64. Notes on Discussions with Indian Consultants to the Secretary of Interior, 15–16 September 1952, Department of Interior Central Files.

65. Frank George to All Tribal Council Chairmen, 26 September 1952, Box 7, Tyler Papers.

66. Dillon S. Myer to All Tribal Council Members, 10 October 1952, Box 2, Myer Papers.

67. House, *Report with Respect to House Resolution Authorizing Investigation*, 1–1593; and Haase, "Termination and Assimilation," 148–49.

68. House, *Report with Respect to House Resolution Authorizing Investigation*, 18, 25, 37–38.

69. House, *Report with Respect to House Resolution Authorizing Investigation*, 28–37.

70. House, *Report with Respect to House Resolution Authorizing Investigation*, 28–37.

71. House, *Report with Respect to House Resolution Authorizing Investigation*, 28–37.

72. Oliver LaFarge, "Helping Elect the Great White Father," copy in Box 37, AAIA Papers; and Alexander Lesser to Oliver LaFarge, 2 February 1953, Box 136, AAIA Papers.

73. Kenneth R. Philp, "Dillon S. Myer and Advent of Termination," 57–59.

74. Philp, "Dillon S. Myer and Advent of Termination," 57–59.

75. Philp, "Dillon S. Myer and Advent of Termination," 57–59.

76. Taylor, *States and Their Indian Citizens*, 61.

77. Prucha, *Great Father*, 2:1048, 1217.

EPILOGUE

1. Cohen, "Erosion of Indian Rights," 917–21. Cohen died on 19 October 1953 at the age of forty-six. Felix Cohen Memorial Service, Indian Claims Commission, 4 December 1953, Box 91, Cohen Papers.

2. Cohen, "Erosion of Indian Rights," 921.

3. Myer, "Cohen Statement," Myer Papers.

4. James E. Curry to Carl Rowan, 29 May 1952, Box 12, NCAI Papers.

5. Felix S. Cohen, "Americanizing the White Man: The Contribution of Indian Culture to the Non-Indian World," Address before the Second Inter-American Conference on Indian Life, Cuzco, Peru, October 1948, Box 8, Doty Papers.

6. Robert F. Berkhofer Jr., *White Man's Indian*, 25–27, 154–57, 185.

7. Myer, *Autobiography*, 264–67; and Cohen, "Americanizing the White Man," Doty Papers.

8. Myer, *Autobiography*, 286–91.

9. Hugh Butler, "What If Immigrants Were Treated like Indians?" *Congressional Record*, 82d Cong., 2d sess., 1952, 98, pt. 2:A4768–69.

10. Charles Russell, "American Indian in Tomorrow's America," 1–5.

11. James E. Officer, "Termination as Federal Policy: An Overview," in Philp, ed., *Indian Self-Rule*, 114–28.

12. Officer, "Termination as Federal Policy"; Taylor, *States and Their Indian Citizens*, 61; and Richard Schifter to Stewart L. Udall, 8 March 1961, Box 10, NCAI Papers.

13. Cornell, *Return of the Native*, 118–20.

14. Felix S. Cohen, Notes on Colonialism, Box 79, Cohen Papers.

15. For a discussion of this topic, consult David Rich Lewis, "Still Native," 203–27.

BIBLIOGRAPHY

ARCHIVAL AND MANUSCRIPT COLLECTIONS

Acheson, Dean. Papers. Harry S. Truman Library. Independence, Missouri.

Association on American Indian Affairs (AAIA). Papers. Seeley G. Mudd Manuscript Library, Princeton University. Princeton, New Jersey.

Bosone, Reva Beck. Papers. Manuscripts Division, Special Collections, Marriott Library, University of Utah. Salt Lake City, Utah.

Brophy, William A. Desk Files. Washington National Records Center. Suitland, Maryland.

Brophy, William A. Papers. Harry S. Truman Library. Independence, Missouri.

Burdick, Usher L. Papers. Orin G. Libby Manuscript Collection, University of North Dakota Library. Grand Forks, North Dakota.

Butler, Hugh. Papers. Nebraska State Historical Society. Lincoln, Nebraska.

Chapman, Oscar L. Office Records of the Secretary of Interior, 1933–53. Record Group 48. National Archives. Washington DC.

Chapman, Oscar L. Papers. Harry S. Truman Library. Independence, Missouri.

Clifford, Clark M. Files. Harry S. Truman Library. Independence, Missouri.

Cohen, Felix S. Papers. Archives and Manuscripts Division, Sterling Memorial Library, Yale University. New Haven, Connecticut.

Collier, John. Office Files. Bureau of Indian Affairs. Record Group 75. National Archives. Washington DC.

Curry, James E. Papers. National Anthropological Archives, Smithsonian Institution. Washington DC.

Davidson, G. G. General Office Files of the Assistant Secretary of Interior. Indian Affairs. Record Group 48. Washington National Records Center. Suitland, Maryland.

Department of Interior. Central Files, 1937–53. Record Group 48. National Archives. Washington DC.

Doty, Dale. Papers. Harry S. Truman Library. Independence, Missouri.

Gardner, Warner W. Papers. Harry S. Truman Library. Independence, Missouri.

Ickes, Harold L. Papers. Library of Congress. Washington DC.

Indian Claims Commission. Papers. Harry S. Truman Library. Independence, Missouri.

Jackson, Boyd J. Papers. University of Oregon Library. Eugene, Oregon.

Krug, Julius A. Papers. Library of Congress. Washington DC.

Langer, William. Papers. Orin G. Libby Manuscript Collection, University of North Dakota Library. Grand Forks, North Dakota.

McCormick, Robert K. Papers. Wisconsin State Historical Society. Madison, Wisconsin.

McCrath, J. Howard. Papers. Harry S. Truman Presidential Library. Independence, Missouri.

Milligan, Edward A. Papers. Montana State University Library. Bozeman, Montana.

Morse, Wayne. Papers. Special Collections, University of Oregon Library. Eugene, Oregon.

Mundt, Karl E. Papers. Karl E. Mundt Library, South Dakota State University. Madison, South Dakota.

Murray, James E. Papers. University of Montana Archives. Missoula, Montana.

Myer, Dillon S. Desk Files. Record Group 75. Washington National Records Center. Suitland, Maryland.

Myer, Dillon S. Papers. Harry S. Truman Presidential Library. Independence, Missouri.

Nash, Philleo. Files. Harry S. Truman Library. Independence, Missouri.

National Congress of American Indians (NCAI). Papers. National Anthropological Archives, Smithsonian Institution. Washington DC.

Nichols, John R. Desk Files. Record Group 75, Washington National Records Center. Suitland, Maryland.

Office of the Solicitor. Records. Office of the Secretary of Interior. Record Group 48. Washington National Records Center. Suitland, Maryland.

O'Mahoney, Joseph C. Papers. University of Wyoming Archives. Laramie, Wyoming.

Searles, Richard. Desk Files. Record Group 48. Washington National Records Center. Suitland, Maryland.

Springharn, Steven. Papers. Harry S. Truman Library. Independence, Missouri.

Truman, Harry S. Papers. Official Files. Harry S. Truman Library. Independence, Missouri.

Tyler, S. Lyman. Papers. Marriot Library, University of Utah. Salt Lake City, Utah.

Washington National Records Center (WNRC). Suitland, Maryland.

Wellington, J. W. Papers. Montana State University Library. Bozeman, Montana.

Wolfsohn, Joel D. Papers. Harry S. Truman Library. Independence, Missouri.

PUBLISHED U.S. GOVERNMENT DOCUMENTS

Goldschmidt, Walter R., and Theodore H. Haas. *A Report to the Commissioner of Indian Affairs: Possessory Rights of the Natives of Southeastern Alaska.* Washington DC: Office of Indian Affairs, 1946.

Haas, Theodore H. *Ten Years of Tribal Government under I.R.A.* Washington DC: Department of Interior, 1947.

Myer, Dillon S. *Program of Bureau of Indian Affairs.* Washington DC: Chilocco Print Shop, 1951.

U.S. Commission on Organization of the Executive Branch of Government. *Hoover Commission Report on Organization of the Executive Branch of the Government.* New York: McGraw-Hill, 1949.

U.S. Commission on Organization of the Executive Branch of Government. *A Report to the Congress on Social Security, Education, and Indian Affairs.* 81st Cong., 1st sess., March 1949. House Document 129.

U.S. Congress. House. *Authorizing and Directing the Secretary of Interior to Study the Respective Tribes, Bands, and Groups of Indians under His Jurisdiction to Determine Their Qualifications to Manage Their Own Affairs without Supervision and Control by the Federal Government.* 82d Cong., 2d sess., 5 May 1952. H. Rept. 1841.

————. House. Committee on Agriculture. *Hearings on H.J.R. 205 to Authorize the Secretary of Agriculture to Sell Timber within the Tongass National Forest.* 80th Cong., 1st sess., 1947.

————. House. Committee on Indian Affairs. Select Committee to Investigate Indian Affairs and Conditions in the United States. *Hearings on H.R. 166: A Bill to Authorize and Direct and Conduct an Investigation to Determine Whether the Changed Status of the Indian Requires a Revision of the Laws and Regulations Affecting the American Indian.* Part 1: 78th Cong., 1st sess., 23 March 1943. Part 2: 78th Cong., 2d sess., 2 February 1944.

————. House. Committee on Indian Affairs. *Hearings on H.R. 1198 to Create an Indian Claims Commission.* 79th Cong., 1st sess., 1945.

————. House. Committee on Interior and Insular Affairs. Subcommittee on Indian Affairs. *Hearings on H.R. 459, H.R. 3235, and H.R. 3624: State Legal Jurisdiction in Indian Country.* 82d Cong., 2d sess., 28–29 February 1952.

————. House. Committee on Public Lands. *Conferring Jurisdiction on the State of New York with Respect to Offenses Committed on Indian Reservations within Such State.* 15 June 1948, 80th Cong., 2d sess. H. Rept. 2355.

————. House. Committee on Public Lands. *H.R. 7002: A Bill to Settle and Extinguish Land Claims to the Public Domain in the Territory of Alaska.* 80th Congress, 2d sess., 19 June 1948.

————. House. Committee on Public Lands. *Authorizing a Survey by the Secretary of Interior Concerning Qualifications of Indian Tribes, Bands, and Groups to Manage Their Own Affairs without Federal Supervision and Control by the Federal Government.* 81st Cong., 2d sess., 24 July 1950. H. Rept. 2723.

————. House. Committee on Public Lands. Subcommittee on Indian Affairs. *Hearings on H.R. 2958, H.R. 2165, and H.R. 1113: Emancipation of Indians.* 80th Cong., 1st sess., 1947.

————. House. *Expressing the Sense of Congress That Certain Tribes of Indians Should Be Freed from Federal Supervision.* 83d Cong., 1st sess., 1953. H. Rept. 841 to Accompany H. Con. Res. 108.

————. House. *Report with Respect to the House Resolution Authorizing the Committee on Interior and Insular Affairs to Conduct an Investigation of the Bureau of Indian Affairs.* Pursuant to H.R. 698, 82d Cong., 2d sess., 15 December 1952. H. Rept. 2503.

————. House. Select Committee to Investigate Indian Affairs and Conditions in the United States. *Report of the Select Committee to Investigate Indian Affairs and Conditions in the United States, Pursuant to H.R. 166.* 78th Cong., 2nd sess., 1944. H. Rept. 2091.

————. Senate. *Attorney Contracts with Indian Tribes.* 83d Cong., 1st sess., 16 January 1953. S. Rept. 8.

————. Senate. Committee on Civil Service. *Hearings on S.R. 41: Officers and Employees of the Federal Government.* 80th Cong., 1st sess., 1947.

————. Senate. Committee on Indian Affairs. *Hearings on H.R. 4497 to Create an Indian Claims Commission.* 79th Cong., 2d sess., 1946.

————. Senate. Committee on Indian Affairs. *Hearings on S.R. 978 to Repeal the Wheeler-Howard Act.* 79th Cong., 2d sess., 1946.

————. Senate. Committee on Indian Affairs. *Hearings on the Nomination of William A. Brophy to Be Commissioner of Indian Affairs.* 79th Cong., 1st sess., 1945.

————. Senate. Committee on Indian Affairs. *Survey of Conditions of the Indians of the United States.* 78th Cong., 1st sess., 1943. S. Rept. 310.

————. Senate. Committee on Interior and Insular Affairs. *Hearings on the Nomination of Oscar L. Chapman to Be Secretary of the Interior.* 81st Cong., 2d sess., 1950.

————. Senate. Committee on Interior and Insular Affairs. Subcommittee on Indian Affairs. *Hearings on H.R. 4386 to Facilitate and Simplify the Administration of Indian Affairs.* 79th Cong., 1st Sess., 1946.

————. Senate. Committee on Interior and Insular Affairs. Subcommittee on Indian Affairs. *Hearings on S.R. 2037 and S.J.R. 162: Repeal Act Authorizing the Secretary of Interior to Create Indian Reservations in Alaska.* 80th Cong., 2d sess., 1948.

————. Senate. Committee on Interior and Insular Affairs. Subcommittee on Indian Affairs. *Hearings on S.R. 2363: A Bill to Promote the Rehabilitation of the Navajo and Hopi Tribes of Indians and the Better Utilization of Resources of the Navajo and Hopi.* 80th Cong., 2d sess., 1948.

————. Senate. Committee on Interstate and Foreign Commerce. Subcommittee. *Hearings on H.R. 1446: A Bill to Authorize the Leasing of Salmon Trap Sites in Alaskan Coastal Waters and for Other Purposes.* 80th Cong., 1st sess., 1947.

————. Senate. Committee on Interstate and Foreign Commerce. House. Committee on

Merchant Marine and Fisheries. *Hearings on S.R. 1446 and H.R. 3859: Bills to Authorize the Leasing of Salmon Trap Sites in Alaska Waters and for Other Purposes.* 80th Cong., 2d sess., 1948.

————. Senate. *Rescinding Certain Orders of the Secretary of Interior Establishing Indian Reservations in the Territory of Alaska.* 80th Congress, 2d sess., 21 May 1948. S. Rept. 1366.

U.S. Department of Interior. Office of Indian Affairs. *Annual Report of the Commissioner, Bureau of Indian Affairs, to the Secretary of the Interior,* 1945–53. Washington DC: Government Printing Office, issued annually.

U.S. Department of Interior. Office of Indian Affairs. *Indian Land Tenure, Economic Status and Population Trends.* Washington DC : Government Printing Office, 1935.

U.S. Library of Congress. *Aspects of Indian Policy: A Review of Current Discussion Prepared by the Legislative Reference Service of the Library of Congress, at the Request of Senator Joseph O'Mahoney, Chairman, Committee on Indian Affairs.* Washington DC: Government Printing Office, 1945.

DISSERTATIONS AND THESES

Cowger, Tom. "Sovereignty and Civil Rights: The National Congress of American Indians, 1944–1961." Ph.D. diss., Purdue University, 1994.

Dixon, Faun. "Native American Property Rights: The Pyramid Lake Reservation Controversy." Ph.D. diss., University of Nevada, 1980.

Franco, Jere. "Native Americans in World War II." Ph.D. diss., University of Arizona, 1990.

Freeman, John L., Jr., "The New Deal for the Indians: A Study in Bureau-Committee Relations in American Government." Ph.D. diss., Princeton University, 1952.

Harvey, Gretchen Grace. "Cherokee and American: Ruth Muskrat Bronson, 1897–1982." Ph.D. diss., Arizona State University, 1996.

Hasse, Larry J. "Termination and Assimilation: Federal Indian Policy, 1943–1961." Ph.D. diss., Washington State University, 1974.

Kalinski, Lynda. "The Termination Crisis: The Menominee Indians versus the Federal Government, 1943–1961." Ph.D. diss., University of Toledo, 1983.

Koppes, Clayton R. "Oscar L. Chapman: A Liberal at the Interior Department." Ph.D. diss., University of Kansas, 1974.

Metcalf, Warren R. "Arthur V. Watkins and the Indians of Utah: A Study of Federal Termination Policy." Ph.D. diss., Arizona State University, 1995.

Orfield, Gary. "Ideology and the Indian: A Study of the Termination Policy." M.A. thesis, University of Chicago, 1965.

Rosenthal, Harvey Daniel. "Their Day in Court: A History of the Indian Claims Commission." Ph.D. diss., Kent State University, 1976.

Stefon, Frederick J. "Native American Education and the New Deal." D.Ed. diss., Pennsylvania State University, 1983.

Underdal, Stanley J. "On the Road to Termination: The Pyramid Lake Paiutes and the Indian Attorney Controversy of the 1950s." Ph.D. diss., Columbia University, 1977.

Webb, Robert D. "The Depression, the New Deal, and the Southern California Indian." M.A. thesis, California State University, Fullerton, 1977.

BOOKS

Anderson, Dewey H., and Walter C. Eells. *Alaska Natives: A Survey of Their Sociological and Educational Status.* Stanford CA: Stanford Univ. Press, 1935.

Anderson, Terry. *Sovereign Nations or Reservations?* San Francisco: Pacific Research Institute for Public Policy, 1995.

Berkhofer, Robert F., Jr. *The White Man's Indian: Images of the American Indian from Columbus to the Present.* New York: Alfred A. Knopf, 1978.

Berman, William C. *The Politics of Civil Rights in the Truman Administration.* Columbus: Ohio State Univ. Press, 1970.

Bernstein, Alison R. *American Indians and World War II: Toward a New Era in Indian Affairs.* Norman: Univ. of Oklahoma Press, 1991.

Biolsi, Thomas. *Organizing the Lakota: The Political Economy of the New Deal on the Pine Ridge and Rosebud Reservations.* Tucson: Univ. of Arizona Press, 1992.

Bordewich, Fergus M. *Killing the White Man's Indian: The Reinventing of Native Americans at the End of the Twentieth Century.* New York: Doubleday, 1996.

Boyce, George A. *When Navajos Had Too Many Sheep: The 1940s.* San Francisco: Indian Historian Press, 1974.

Bronson, Ruth, Muskrat. *Indians Are People Too.* New York: Friendship Press, 1944.

Brophy, William, and Sophie Aberle. *The Indian: America's Unfinished Business.* Norman: Univ. of Oklahoma Press, 1966.

Clarke, Anne N. *Roosevelt's Warrior: Harold L. Ickes and the New Deal.* Princeton: Princeton Univ. Press, 1996.

Clopton, Beverly Bosone. *Her Honor, the Judge: The Story of Reva Beck Bosone.* Ames: Iowa State Univ. Press, 1980.

Cohen, Felix S. "Politics and Economics." In *Socialist Planning and a Socialist Program,* ed. Henry W. Laider. New York: Falcon Press, 1932.

———, ed. *Handbook of Federal Indian Law.* Washington DC: Government Printing Office, 1945.

Cohen, Lucy Krammer, ed. *The Legal Conscience: Selected Papers of Felix S. Cohen.* New Haven: Archon Books, 1970.

Colby, Merle. *A Guide to Alaska: Last American Frontier.* New York: Macmillan, 1942.

Coombs, Madison L. *Doorway toward the Light: The Story of the Special Navajo Education Program.* Washington DC: Bureau of Indian Affairs, 1962.

Cornell, Stephen. *The Return of the Native: American Indian Political Resurgence.* New York: Oxford Univ. Press, 1988.

Daniels, Walter M., ed. *American Indians.* New York: H. W. Wilson, 1957.

Deloria, Vine, Jr., ed. *American Indian Policy in the Twentieth Century.* Norman: Univ. of Oklahoma Press, 1985.

Deloria, Vine, Jr., and Clifford M. Lytle. *American Indians, American Justice.* Austin: Univ. of Texas Press, 1983.

———. *The Nations Within: The Past and Future of American Indian Sovereignty.* New York: Pantheon Books, 1984.

Donovan, Robert J. *Conflict and Crisis: The Presidency of Harry S. Truman, 1945–1948.* New York: W. W. Norton, 1977.

Drinnon, Richard. *Keeper of Concentration Camps: Dillon S. Myer and American Racism.* Berkeley: Univ. of California Press, 1987.

Drucker, Philip. *The Native Brotherhoods: Modern Intertribal Organizations on the Northwest Coast.* Bureau of American Ethnology Bulletin 168. Washington DC: Government Printing Office, 1958.

Edmunds, David, ed. *Studies in Diversity: American Indian Leaders.* Lincoln: Univ. of Nebraska Press, 1980.

Edwards, Jerome E. *Patrick McCarran: Political Boss of Nevada.* Reno: Univ. of Nevada Press, 1983.

Ferrell, Robert. *Harry S. Truman: A Life.* Columbia: Univ. of Missouri Press, 1994.

Fey, Harold E., and D'Arcy McNickle. *Indians and Other Americans: Two Ways of Life Meet,* rev. ed. New York: Harper and Row, 1966.

Fixico, Donald L. *Termination and Relocation: Federal Indian Policy, 1945–1960.* Albuquerque: Univ. of New Mexico Press, 1986.

———, ed. *Re-thinking American Indian History.* Albuquerque: Univ. of New Mexico Press, 1997.

Gruening, Ernest. *The State of Alaska,* rev. ed. New York: Random House, 1968.

Haas, Theodore H., ed. *Felix S. Cohen: A Fighter for Justice.* Washington DC: Washington DC Chapter of the Alumni of the City College of New York, 1956.

Hagan, William T. *Indian Police and Judges: Experiments in Acculturation and Control.* New Haven: Yale Univ. Press, 1966.

Hamby, Alonzo L. *Beyond the New Deal: Harry S. Truman and American Liberalism.* New York: Columbia Univ. Press, 1973.

Hartmann, Susan M. *Truman and the 80th Congress.* Columbia: Univ. of Missouri Press, 1971.

Hauptman, Laurence M. *Formulating American Indian Policy in New York State, 1970–1986.* Albany: State Univ. of New York Press, 1988.

———. *The Iroquois and the New Deal.* Syracuse: Syracuse Univ. Press, 1981.

Haycox, Stephen W. "Economic Development and Indian Land Rights in Modern Alaska." In *An Alaska Anthology: Interpreting the Past,* ed. Stephen W. Haycox and Mary Childers Mangusso, 336–63. Seattle: Univ. of Washington Press, 1996 (reprinted from *Western Historical Quarterly*).

Hecht, Robert A. *Oliver LaFarge and the American Indian: A Biography.* Metuchen NJ: Scarecrow Press, 1991.

Hertzberg, Hazel W. *The Search for an American Indian Identity: Modern Pan-Indian Movements.* Syracuse: Syracuse Univ. Press, 1971.

Hoxie, Frederick E. *A Final Promise: The Campaign to Assimilate the Indians, 1880–1920.* Lincoln: Univ. of Nebraska Press, 1984.

Hurtado, Albert L., and Peter Iverson, eds. *Major Problems in Indian History.* Lexington MA: D. C. Heath, 1994.

Iverson, Peter. *Carlos Montezuma and the Changing World of American Indians.* Albuquerque: Univ. of New Mexico Press, 1982.

———. *The Navajo Nation.* Westport CT: Greenwood Press, 1981.

———, ed. *The Plains Indians of the Twentieth Century.* Norman: Univ. of Oklahoma Press, 1985.

Josephy, Alvin M., Jr. *Now That the Buffalo's Gone: A Study of Today's American Indians.* New York: Alfred A. Knopf, 1982.

Kappler, C. *Laws and Treaties.* Washington DC: Government Printing Office, 1903.

Kelly, Lawrence. *The Assault on Assimilation: John Collier and the Origins of Indian Policy Reform.* Albuquerque: Univ. of New Mexico Press, 1983.

Kelly, William H., ed. *Indian Affairs and the Indian Reorganization Act: The Twenty Year Record.* Tucson: Univ. of Arizona Press, 1954.

Kersey, Harry A. *The Florida Seminoles and the New Deal, 1933–1942.* Boca Raton: Florida Atlantic Univ. Press, 1989.

Kinney, J. P. *Facing Indian Facts.* Laurens NY: Press of the Village Printer, 1973.

Kvasnicka, Robert M., and Herman Viola, eds. *The Commissioners of Indian Affairs, 1824–1977.* Lincoln: Univ. of Nebraska Press, 1979.

LaFarge, Oliver, ed. *The Changing Indian.* Norman: Univ. of Oklahoma Press, 1942.

Lawson, Michael L. *Dammed Indians: The Pick-Sloan Plan and the Missouri River Sioux, 1944–1980.* Norman: Univ. of Oklahoma Press, 1982.

Lear, Linda J. *Harold L. Ickes: The Aggressive Progressive, 1874–1933.* New York: Garland, 1981.

Leighton, Alexander. *The Governing of Men: General Principles and Recommendations*

Based on Experience at a Japanese Relocation Camp. Princeton NJ: Princeton Univ. Press, 1945.

Lindquist, G. E. E. *Indian Wardship.* New York: Home Missions Council of North America, 1943.

Lowitt, Richard. *The New Deal and the West.* Bloomington: Indiana Univ. Press, 1984.

McCoy, Donald R., and Richard T. Ruetten. *Quest and Response: Minority Rights and the Truman Administration.* Lawrence: Univ. Press of Kansas, 1973.

McNickle, D'Arcy. *Indian Man: A Life of Oliver LaFarge.* Bloomington: Indiana Univ. Press, 1971.

Meriam, Lewis, et al. *The Problem of Indian Administration.* Baltimore: Johns Hopkins Univ. Press, 1928.

Myer, Dillon S. *Uprooted Americans: The Japanese-Americans and the War Relocation Authority during World War II.* Tucson: Univ. of Arizona Press, 1971.

Nash, Gerald D. *The American West Transformed: The Impact of the Second World War.* Bloomington: Indiana Univ. Press, 1985.

Neils, Elaine, *Reservation to City: Indian Migration and Federal Relocation.* Chicago: Department of Geography, University of Chicago, 1971.

Norgren, Jill. *The Cherokee Cases: The Confrontation of Law and Politics.* New York: McGraw-Hill, 1996.

O'Brien, Sharon. *American Indian Tribal Governments.* Norman: Univ. of Oklahoma Press, 1989.

Orfield, Gary. *A Study of the Termination Policy.* Denver: National Congress of American Indians, 1965.

Ourada, Patricia. "Dillon S. Myer, 1950–1953." In *The Commissioners of Indian Affairs, 1824–1977,* ed. Robert Kvasnicka and Herman Viola. Lincoln: Univ. of Nebraska Press, 1979.

————. *The Menominee Indians: A History.* Norman: Univ. of Oklahoma Press, 1979.

Parker, Dorothy R. *Singing an Indian Song: A Biography of D'Arcy McNickle.* Lincoln: Univ. of Nebraska Press, 1992.

Parman, Donald L. *Indians and the American West in the Twentieth Century.* Bloomington: Indiana Univ. Press, 1994.

————. *The Navajos and the New Deal.* New Haven: Yale Univ. Press, 1976.

Paterson, Thomas G. *On Every Front: The Making of the Cold War.* New York: Norton, 1979.

Paul, Justus F. *Senator Hugh Butler and Nebraska Republicanism.* Lincoln: Nebraska State Historical Society, 1976.

Pearson, Drew. *Diaries, 1949–1959.* New York: Holt, Rinehart & Winston, 1974.

Pemberton, William E. *Bureaucratic Politics: Executive Reorganization during the Truman Administration.* Columbia: Univ. of Missouri Press, 1979.

Peroff, Nicholas. *Menominee Drums: Tribal Termination and Restoration, 1954–1974.* Norman: Univ. of Oklahoma Press, 1982.

Philp, Kenneth R. *John Collier's Crusade for Indian Reform, 1920–1934.* Tucson: Univ. of Arizona Press, 1977.

———, ed. *Indian Self-Rule: First-Hand Accounts of Indian-White Relations from Roosevelt to Reagan.* Salt Lake City: Howe Brothers, 1986.

Price, Daniel O., and Melanie Sikes. *Rural-Urban Migration Research in the United States.* Washington DC: Government Printing Office, 1975.

Prucha, Francis Paul. *American Indian Treaties: The History of a Political Anomaly.* Berkeley: Univ. of California Press, 1994.

———. *The Great Father: The United States Government and the American Indians.* Vol. 2. Lincoln: Univ. of Nebraska Press, 1984.

Purdy, John. *The Legacy of D'Arcy McNickle: Writer, Historical Activist.* Norman: Univ. of Oklahoma Press, 1996.

Roessel, Ruth, and Broderick Johnson. *Navajo Livestock Reduction: A National Disgrace.* Tsaile AZ: Navajo Community College Press, 1974.

Rosenthal, Harvey D. *Their Day in Court: A History of the Indian Claims Commission.* New York: Garland, 1990.

Sanchez, George I. *The People: A Study of the Navajos.* Lawrence KS: Haskell Institute, United States Indian Bureau, 1948.

Schmeckebier, Lawrence F. *The Office of Indian Affairs: Its History, Activities, and Organization.* Baltimore: Johns Hopkins Univ. Press, 1927.

Spicer, Edward, Asael T. Hansen, Katherine Luomara, and Marvin Opler. *Impounded People: Japanese-Americans in the Relocation Centers.* Reprint of 1946 report of War Relocation Authority. Tucson: Univ. of Arizona Press, 1969.

Stern, Theodore. *The Klamath Tribe: A People and Their Reservation.* Seattle: Univ. of Washington Press, 1965.

Szasz, Margaret Connell. *Education and the American Indian: The Road to Self-Determination, 1928–1973.* Albuquerque: Univ. of New Mexico Press, 1974.

Taylor, Graham D. *The New Deal and American Indian Tribalism: The Administration of the Indian Reorganization Act, 1934–45.* Lincoln: Univ. of Nebraska Press, 1980.

Taylor, Theodore W. *American Indian Policy.* Mt. Airy MD: Lomond, 1983.

———. *The States and Their Indian Citizens.* Washington DC: Bureau of Indian Affairs, 1972.

Thompson, Hildegard. *The Navajos Long Walk for Education: A History of Navajo Education.* Tsaile AZ: Navajo Community College Press, 1975.

Tyler, S. Lyman. *A History of Indian Policy.* Washington: Bureau of Indian Affairs, 1973.

Watkins, T. H. *Righteous Pilgrim: The Life and Times of Harold Ickes.* New York: Henry Holt, 1990.

White, Richard. *The Roots of Dependency: Subsistence, Environment, and Social Change among the Choctaws, Pawnees, and Navajos.* Lincoln: Univ. of Nebraska Press, 1983.

Wilkinson, Charles F. *American Indians, Time, and the Law: Native Societies in a Modern Constitutional Democracy.* New Haven: Yale Univ. Press, 1987.

Wilson, Raymond. "The New Assault on Tribalism." In *The United States in the 20th Century,* vol. 2, ed. James S. Olson, Robert D. Marcus, and David Burner. New York: St. Martin's Press, 1995.

Wunder, John R. *"Retained by the People": A History of American Indians and the Bill of Rights.* New York: Oxford Univ. Press, 1994.

ARTICLES

Armstrong, O. K. "Let's Give the Indians Back to the Country." *Reader's Digest* 52 (April 1948): 129–32.

———. "Set the American Indians Free." *Reader's Digest* 47 (August 1945): 47–50.

Barker, Robert. "The Indian Claims Commission: The Conscience of the Nation in Its Dealings with the Original American." *Federal Bar Journal* 20 (1960): 233–39.

Barney, Ralph. "Legal Problems Peculiar to Indian Claims Litigation." *Ethnohistory* 11 (fall 1955): 315–20.

Benge, William B. "Law and Order on Indian Reservations." *Federal Bar Journal* 20 (1960): 223–29.

Berkhofer, Robert T. "The Political Context of a New Indian History." *Pacific Historical Review* 40 (1971): 357–75.

Black, Charles L. "Counsel of Their Own Choosing." *American Indian* 6 (fall 1951): 3–17.

Bronson, Ruth Muskrat. "Plundering the Indians of Alaska." *Christian Century* 64 (8 October 1947): 1204.

———. "Shall We Repeat Indian History in Alaska?" *Indian Truth* 24 (January–April 1947): 1–11.

Brophy, William A. "An Address before the Sixty-Third Annual Meeting of the Indian Rights Association." *Indian Truth* 23 (January–February 1946): 1–8.

Bruce, Louis R., Jr. "Indian Trail to Success." *Reader's Digest* 55 (November 1949): 77–80.

Carmer, Carl, ed. Editorial. "Navajo Institute Report." *American Indian* 4 (1947): 1–3.

Cohen, Felix S. "Alaska's Nuremberg Laws: Congress Sanctions Racial Discrimination." *Commentary* 6 (August 1948): 136–43.

———. "Americanizing the White Man." *American Scholar* 21 (spring 1952): 177–91.

———. "Breaking Faith with Our First Americans." *Indian Truth* 25 (March 1948) 1–8.

———. "The Civil Rights Report." *Review of General Semantics* 4 (spring 1948): 161–67.

———. "Colonialism: U.S. Style." *Progressive* 15 (February 1951): 16–18.

———. "The Erosion of Indian Rights, 1950–1953: A Case Study in Bureaucracy." *Yale Law Journal* 62 (February 1953): 348–90.

———. "Indians Are Citizens, Too." *American Indian* 1 (summer 1944): 12–22.

———. "Indian Rights and the Federal Courts." *Minnesota Law Review* 24 (January 1940): 146–67.

———. "Indian Self-Government." *American Indian* 5 (1949): 3–12.

———. "Indian Wardship: Twilight of a Myth." *American Indian* 6 (summer 1953): 8–14.

———. "Open Season on Alaskan Natives." *Newsletter, Institute of Ethnic Affairs* 3 (April 1948) 4–8.

———. "Our Country's Shame!" *Progressive* 13 (May 1949): 9–10.

———. "Socialism and the Myth of Legality." *American Socialist Quarterly* 4 (November 1935): 3–33.

Cohen, Lucy Krammer. "Biography of Felix S. Cohen." *Rutgers Law Review* 9 (winter 1954): 345–50.

Collier, John. "The Indian Bureau and Self-Government: A Reply to John F. Embree." *Human Organization* 8 (summer 1949) 22–26.

Crichton, K. "Storm over Alaska: Department of Interior Settles Indians on Reservations." *Colliers* 115 (31 March 1945): 20–22.

Curry, James E. "Displaced Alaskans." *Commonwealth* 46 (1 August 1947): 381–83.

Danforth, Sandra C. "Repaying Historical Debts: The Indian Claims Commission." *North Dakota Law Review* 49 (winter 1973): 359–403.

Dobyns, Henry F. "The Indian Reorganization Act and Federal Withdrawal." *Applied Anthropology* 7 (spring 1948): 35–44.

Editorial. "Indians Might Do Better with Less Protection." *Saturday Evening Post* 223 (29 July 1950): 10+.

Editorial. "New Trails for Indians?" *Economist*, 1 September 1951, 507–8.

"Editorial Notes: Section 2 of the Indian Claims Commission Act." *George Washington Law Review* 16 (June 1947): 389.

Elkus, Charles de Y. "Whither the California Indians." *American Indian* 3 (fall 1946): 7–13.

Embree, John F. "The Indian Bureau and Self-Government." *Human Organization* 8 (spring 1949): 11–14.

Emerson, Haven. "Freedom as Exploitation." *American Indian* 1 (fall 1945): 3–7.

Goldberg, Carole E. "Public Law 280: The Limits of State Jurisdiction over Reservation Indians." *UCLA Law Review* 22 (fall 1975): 535–94.

Guthals, Joel E. "State Civil Jurisdiction over Tribal Indians: A Re-examination." *Montana Law Review* 35 (summer 1974), 340–47.

Haas, Theodore H. "Administration and Self-Government," *American Indian* 5 (spring 1950): 40–43.

———. "The Legal Aspects of Indian Affairs from 1887 to 1957." *Annals of the American Academy of Political and Social Science* 311 (May 1957): 12–22.

Harper, Allen G. "Economic Factors in Self-Government." *American Indian* 5 (1949): 18–21.

Hassrick, Royal B. "The American Indian in Tomorrow's America." *American Indian* 2 (winter 1944–45): 3–12.

Hauptman, Laurence M. "Africa View: John Collier, the British Colonial Service and American Indian Policy, 1933–1945." *Historian* 48 (May 1986): 359–74.

———. "Alice Jemison: Seneca Political Activist, 1901–1964." *Indian Historian* 12 (summer 1979): 15–22.

———. "The American Indian Federation and the New Deal: A Reinterpretation." *Pacific Historical Review* 52 (1983): 378–402.

Haycox, Stephen W. "Economic Development and Indian Land Rights in Modern Alaska: The 1947 Tongass Timber Act." *Western Historical Quarterly* 21 (February 1990), 20–46.

Hertzberg, Stephen J. "The Menominee Indians: From Treaty to Termination." *Wisconsin Magazine of History* 60 (summer 1977): 267–329.

Hoebel, E. Adamson. "The Problem of Iroquois Law and Order." *American Indian* 2 (spring 1945): 12–19.

Holm, Tom. "Fighting a White Man's War: The Extent and Legacy of American Indian Participation in World War II." *Journal of Ethnic Studies* 9 (summer 1981): 75–78.

Hood, Susan. "Termination of the Klamath Tribe in Oregon." *Ethnohistory* 19 (fall 1972): 379–92.

Hoxie, Frederick E. "War of the Worlds: History versus the Law in Charles Wilkinson's *American Indians, Time and the Law*." *Law and Social Inquiry* 13 (fall 1988): 791–99.

Ickes, Harold L. "Farewell Secretary Krug." *New Republic* 121 (28 November 1949): 17.

———. "Indians Have a Name for Hitler." *Colliers* 114 (January 1944): 41–45.

———. "Justice in a Deep Freeze." *New Republic* 124 (21 May 1951): 17.

———. "New Low in Indian Education." *New Republic* 121 (24 October 1949): 15–16.

———. "On Frisking the Alaska Indians." *New Republic* 120 (9 May 1949): 19.

Iverson, Peter. "Building toward Self-Determination: Plains and Southwestern Indians in the 1940's and 1950's." *Western Historical Quarterly* 16 (1985): 163–73.

Jay, Martha. "Witnesses Unanimous in Opposition." *Southwest Indian Newsletter* 1 (January–February 1952): 1.

Johnson, Napoleon Bonaparte. "The National Congress of American Indians." *Chronicles of Oklahoma* 30 (summer 1952): 140–48.

Kelly, Lawrence C. "Anthropology and Anthropologists in the Indian New Deal." *Journal of the History of Behavioral Sciences* 16 (January 1980): 6–24.

———. "The Indian Reorganization Act: The Dream and the Reality." *Pacific Historical Review* 44 (August 1975): 291–312.

Kirk, Ruth. "The Navajos' Tragedy." *Chicago Jewish Forum* 6 (spring 1948): 176–81.

Koppes, Clayton R. "From New Deal to Termination: Liberalism and Indian Policy, 1933–53." *Pacific Historical Review* 46 (November 1977): 543–66.

LaFarge, Oliver. "Helping Elect the Great White Father." *Reporter* (28 October 1952): 31–34.

————. "Termination and Federal Supervision: Disintegration and the American Indians." *Annals of the American Academy of Political and Social Science* 311 (May 1957): 41–46.

LeDuc, Thomas. "The Work of the Indian Claims Commission under the Act of 1946." *Pacific Historical Review* 26 (February 1957): 1–16.

Lewis, David Rich. "Still Native: The Significance of Native Americans in the History of the Twentieth-Century American West." *Western Historical Quarterly* 24 (May 1993): 203–27.

Lindquist, G. E. E. "Indian Treaty Making." *Chronicles of Oklahoma* 26 (winter 1948–49): 416–48.

Lurie, Nancy O. "The Indian Claims Commission." *Annals of the American Academy of Political Science* 436 (March 1978): 97–110.

————. "The Indian Claims Commission Act." *Annals of the American Academy of Political and Social Science* 311 (May 1957): 56–70.

MeKeel, Scudder. "An Appraisal of the Indian Reorganization Act." *American Anthropologist* 46 (April–June 1944): 209–17.

————. "The American Indian as a Minority Group Problem." *American Indian* 2 (fall 1944): 3–11.

Myer, Dillon S. "Indian Administration: Problems and Goals." *Social Science Review* 27 (June 1953): 193–200.

————. "The Program of the Bureau of Indian Affairs." *Journal of Negro Education* 20 (summer 1951): 346–53.

Officer, James E. "The Bureau of Indian Affairs since 1945: An Assessment." *Annals of the American Academy of Political and Social Science* 436 (March 1978): 61–72.

Parker, Dorothy. "D'Arcy McNickle: Native Author, Montana Native Son." *Montana: The Magazine of Western History* 45 (spring 1995): 2–17.

Parman, Donald L. "Inconsistent Advocacy: The Erosion of Indian Fishing Rights in the Pacific Northwest, 1933–1956." *Pacific Historical Review* 53 (May 1984): 163–89.

————. "J. C. Morgan: Navajo Apostle of Assimilation." *Prologue: Journal of the National Archives* 4 (summer 1972): 83–98.

Philp, Kenneth R. "Dillon S. Myer and the Advent of Termination, 1950–53." *Western Historical Quarterly* 19 (January 1988): 37–59.

————. "The New Deal and the Alaska Natives, 1936–1945." *Pacific Historical Review* 50 (August 1981): 309–27.

———. "Stride toward Freedom: The Relocation of Indians to Cities, 1952–1960." *Western Historical Quarterly* 16 (April 1985): 175–90.

———. "Termination: A Legacy of the New Deal." *Western Historical Quarterly* 14 (April 1983): 165–80.

Prucha, Francis Paul. "American Indian Policy in the 20th Century." *Western Historical Quarterly* 15 (January 1984): 5–18.

Quinn, William W. "Federal Acknowledgement of American Indian Tribes: The Historical Development of a Legal Concept." *American Journal of Legal History* 34 (October 1990): 331–61.

Ray, Verne F. "The Klamath Oppose Liquidation." *American Indian* 4 (1948): 15–22.

Rogers, Will, Jr. "Starvation without Representation." *Look Magazine* 12 (3 February 1948): 33+.

Russell, Charles. "The American Indian in Tomorrow's America." *Indian Truth* 30 (January–February 1953): 1–5.

Selander, K. J. "Section 2 of the Indian Claims Commission Act." *George Washington Law Review* 16 (June 1947): 388–425.

Schuete, Steven C. "Removing the Yoke of Government: E. Y. Berry and the Origins of Indian Termination Policy." *South Dakota History* 14 (1984), 49–67.

Steere, Jonathan M. "Alaska Statehood Bill Jeopardizes Land Rights of Alaskan Natives." *Indian Truth* 27 (April–August 1950): 1–2.

———. "Appropriations–1953." *Indian Truth* 29 (autumn 1952): 5.

———. "Arizona and New Mexico Indians Get Right to Vote." *Indian Truth* 25 (May–August 1948): 1.

———. "Arizona Discriminates against Crippled Indian Children." *Indian Truth* 27 (January–March 1950): 1–2.

———. "Crucial Needs of Navajo Indians Presented by Superintendent Allan Harper." *Indian Truth* 28 (January–February 1951): 1–3.

———. "Emancipating the Indian." *Indian Truth* 25 (May–August 1948): 4–5.

———. "Governors' Conference on Indian Affairs." *Indian Truth* 27 (January–March 1950): 3–5.

———. "Hoover Commission Report on Indian Affairs." *Indian Truth* 26 (January–May 1949): 5–7.

———. "Impoverished Navajo Indians Hard Hit by Two-Year Drought." *Indian Truth* 28 (June–August 1951): 1–3.

———. "Indian Bureau Policy Jeopardizes Indian Rights and Welfare." *Indian Truth* 29 (autumn 1952): 1–4.

———. "Indians' Free Choice of Attorneys Threatened." *Indian Truth* 28 (January–February 1951): 4–5.

———. "Indians Should Share in Planning." *Indian Truth* 28 (January–February 1951): 6–7.

———. "National Congress of American Indians." *Indian Truth* 21 (December 1944): 6.

———. "Navajo Rehabilitation: A National Responsibility." *Indian Truth* 25 (January–February 1948): 1–7.

———. "New Commissioner of Indian Affairs." *Indian Truth* 27 (January–March 1950): 2–3.

———. "Proposed Hasty End of Federal Supervision Threatens Indian Welfare." *Indian Truth* 29 (May–June 1952): 1–3.

———. "Zimmerman Transferred from Indian Service." *Indian Truth* 27 (April–August 1950): 5–6.

Stefon, Frederick J. "The Irony of Termination: 1943–1958." *Indian Historian* 11 (summer 1978): 3–14.

Steinberg, Alfred. "McCarran: Lone Wolf of the Senate." *Harper's Magazine* 201 (November 1950): 89–95.

Taylor, Graham. "Anthropologists, Reformers and the Indian New Deal." *Prologue: The Journal of the National Archives* 7 (fall 1975): 151–62.

———. "The Tribal Alternative to Democracy: The Indians' New Deal, 1933–1945." *Journal of the West* 13 (January 1974): 128–42.

Vance, John T. "The Congressional Mandate and the Indian Claims Commission." *North Dakota Law Review* 45 (1969): 327–35.

Villard, O. G. "Wardship and the Indian." *Christian Century* 61 (29 March 1944): 397–98.

Warne, William E. "The Plight of the American Indian." *Talks: A Quarterly Digest of Addresses* 14 (July 1949): 45+.

———. "The Public Share in Indian Assimilation." *American Indian* 4 (1948): 3–11.

Watkins, Arthur V. "Termination of Federal Supervision: The Removal of Restrictions over Indian Property and Person." *Annals of the American Academy of Political and Social Science* 311 (May 1957): 47–55.

Wesley, Clarence. "San Carlos Apache Tribe Seeks Equal Rights." *Southwest Indian Newsletter* 1 (February 1951): 1.

Wilkinson, Charles F., and Eric R. Biggs. "The Evolution of the Termination Policy." *American Indian Law Review* 5 (1977): 139–84.

Williams, Julian. "The Socialization of U.S. Law." *Christian Crusade Weekly*, 9 June 1974, 11–12.

Willis, Purl. "California Indians Win Partial Victory in Court of Claims." *Indian: The First American* 6 (November 1945): 4–6.

Zimmerman, William, Jr. "Economic Status of Indians in the United States." *Journal of Religious Thought* 7 (spring–summer 1950): 108–20.

INTERVIEWS AND ORAL HISTORIES

Hess, Jerry. Oral History Interview by Warner W. Gardner, 22 June 1972. Harry S. Truman Library.

Krammer, Lucy Cohen. Telephone Interview by Kenneth R. Philp. Washington DC, May 1996.

Myer, Dillon S. *An Autobiography of Dillon S. Myer.* Berkeley: University of California, Regional Oral History Office, 1970.

Nash, Philleo. Interview by Kenneth R. Philp. Conference on Indian Self-Rule, Institute of American West, Sun Valley, Idaho, 19 August 1983.

Wilson, Dean Frank T. "Interview with Dillon S. Myer." *Journal of Religious Thought* 7 (spring–summer 1950): 93–100.

INDEX

AAIA (Association on American Indian Affairs): and attorney contracts, 113, 116–17, 121–22; and claims syndicate, 109; and economic rehabilitation of tribes, 82; and federal withdrawal, 13, 82; and law enforcement legislation, 141–42, 149–50; and Navajos, 53, 65; on reorganization of Indian Bureau, 12; on self-determination, 12, 47, 82; on state jurisdiction, 13; on termination, 13, 68, 86, 161; and tribal claims, 12, 20

Acheson, Dean, 79

Adams, George, 166

Adams, Lucy, 58

Agua Caliente Band, 161

Ahkeah, Sam: and attorney contracts, 121; as consultant, 164; criticizes federal paternalism, 61; and Navajo Advisory Committee, 65; and Navajo Coordinating Committee, 55; and Navajo-Hopi rehabilitation bill, 64–65; and off-reservation Navajos, 62; and political activism of, 49–50, 55, 57, 61, 121, 174; and right to vote, 52; and San Juan Irrigation Project, 55; and self-determination, 52, 61; on social security benefits, 52; and state jurisdiction, 64; and Treaty of 1868, 61; and universal education, 50; and W. Zimmerman, 61

Aid-to-Dependent Children, 143

AIF (American Indian Federation), 9, 18–19, 29, 105

Akers, Dolly, 108, 120

Alabama and Coushatta Indians, 163

Alaska Native Brotherhood, 35, 45, 47

Alaska Native Sisterhood, 35, 45

Alaska Reorganization Act. *See* ARA

Alaska Territory: administrative hearings for, 35, 37, 41, 46; economic development of, 34, 36–44; and fish traps, 35–39; forestry service in, 35, 40, 43, 46; Haidas and Tlingits in, 32, 35–42, 44, 46–48; Indians in, compared to Irish and Israelis, 49; Inuits in, 34–35; land allotment for, 35, 46–48; movement toward statehood in, 46–47, 172; and NCAI, 30–40, 42, 45, 49; political activism of Indians in, 34–35, 40, 42–45, 47–49; possessory rights in, 35–36, 38, 41, 46–48, 167, 173; salmon packers in, 34, 36, 38–40; and self-determination, 39, 43–45, 47–49; Tongass National Forest in, 34–37, 40–47; and solicitors' rulings, 35, 44

Albuquerque boarding school, 52

Alcea Band of Tillamooks v. U. S. (1946), 41

Aleck, Albert, 117–18

Aleuts, 35, 37

Alk, Isadore, 118

Allard, John, 101–2

All Pueblo Council, 60, 103, 114, 158

American Bar Association, 4, 115, 118, 121–22, 124

American Citizens' League, 58

American Friends Service Committee, 57, 113

American Indian Federation. *See* AIF

American Restitution and Righting Old Wrongs. *See* ARROW

American Socialist Quarterly, 4

Anderson, Clinton P., 80, 118–19, 122–24, 162

Angoon AK, 111

Apaches, 30–31, 101–3

Printed in the United States
3643